1096

ESSENTIAL

Trusts

Titles in the series:

Company Law
Constitutional & Administrative Law
Contract Law
Criminal Law
EC Law
English Legal System
Family Law
Jurisprudence
Land Law
Tort
Trusts

ESSENTIAL

Trusts

by

Andrew Iwobi LLB LLM
Lecturer in Law
Swansea Law School

First published in Great Britain 1995 by Cavendish Publishing Limited, The Glass House, Wharton Street, London WC1X 9PX

Telephone: 0171-278 8000   Facsimile: 0171-278 8080

British Library Cataloguing in Publication Data

Iwobi, Andrew
Essential Trusts Law –
(Essential Law Series)
I Title II Series
344.2064

ISBN 1-85941-119-3
Printed and bound in Great Britain

To Uzoamaka and Ifunanyachukwu
with love

Foreword

This book is part of the Cavendish Essential series. The books in the series are designed to provide useful revision aids for the hard-pressed student. They are not, of course, intended to be substitutes for more detailed treatises. Other textbooks in the Cavendish portfolio must supply these gaps.

Each book in the series follows a uniform format of a checklist of the areas covered in each chapter, expanded treatment of 'Essential' issues looking at examination topics in depth, followed by 'Revision Notes' for self-assessment.

The team of authors bring a wealth of lecturing and examining experience to the task in hand. Many of us can even recall what it was like to face law examinations!

Professor Nicholas Bourne
General Editor, Essential Series
Swansea Law School

Table of contents

1 **The general nature of the trust** 1
 Some definitions 1
 Trusts and related concepts 3
 Revision Notes 9

2 **Creation of express private trusts** 13
 The three certainties 13
 Formalities for the creation of trusts 25
 Testamentary trusts 29
 Revision Notes 39

3 **The constitution of trusts** 45
 Vesting of property as a condition for enforcement of trusts . . .45
 Declaration of self as trustee 46
 Transfer to trustees and outright gifts 47
 The position where every effort is made to vest the property . .48
 The position where vesting occurs by other means 49
 Circumstances in which a gift is enforceable
  without vesting 49
 Revision Notes 55

4 **Resulting and constructive trusts** 59
 Resulting trusts 59
 Purchase in the name of another 61
 The presumption of advancement 62
 Rebutting the presumptions of resulting
  trust and advancement 64
 Automatic resulting trusts 66
 Constructive trusts 70
 The 'new model' approach 72
 The main categories of traditional constructive trusts 75
 Trusts of the family home 86
 Revision Notes 91

5 **Charitable trusts** 99
 The significance of charitable status 99
 The requirements of a valid charitable trust 100

The relief of poverty 101
The advancement of education 103
The advancement of religion 106
Other purposes beneficial to the community 108
The requirement of public benefit 114
The requirement that the trust must be exclusively charitable .118
The cy-pres doctrine 122
The scope of the doctrine 122
Initial and subsequent failure 124
Subsequent failure 128
Revision Notes 129

6 The administration of trusts 139
The appointment, retirement and removal of trustees 139
Formalities for appointment 143
Appointment by the Court 143
Accepting the appointment 144
The main duties and powers of trustees 147
The trustee's duties 150
The trustee's powers 164
Variation of trusts 176
Variations authorised by statute 178
Revision Notes 185

7 Breach of trust 195
General 195
Remedies for breach of trust 196
The measure of liability 198
Defences to an action for personal liability 201
The proprietary remedy of tracing 205
Tracing in equity 207
Property in a traceable form 208
No inequitable results 215
Revision Notes 217

Index 225

1 The general nature of the trust

Some definitions

The leading textbooks contain various definitions of the trust. For example:

Underhill

A trust is an equitable obligation binding on a person (who is called a trustee) to deal with property over which he has control (which is called the trust property), for the benefit of persons (who are called the beneficiaries or *cestuis que trust*) of whom he may be one and any of whom may enforce the obligation.

Keeton and Sheridan

A trust is the relationship which arises wherever a person called the trustee is compelled in equity to hold property, whether real or personal and whether by legal or equitable title, for the benefit of some persons (of whom he may be one and who are termed the beneficiaries) or for some objects permitted by law in such a way that the real benefit of the property accrues not to the trustee, but to the beneficiaries or other objects of the trust.

1

The main elements of the trust

It has been observed in Hanbury's *Modern Equity* that of the many attempts which have been made at defining a trust none has been entirely successful. This is scarcely surprising as the trust is such a multi-faceted device which has been employed in a diverse range of settings. Various commentators have therefore suggested that it is more instructive to describe than to define the trust. A convenient way of describing the trust is to elaborate on the key elements which emerge from the various definitions.

Equity/equitable jurisdiction

This is an acknowledgment of the historical fact that the trust is a creature of equity rather than the common law. It owes its origin and present-day existence to the willingness of the Chancellors to compel any person who undertook to hold property on behalf of another to give effect to his undertaking in circumstances where the common law judges refused to intervene. The involvement of the Chancellors in the evolution of the trust and its forerunner the use has been well documented and reference may be made to Hanbury 's *Modern Equity* (14th ed pp 5-14; or Pettitt's *Equity and The Law of Trusts* (7th ed pp 1-4 and 11-16 for fuller accounts).

Obligation/compelled

A trust gives rise to duties which are imperative such that failure to carry them out renders a trustee liable for breach of trust.

Trustee-beneficiary (or *cestui que trust*)

The existence of a trust involves a relationship which in most definitions is presented as a simple bi-partite one between trustees and beneficiaries. In reality, however, trusts, particularly in the commercial sphere, often involve more complex multi-partite relationships. Unit Trusts for instance normally entail a tri-partite relationship between trustees, fund managers and investors.

It is noteworthy that Keeton and Sheridan's definition refers not only to human beneficiaries but also to objects permitted by law. This reflects the emergence of the charitable trust as a vehicle for fulfilling purposes beneficial to the community at large.

Property

Trusts do not exist in a vacuum but by reference to some specie of real or personal property which constitutes the subject-matter of the trust. Any object, tangible or intangible, which in the eyes of the law is capable of being owned is also capable of being held on trust.

Moreover, a trust is capable of coming into being whether the party creating it (known as the settlor or the testator) owns a legal estate or interest or an equitable interest in the property to be held on trust. Where the subject-matter of the trust consists of a legal estate or interest, it is commonly but not invariably the case that this becomes vested in the trustee.

The beneficial interest

It is clear from all the definitions that notwithstanding the fact that the trustee ordinarily becomes the legal owner of the trust property he derives no material advantage or benefit for himself. Instead, equity decrees that it is the beneficiary or *cestui que trust* who is entitled to enjoy the benefits which flow from the property. On account of this, the beneficiaries are said to have an equitable or beneficial interest in the trust property.

The proprietary character of the beneficial interest

Originally, the rights of beneficiaries under a trust were regarded as personal rights enforceable only against the trustee. Over the centuries, however, the beneficiary's entitlement has assumed the character of a proprietary interest as distinct from a mere personal right. The implications of this are three-fold:

- beneficial interests can be bought, sold or otherwise disposed of like any other form of property;
- beneficial interests like all proprietary interests are enforceable not merely *in personam* against the trustee but *in rem* against the whole world except a bona fide purchaser for value without notice.
- the hierarchy of legal estates/interests evolved by the common law judges was replicated by the Chancellors in the context of beneficial ownership under the trust.

Trusts and related concepts

In seeking to understand the nature of the trust it is useful to compare it with various other concepts familiar to English law.

Trusts and bailment

Bailment entails delivery of goods for specified purposes on the condition that on the fulfilment of such purposes the bailee will return them to the bailor or deliver them according to his directions. For example, hire of a car; deposit of an item for repair or safekeeping; consignment of goods for delivery to a third party.

As with a trust a bailment entails the reliance by one person on another person to whom he has entrusted his property. Thus, for instance, a direction by A to B to keep a piano for A's infant son C until C turns 21, may give rise to a trust in some circumstances and a bailment in others.

In spite of this, the trust and bailment differ materially in a number of respects:

• bailment originated from the common law; trusts from equity;
• the subject-matter of any bailment consists of goods but the subject-matter of a trust may be any form of property whatsoever;
• bailment passes special property (possession) while the trust ordinarily requires the settlor to divest himself of general property (ownership) in favour of the trustee;
• by virtue of such ownership the trustee can pass a good title to a purchaser in good faith and for value. Except in certain instances allowed by statute (eg under the Factors Act 1889) the bailee is incapable of passing a good title to a third party.

Trusts and contract

A contract is an agreement between parties which is intended to create legal relations. Unlike trusts which are enforceable only in equity, contracts are recognised and enforced both at law and in equity by means of such remedies as damages, specific performance and injunctions.

Furthermore, whereas a trust imposes an obligation on one person to hold property for the benefit of another, the obligations imposed by a contract do not always relate to property. For example, A may agree to give B music lessons if B does A's weekly laundry.

Because of the rules of privity, a contract is generally enforceable only by a party to the agreement. Moreover, the party must have furnished some consideration unless the contract is under seal. By contrast, absence of an agreement and lack of consideration will not in themselves render a trust unenforcable. For example, X may in his will leave Blackacre to Y to hold on trust for Z without consulting either Y or Z and without demanding anything in return from Z. When X dies, the legal title to Blackacre will pass to Y but equity will give effect to Z's interest.

There are, however, certain situations in which the distinction between contractual relationships and relationships founded on trusts tend to be somewhat blurred. This is often the case, where A enters into an agreement with B under which B in return for consideration given by A undertakes to confer some benefit on C. Ordinarily C will be unable to enforce the agreement in contract as he was not privy to it. See *Tweddle v Atkinson* (1861) *Dunlop v Selfridges* (1915) *Scruttons v Midland Silicones* (1962).

In such instances, however, equity sometimes provides an avenue for enforcement by C by finding that either A or B contracted as a trustee of the benefit of C. Where the court is able to import a trust into the agreement and C does not receive the benefit due to him, the party who contracted as a trustee for C is obliged in equity to take legal action on C's behalf. If no such action is taken, it has been established in such cases as *Lloyds v Harper* (1880) and *Les Affreteurs Reunis Societe Anonyme v Leopold Walford* (1919) that C himself may enforce the benefit by virtue of the trust.

It does not follow that a trust is automatically imported into every agreement under which A contracts with B for C's benefit. On the contrary, it is clear from cases such as *Vanderpitte v Preferred Accident Insurance Corp* (1933) and *Re Schebsman* (1944) that it is only where it is established that A and B intended that the benefit of the contract was to be held on trust for C, that the courts will allow C to enforce the benefit himself.

Trusts and agency

The relationship of a principal and his agent bears a close resemblance to that of a trustee and beneficiary. In particular:

- the trustee and agent are both fiduciaries who must exercise utmost good faith in carrying out the trust or agency;
- each must account for any unauthorised profits or benefits received by virtue of his office;
- each is enjoined by law to perform his responsibilities personally, instead of delegating them.

There are, however, notable differences between the two concepts:

- Agency is founded on agreement (except agency of necessity); whereas agreement is not a pre-requisite for declaring a trust.

- Agency is in the nature of a personal relationship under which any property which the principal entrusts to the agent is held in possession with no attendant transfer of ownership. A trust on the other hand is a proprietary relationship, albeit one in which the trustee's ownership is no more than nominal or custodial.
- In the event of insolvency, the beneficiary is in a more secure position as against trustee than the principal is *vis-à-vis* the agent. Where money or the monetary equivalent of property is due from the trustee to the beneficiary and the trustee is adjudicated bankrupt, the beneficiary's proprietary interest often gives him a prior claim to the trustee's assets as against other creditors. On the other hand where the principal is placed in the same situation, he is treated on the same footing as any unsecured creditor since the agency relationship is personal rather than proprietary. This difference between personal and proprietary relationships was clearly brought out in *Lister v Stubbs* (1890).

Trusts and powers

A power, as explained in *Freme v Clement* (1881), is an authority conferred by a donor on a donee to deal with or dispose of property owned by the donor.

Different types of powers may be conferred on donees for various purposes. The most notable of these is the power of appointment. Under such a power the donee (also called the appointor) is authorised to nominate persons (who are called appointees) in whom interests in specified property will vest.

Trusts bear an unmistakable resemblance to powers of appointment insofar as both trustees and appointors are authorised to deal with/dispose of property. Whether a trust or power of appointment has come into being is largely determined by construing the instrument creating it. It is important that this should be framed in terms which make it clear which of the two was intended as there are several notable differences between them.

In the first place, trusts operate exclusively in the domain of equity whereas powers may be legal or equitable. Note, however, that under the Law of Property Act 1925 powers of appointment can now exist only as equitable powers under a trust.

Secondly and more significantly, the essential distinction between trusts and power stems from the fact that trusts are imperative whereas powers are discretionary.

On account of the imperative nature of the trust equity has long maintained that the beneficiaries who are the objects of a trust are in substance the owners of the trust property. On the other hand, the objects of a power are deemed to own absolutely nothing unless and until the appointor chooses to appoint any part of the property to them. Until then, all they have is an expectancy that the power will be exercised in their favour. At this point, equitable ownership is deemed to vest in whosoever is entitled to the property in default of appointment, although the latter is liable to be divested upon the exercise of the power.

One notable consequence of this is that in the case of a trust, where all the intended beneficiaries are *sui juris* it is open to them to bring the trust to an end and require the property to be conveyed to them under the rule in *Saunders v Vautier* (1841). The objects of the power on the other hand are in no position to direct the appointor to transfer the property which is the subject of the power to them.

Furthermore, where a trustee fails to carry out the terms of the trust he can be compelled to do so by the court on the insistence of the beneficiaries, and the court will as a last resort carry out the trust itself (eg where the trustee dies without performing the trust and there are no other trustees). In the case of a power of appointment, however, the court will neither compel the appointor to make an appointment nor will the court undertake to exercise the power if the appointor refuses to or dies without having done so.

The distinction between trusts and powers of appointment has however become somewhat blurred in a number of material respects.

Powers of appointment and discretionary trusts

Under a discretionary trust, the settlor typically entrusts the trustees with the responsibility for determining the manner in which property should be distributed among the members of a specified class. This bears some resemblance to the power of appointment under which the appointor is similarly authorised to employ his discretion in distributing property among members of a class.

A common characteristic of discretionary trusts and powers of appointment is that in order for either to be valid, the class of objects must be sufficiently certain to enable the trustee or appointor to ascertain whether any particular person is or is not within the class. See *Re Gulbenkian* (1970) and *Mcphail v Doulton* (1971). As shall be seen in Chapter 2, the position is different with regard to fixed trusts in favour of members of a class.

Mere powers and trust powers

The distinction between trusts and powers is further blurred by the emergence of what has been variously labelled the trust power or power in the nature of a trust. The trust power is an arrangement which on its face appears to give rise to an ordinary power of appointment, but which in substance is treated as a trust by the courts.

This super-imposition of trusts on arrangements which would otherwise be regarded as powers is exemplified by a line of cases going back to *Burrough v Philcox* (1840). T had left property to S and D specifying that the survivor of the two was to dispose of the property in their will amongst such of T's nephews and nieces as the survivor saw fit. S who survived D, eventually died without making any disposition and the nephews and nieces sought an order that the property should be divided among them. The material clause in T's will was framed in terms indicative of a power and it might therefore have been expected that as no appointment had been made, the objects would have no claim. Their claim nevertheless succeeded since the court felt able to discern an underlying intention on T's part that a trust would arise in favour of the whole class in the absence of any appointment. Note, however, subsequent cases like *Re Weekes* (1897); *Re Combes* (1925) and *Re Perowne* (1951) which emphasise that the decision in *Burrough v Philcox* will not apply unless there is evidence that the donor intended the members of the specified class to benefit in any event even if the selection was not made.

The proposition that trusts are imperative and powers discretionary does has not always strictly been maintained

On the one hand, it was seen that because powers are discretionary, the courts are not prepared to take any action where a power is not exercised. This must now be qualified in the light of the recent decision in *Mettoy Pensions Trustees Ltd v Evans* (1990) where it was signified that in certain circumstances, the court may intervene to exercise a fiduciary power where there is nobody else to exercise it.

On the other hand, it is noticeable that trusts for certain purposes (such as the upkeep of animals) are recognised as valid, even where there are no human beneficiaries to compel the trustees to perform them. The willingness of the courts to uphold these so-called trusts of imperfect obligation contradicts the fundamental distinction between the imperative character of trusts and the discretionary nature of powers.

Revision Notes

In its typical form, a trust arises where equity obliges a party called the trustee to hold property or an interest in property for the benefit of another person called the beneficiary or to apply such property towards a purpose recognised by law.

For historical reasons, the trustee is treated as the owner of the property under the common law. In substance, he is a nominal owner who is bound to administer the property for the benefit of the beneficiary or devote it to the purpose of the trust.

The beneficiary, for his part, is the equitable owner of the trust property who for centuries has been entitled to enforce his proprietary interest against the whole world except a bona fide purchaser for value without notice.

Trust and bailment

There are certain parallels between trusts and bailment. Both commonly arise where one person entrusts his property to another with directions as to what should be done with the property.

There are, however, material differences between the two:

- bailment is a common law creation while trusts are equitable;
- bailment covers only goods while trusts encompass all property;
- a bailee obtains special property but a trustee obtains general property/ownership. On account of this a trustee can pass a good title to property to a bona fide purchaser for value, whereas a bailee cannot except under such legislation as the Factors Act.

Trust and contract

Both the common law and equity have always recognised and given effect to contractual rights and obligations whereas trusts are enforceable only in equity.

Another notable difference is that trusts exist by reference to property but many contracts have nothing to do with property.

Most importantly the enforceability of a contract generally depends on the existence of agreement and consideration, which are not crucial requirements for the enforceability of trusts.

However, the distinction between contracts and trusts is not always entirely clear-cut especially where two parties enter into a contract for the benefit of a third. Sometimes, the courts find that one of the contracting parties did so as a trustee for the third party (*Lloyds v Harper* and the *Leopold Walford Case*). But before a trust is imported into a contract in this manner it must proved that this was intended by the contracting parties (*Re Schebsman* and the *Vanderpitte Case*).

Trust and agency

Trustees like agents are fiduciaries. This means that they must both act in good faith, account for unauthorised profits and cannot ordinarily delegate their responsibilities.

There are, however, differences between the two. The most notable is that agency is a personal relationship while the trust gives rise to a proprietary relationship (see *Lister v Stubbs*). The main significance of this is that where the agent becomes bankrupt, his principal is in the same position as an ordinary creditor in respect of money entrusted to the agent. By contrast, where the trustee becomes bankrupt, the beneficiaries have a prior claim over other creditors to trust funds in his hands.

Trusts and powers

A power is an authority to deal with or dispose of property (*Freme v Clement*). It resembles a trust since a trustee, like a donee of a power, has authority to deal with/dispose of property.

The main differences between trusts and powers are that:

- trusts are equitable but powers may be legal or equitable;
- the trust is imperative whereas the power is discretionary. In this connection, contrast eg a trust for sale and a power of sale or a discretionary trust and a power of appointment.

In spite of this the dividing line between trusts and powers is not always easy to draw for a variety of reasons:

- discretionary trusts are now dealt with on the same basis as powers of appointment as far as the issue of certainty of objects is concerned (*Re Gulbenkian; Mcphail v Doulton*);
- certain arrangements which appear to be framed as powers of appointment have been construed by the courts as trusts (or powers in the nature of a trust) (*Burrough v Philcox*);
- the fundamental premise that trusts are imperative and powers discretionary has been undermined by:

(a) the decision in *Mettoy Pensions v Evans* that the court may give effect to a fiduciary power where no one is available to exercise it;

(b) the judicial recognition of trusts of imperfect obligation.

2 Creation of express private trusts

The three certainties

The basic principles

In creating an express trust the settlor must ensure that his declaration is framed in clear, unambiguous terms in order to allow the trustees to discharge their duties properly, minimise the scope for controversy and litigation and enable the courts to carry out the trust if this becomes necessary. It was thus laid down in such cases as *Wright v Atkyns* (1823) and *Knight v Knight* (1840) that the declaration must be certain in three respects:

- the intention to create a trust must be manifest – *certainty of intention (or words)*;
- the property to be held on trust must be certain – *certainty of subject-matter*;
- the beneficiaries must be certain – *certainty of objects*.

Certainty of intention (or words)

A trust imposes an obligation on the trustee to hold property in accordance with the settlor's directions. Consequently, a trust will be deemed to have been validly declared only where it is certain that the settlor intended to create such an obligation.

Ascertaining the settlor's intention

The settlor's words

Where it has to be determined whether a trust was intended in any given case, the starting point is to consider the language in which the declaration was framed to see whether the settlor's words are sufficiently *imperative* to reflect the obligatory character of a trust.

'Trust'

The most obvious way for a settlor to denote his intention to create a trust is to employ the words 'trust' or 'trustee' in his declaration. At the same time it is evident from the decision in *Tito v Waddel (No 2)* (1977), that it is not in every conceivable instance where assets are expressed to be held on trust that the courts will conclude that a trust in the conventional sense has been created.

Other imperative words

Given that equity is more concerned with substance than form, the courts have made it clear in such cases as *Re Kayford* (1975), *Re Multi Guarantee Co Ltd* (1987) and *Re English & American Insurance Co Ltd* (1993), that a settlor may express an intention to create a trust without using the word 'trust' or its derivatives. Alternative expressions such as *beneficial interest* are recognised as appropriate words for creating a trust (see *Re London Wine Co (Shippers) Ltd* (1975)). Equally, where the settlor uses such words as 'I require' or 'I direct' this usually indicates an intention to create a trust.

The effect of precatory words

Where a person transfers property and in so doing employs words such as 'I request/suggest/wish/hope/desire/believe' such words do not convey an imperative command and are said to be *precatory* in nature.

Before Lambe v Eames

Until the latter part of the 19th century the Chancellors tended to regard a gift accompanied by precatory words as being indicative of an intention to impose a trust on the donee (See eg *Harding v Glyn* (1739); *Palmer v Simmonds* (1854); *Hart v Tribe* (1854) and *Gully v Cregoe* (1857).

The turning of the tide

A change of approach was, however, heralded by the case of *Lambe v Eames* (1871), where a testator left property to his widow, specifying that 'it is to be at her disposal as she thinks fit for herself and her family'. The court took the view that these words were not intended to create a trust and held accordingly that the widow was absolutely entitled to the property with no more than a moral obligation in favour of her family.

This decision has been re-inforced by a host of subsequent cases in which the courts have refused to enforce as trusts, gifts accompanied by one form of precatory words or another including:
- *Mussoorie Bank v Raynor* (1882): 'Feeling confident that she will act justly toward our children';
- *Re Adams & Kensington Vestry* (1884): 'In full confidence that she will do what is right as to the disposal...as between my children';
- *Re Diggles* (1888): 'It is my desire ...';
- *Re Hamilton* (1895): 'I wish them ...';
- *Re Williams* (1897): 'Absolutely, in the fullest confidence that she will carry out my wishes';
- *Re Conolly* (1910): 'I specifically desire'; and
- *Re Johnson* (1939): 'I request that ...'.

Exceptional cases where precatory words give rise to trusts
It is not an absolute rule that the use of precatory words in making a gift invariably precludes the possibility of a trust. The true position as summed up by Lopes LJ in *Re Hamilton* is that the court will not ordinarily enforce a declaration framed in precatory terms as a trust 'unless on the consideration of all the words employed it comes to the conclusion that it was the intention of the testator to create a trust'.

This position is well illustrated by *Comiskey v Bowring-Hanbury* (1905). Here T left property to W 'absolutely, in full confidence' that W would make such use of it as T would have done and that at W's death she would leave it to one or more of T's nieces as W saw fit. The words 'in full confidence' would ordinarily have been construed as precatory (see *Re Adams & KV*). However, T also specified that if W did not leave the property to one or more niece, there would be a gift over to all of them. This, in the court's view, signified that T intended to create a trust rather than an outright gift in W's favour (see also *Re Steele's WT* (1948)).

Conduct indicative of an intention to create a trust
Occasionally, the courts have been able to deduce an intention to declare a trust from a combination of words and conduct, where words alone would be insufficient. In *Paul v Constance* (1977), C was co-habiting with P having separated from his wife, D. He received £950 as

damages for personal injury which he put in a deposit account. The account was in C's name but he repeatedly told P it was as much hers as his. After C's death both P and D claimed the balance in the account. It was held that C's statements coupled with the fact that the account was in practice operated by him and P as a joint account indicated that he intended to hold the money on trust for himself and P.

Other cases such as *Re Kayford* and *Re English & American Insurance Co* establish that where a company receives funds from customers on the footing that it will segregate the funds from its other income and assets, this signifies an intention to hold such funds on trust for the customers even where no trust has been specifically declared (contrast, however, with *Re Multi Guarantee Co*).

Certainty of subject-matter

Certainty of subject-matter involves two requirements. Outlining these requirements, Oliver J declared in *Re London Wine Co* that:

To create a trust it must be possible to ascertain with certainty not only what the *interest of the beneficiary* is, but also to what *property* it is to attach.

Certainty as to the trust property

Once it is established that a trust was intended it is necessary to determine what property is held on trust. The trust is liable to fail unless the property is clearly identifiable. For example, if a testator who owns several houses in Swansea is unwise enough to devise 'my house in Swansea' to T to hold on trust for B', the trust is unlikely to be enforced by the court.

Uncertainty regarding the trust property is most likely to present problems in the following contexts.

Where the trust relates to property forming part of a larger quantity
This type of situation is liable to arise where, for instance:

- A who has just won £100,000 on the football pools declares that he will hold of £50,000 out of this amount on trust for his son B without setting the £50,000 apart; or
- S who owns £10,000 worth of shares in British Telecom puts them in T's name, directing T to hold £5,000 worth of these shares on trust for C without specifying the actual shares.

It appears from *Re London Wine Co* that declarations made in these terms do not operate to create a trust. Here a company sold wine to customers on the understanding that pending delivery it would store the wine in warehouses at the customer's expense. Customers paid in advance for their orders and were given certificates of title describing them as beneficial owners of particular consignments but the company did nothing to segregate the consignment from the rest of its stock until delivery was due. It was decided that these consignments were not held on trust for the various customers. The court's reasoning was that even if the company sought by this arrangement to create a trust, the subject-matter was uncertain since the actual consignments were not set apart from the company's other stock and the trust would therefore fail (note also *Re Goldcorp Exchange Ltd* (1994)).

A different conclusion was, however, reached in *Hunter v Moss* (1993). M, the registered owner of 950 shares in ME Ltd which had an issued share capital of 1,000 shares declared himself a trustee of 5% of the issued share capital in favour of H, without stating which shares out of his 950, would be held on trust. M subsequently repudiated the trust claiming on the authority of *Re London Wine Co* that it was invalid for uncertainty of subject-matter. The trial court accepted that where tangible assets such as wine were concerned, specific appropriation, in the manner contemplated by *Re London Wine*, was required since it was quite possible that different batches of the same stock might vary in quality or condition. By contrast, intangible assets such as the shares in the present case all carried identical rights and it made no difference which of M's 950 shares were held on trust for H. Consequently, the court had no difficulty in holding that the subject-matter of the trust was sufficiently certain even though M had not identified the particular shares involved. This decision has recently been upheld by the Court of Appeal.

Where relative words are employed in defining the property

A trust is liable to fail for uncertainty where the property is defined in terms that are susceptible to variable interpretations.

This was the case for instance in *Palmer v Simmonds* where T directed that the bulk of her residuary estate was to go to specified beneficiaries since it was impossible to determine what T meant by the term 'bulk'. A similar line of reasoning was adopted in *Re Kolb* (1962), where T's will contained a clause directing his trustees to invest in 'blue chip' securities. The court considered the expression 'blue chip' to be subjective and as T had given no indication as to what he meant by the expression in the present context, the clause was held to have failed for uncertainty.

A more flexible approach was adopted in *Re Golay's WT* (1965) where T made a will directing his executors to pay a 'reasonable income' to B without specifying what he meant by this. The court refused to hold that the subject-matter was uncertain since 'reasonable income' imported an objective standard capable of being measured by the court having regard to the standard of living to which B was accustomed.

Where property is given to one person subject to a gift over of an unspecified part of the property to some other person
A situation of this nature arose in *Sprange v Barnard* (1789), where T left a sum of money to H directing that at H's death any part of this sum which he did not require was to go to A, B and C equally. Because of the uncertainty regarding what part of the sum would remain unused when H eventually died, the court held that there was no valid trust in favour of A, B and C. Contrast this, however, with *Re Last* (1958).

Certainty as to beneficial interests
If the trust makes provision for more than one beneficiary, the declaration must be framed in terms which makes it possible to ascertain their respective beneficial entitlements.

The issue of certainty of beneficial interest arose in *Boyce v Boyce* (1849), where T devised his houses to trustees on trust to convey to his daughter M whichever one she might choose with the others to go to his other daughter C. M died before choosing and it was held that the trust in C's favour would fail because M's death made it was impossible to ascertain which of the houses constituted C's share of the trust property.

Another instructive case is *Curtis v Rippon* (1820), where T left property to W trusting that W would make such use of it as would be for her own good and that of their children and remembering the church and the poor. It was held that there was no trust for the children, the church or the poor as it was uncertain which part of the property W was obliged to hold for their benefit.

Exceptions
It is not in every instance where the beneficial interests have not been specified with sufficient precision that a trust will fail:

• The trust will not fail where the testator or settlor has given the trustees the discretion to determine the entitlements of the respective beneficiaries in any manner they think fit.

* In some instances, the courts are prepared to save the trust from failure by invoking the maxim 'equality is equity' as the basis for determining the shares of the beneficiaries.

Certainty of objects

The beneficiary principle
The requirement that the objects of a trust must be certain is based on the recognition that 'a trustee would not be expected to be subject to an equitable obligation unless there was somebody who could enforce a correlative equitable right' per Roxburgh J in Re Astor's ST (1952). In the same vain, Evershed MR declared in Re Endacott (1960) that 'a trust not being a charitable trust in order to be effective must have ascertained or ascertainable beneficiaries.

A notable consequence of the beneficiary principle is that trusts which are expressed to be for purposes rather than persons will generally be unenforceable. For example, as Russell J signified in Re Hummeltenberg (1923), a trust for the purpose of training poodles to dance will fall in this account.

Purpose trusts are however enforceable, where:
* the purpose is charitable (see Chapter 5);
* the purpose is one that benefits ascertained or ascertainable persons: see Re Osoba (1978); Re Denley's DT (1969);
* the trust is a trust of imperfect obligation: eg a trust for the upkeep of particular animals (see Re Dean (1899); Milton v Reynolds (1848)); or a trust for the erection or maintenance of a specified tomb or monument (see Mussett v Bingle (1876); Pirbright v Salwey (1896); Re Hooper (1932)).

It is only in a few exceptional circumstances which are dealt with in Chapter 6 that the courts will give effect to a trust which is expressed to be for a non-charitable purpose.

Determining whether the beneficiaries are sufficiently certain gifts to named individuals
Where the settlor or testator, in declaring the trust has specifically named the beneficiary or beneficiaries (eg '£10,000 to T on trust for my friend John Doe') there is little likelihood that the gift will fail unless there is evidence that he knows two or more persons so named. For example, £10,000 to X on trust for John Doe.

Gifts to individuals identified by description

Where a settlor does not name the object of his bounty but employs a descriptive term, the issue at stake is whether the description indisputably fits a particular person. A gift of this nature is unlikely to fail for uncertainty, where, for instance, T in his will leaves £10,000 on trust for A's eldest son and at T's death A has two sons aged 21 and 18. By contrast, there would be uncertainty if T leaves £10,000 on trust for A for life, reminder to his wife, and at the time of the gift A is not married but later marries and divorces twice and remains a divorcee at the time of his death.

Gifts to persons as members of a class

Where property is left on trust, not for specified individuals, but for members of a class, the requirement of certainty dictates that the trustees must be in a position to tell who belongs to the class.

In many cases, this requirement is easily fulfilled. There will be no difficulty, for instance, where T in his will devises Blackacre to trustees on trust for his children and it is well known that T was survived by two sons and a daughter. Equally, where T leaves £10,000 on trust for the surviving members of the England football squad who won the 1966 World Cup there is every likelihood that the identities and whereabouts of the intended beneficiaries can be discovered by delving into official records.

However, it is not every gift expressed to be for the benefit of the members of a class that will be attended by such certainty. In this context, lack of certainty may be evident on a number of different levels:

- the language used to define the class may be susceptible to several meanings thus giving rise to *conceptual uncertainty*;
- the language which is used may be certain but the means of discovering who falls within the class may be unavailable thus giving rise to *evidential uncertainty*;
- there may be no difficulty in identifying every member of the class but the element of *ascertainability* may be lacking in the sense that it is impossible to determine the whereabouts of every single member of the class;
- the class as defined may be so wide and amorphous that the trust is rendered *administratively unworkable*.

In determining whether the objects of a trust are sufficiently certain the courts are guided by different tests depending on whether the trust is *fixed* or a *discretionary trust*.

Fixed trusts

There is a fixed trust where the settlor or testator prescribes the interests or shares of the beneficiaries.

The fixed trust may be in favour of named persons; eg £10,000 on trust for A, B, C and D in equal shares; or £10,000 on trust for E and F for life remainder to G and H. In such instances the requirement of certainty of objects presents no problems.

On the other hand, a fixed trust may be declared in favour of the members of a designated class; eg £100,000 on trust for all the employees of a specified organisation in equal shares. In trusts of this nature the settlor's directions can only be carried out where the size of the class and identities of all the members are known to the trustees or capable of ascertainment. It has accordingly held in such cases as *IRC v Broadway Cottages Trust* (1955); *Re Gulbenkian's ST* (1970) and *Mcphail v Doulton* (1971) that for such trusts, the test for certainty is whether it is possible to make a *comprehensive list*, which accurately includes the names of all those who are beneficially entitled, while excluding all those who fall outside the class.

Where it is not possible to draw up such a list, the trust will fail, whether this is due to *conceptual* or *evidential uncertainty*. For example, a gift of £10,000 on trust for 'my old friends' in equal shares will fail on the basis of conceptual uncertainty (see *Re Gulbenkian* and *Brown v Gould* (1972)); as would a gift on the same terms for the benefit of 'all those persons who have a moral claim on me' (see *Re Baden's Deed Trusts (No 2)* (1973)). On the other hand, where trustees are given £100,000 to be divided equally among all those who were pupils of a named school between 1930 and 1939 there will be no conceptual uncertainty regarding the class. Assuming, however, the school's records were all destroyed in a bombing raid during World War II, the gift may fail on account of evidential uncertainty unless the material information can be derived from some other source.

By contrast, where there is conceptual as well as evidential certainty but the whereabouts or continued existence of some of the beneficiaries cannot be *ascertained*, it has been argued that this will not make the gift fail since the share of such beneficiaries can be paid into court. See CT Emery (1982) 98 LQR 551.

Discretionary trusts

A settlor who declares a trust in favour of a class may, instead of fixing the shares to be taken by individual members, confer a discretion on the trustee to determine their shares. Prior to 1970 the test for certainty for such discretionary trusts was that applicable to fixed trusts.

See *Re Ogden* (1933); *IRC v Broadway Cottages* and *Re Sayer* (1957). This meant that even if the trustee was content to distribute the trust property among a limited section of the discretionary class already identified by them, the trust was nevertheless liable to fail if it was impossible to list every member of the class.

Mcphail v Doulton

Since 1970, when the House of Lords delivered judgment in this case, discretionary trusts have been subject to a different test. In this case, B executed a deed establishing a fund for the benefit of the employees of a company. By Clause 9 of the deed the trustees were given a discretion to apply the income of the fund in making grants to or for benefit of officers and employees or ex-officers and ex-employees of the company and their relatives and dependants. It was common ground in the trial court and the Court of Appeal that if Clause 9 created a discretionary trust it would fail for uncertainty of objects since it would prove impossible to draw up a comprehensive list of all the relatives and dependants of employees. To avert this possibility both courts found that Clause 9 did not create a discretionary trust but a power. This enabled them to hold that it did not fail for uncertainty since a less stringent test had been formulated for powers in such cases as *Re Gestetner* (1953) and *Re Gulbenkian*. These authorities had established that where a power was concerned, the decisive issue was *whether it could be said with certainty that any individual is or is not a member of the class in whose favour the power was exercisable*. By contrast, the House of Lords found that Clause 9 created a discretionary trust rather than a power. By a majority of three to two, the House rejected the prevailing view that the test for certainty for a discretionary trust ought to be the 'comprehensive list test' preferring instead, to adopt the 'is-is not' test applicable to powers. Elaborating on this, Lord Wilberforce, explained that trustees of a discretionary trust were not bound to consider every potential beneficiary and thus it was not necessary to be able to ascertain all the beneficiaries for the trust to be valid. All that was required was for the trustees to be able to *survey the whole field* to gain a general impression as to its size and for them to be able to say whether any given claimant fell within or outside the field.

The case was then remitted to the High Court (under the name *Re Baden's Deed Trust (No 2)* to determine whether Clause 9 and in particular the terms 'relatives' and 'dependants' satisfied the new test and Brightman J held that they did. In the ensuing appeal it was contended that even on the basis of the 'is-is not' test, the term 'relation' was uncertain since it could not be conclusively determined that one person was *not* the relation of another. In rejecting this contention, the Court of Appeal indicated that the term 'relation' was not *conceptually uncertain* which would undoubtedly have invalidated the trust. In the view of Sachs and Megaw LJ even if there was a measure of *evidential uncertainty* surrounding whether a person was not the relation of another this did not mean that the trust would fail on the basis of the 'is-is not test'. According to Sachs LJ whether a person fell within the class of relations of employees was a question of fact and if a person was not proved to be a relation of an employee then he should be treated as not being within the class for purposes of the trust. For his part Megaw LJ reasoned that when dealing with a class such as relations, once it was possible to say that a substantial number of persons are within the class the trust would be deemed valid even if it could not be said whether some other persons fell within or outside it. By contrast, Stamp LJ chose to adopt a strict literal approach to the 'is-is not' test. In his view, if the term relation was construed as persons descended from the same ancestor the trust would have failed for uncertainty as the appellants contended. He, however, took the term to mean next-of-kin or nearest blood relations and held that the class as so defined was sufficiently certain since it could be said of any given person whether he was within or outside it.

Curing uncertainty by reference to opinions of third parties
Commentators like Hanbury and Martin maintain that where the class of beneficiaries is defined in terms that import an element of conceptual uncertainty into the trust, this uncertainty may be cured where the settlor provides that the trustee or some third party is to determine the meaning to be ascribed to such terms. In *Re Tuck's ST* (1978), for instance, a settlor made a gift for the benefit of persons of Jewish blood who continued to worship according to the Jewish faith, directing that in case of dispute or doubt as to who would qualify the opinion of the Chief Rabbi would be conclusive. It was held that even if there was uncertainty as to what was meant by worshipping according to the Jewish faith, this direction made the gift valid.

On the other hand, other commentators (such as Matthews (1983) NLJ 913 and Riddall in *Law Of Trusts*) express doubts as to whether conceptual uncertainty can be cured arguing that:

if the description of the class was conceptually uncertain then it would be no more possible for a private person to make a rational decision ... than it would be for the court to do so.

Failure on the ground of administrative unworkability

Another important dimension of Lord Wilberforce's judgment in *Mcphail* was his assertion that a discretionary trust would be void if the meaning of the words used in defining the objects though conceptually certain 'is so hopelessly wide as not to form anything like a class so that the trust is administratively unworkable' (eg a discretionary trust in favour of all the residents of Greater London). Lord Wilberforce did not proffer any persuasive reason why a discretionary trust should be void on this account and McKay suggested in (1974) 38 Conv 269 that there was no justification for his view on the basis of either administrative feasibility or judicial execution. Despite such reservations the notion of administrative unworkabilty was adopted in *R v District Auditor Ex p West Yorkshire Metropolitan CC* (1986), where Lloyd J held that a trust in favour of any or all or some of the inhabitants of West Yorkshire was void on this basis.

Although the criterion of administrative unworkabilty was formulated in the context of discretionary trusts it seems that it will also be material where a fixed trust is declared in favour of a class which is so hopelessly wide that it would be entirely impracticable for the trustees to share the property among the class (see Riddall p 29).

Trusts with a power of selection

Where the trustee or a third party is empowered to select beneficiaries from a specified class the settlor will sometimes be deemed to have intended that the members of the class should take equally in default of selection (as happened for instance in *Burrough v Philcox* (1840)). In such cases, the test for powers/discretionary trusts will at the outset determine whether the class is sufficiently certain. But if the selection is not made, a fixed trust comes into being and whether or not the class is sufficiently certain will now depend on the stricter test laid down in *IRC v Broadway Cottages*.

Gifts which are expressed to be subject to a condition precedent

A distinction is drawn between a discretionary trust in favour of a class and a gift or series of individual gifts subject to a condition precedent. The latter is a gift which does not confer on the prospective donee an interest in the property unless and until he has met a particular condition or qualification. For instance where a settlor gives £500,000 to trustees with instructions to pay £100 to each of the settlor's old friends, these are individual gifts of a specified amount in favour of every person who fulfils a condition or description prescribed by the settlor.

Where a gift of this nature is concerned, the basis for determining whether the objects of the gift are sufficiently certain is to consider *whether it is possible to say of at least one person that he or she satisfies the condition or description.* This test which is less rigorous than the test for discretionary trusts was laid down in *Re Allen* (1953) and endorsed in *Re Barlow's WT* (1979). Here T had directed her executors to allow any member of her family or any friends of hers to purchase any paintings belonging to her at prices below their true value. Ordinarily, 'friend' would be regarded as a conceptually uncertain word. However, Browne-Wilkinson J held that friendship as employed here was no more than a condition or qualification for exercising the option to purchase and that once there were any persons who on account of their long-standing social connection with T fitted the description, the gift would be valid.

Formalities for the creation of trusts

The process of establishing the existence and terms of a trust is greatly facilitated where it is embodied in writing or supported by documentary evidence. However, equity did not at the outset require writing or any other formalities were necessary for the creation of express trusts.

Statute has since intervened with the result that writing is now a formal requirement with regard to both *inter vivos* and *testamentary trusts*. The most important of these provisions are set out in the Law of Property Act (LPA) 1925 (*inter vivos* trusts) and the Wills Act 1893 (testamentary trusts).

Inter vivos trusts

Trusts of pure personality
Where the subject-matter of a proposed trust is personality, writing is not required for the declaration of trust to be effective (see *Petty v Petty* (1853); *Re Kayford* (1975) and *Paul v Constance*).

Trusts of land
For centuries, land was the most valuable asset a person could own and a high premium has traditionally been placed on the prevention of fraud in dealings connected with land. To this end, it has been a feature of English law since the enactment of the Statute of Frauds 1677 that must either be done in writing or supported by written evidence.

With specific reference to trusts of land, s 53(1)(b) LPA provides that: a declaration of trust respecting land or an interest in land must be manifested and proved by some writing signed by some person able to declare the trust.

This requirement is especially important to purchasers of land held on trust in the light of the provision in s 14(2) Trustee Act 1925 that the purchase price must be paid to at least two trustees. This is because it helps ensure that such purchasers are aware that the land is held on trust and reduces the risk of inadvertent non-compliance with the 'two trustee' rule.

It is noteworthy that the actual declaration need not be in writing. A document acknowledging a prior oral declaration will be admissible under s 53(1)(b) if executed before the date legal action is taken to enforce the declaration (see *Forster v Hale* (1798); *Childers v Childers* (1857) and *Mcblain v Cross* (1871)).

The relevant document must show that a trust was intended but it need not contain all the terms of the trust (see *Re Tyler's Fund Trust* (1967)).

The proper party to sign the document is the person able to declare the trust (ie the owner of the land or interest therein which is the subject matter of the trust). The signature of an agent will not suffice (see *Re Northcliffe* (1925)).

Given that the requirement of writing was introduced to prevent fraud, the courts have been prepared to dispense with it in cases where they find that it is being used as a cloak for fraud. Thus in *Rochefoucauld v Bousted* (1897) A was the mortgagor of property in Ceylon. The mortgagee sold the property to B who then sold it for a larger sum than he paid for it. A claimed that B held the property on trust for her and was liable to account to her for the proceeds of the subsequent sale. There was no written evidence of the trust but the court found sufficient proof that B had orally undertaken to hold the property on trust for A and concluded that it would be fraudulent for B to deny the trust because writing was absent. To prevent this, the undertaking was enforced as an *express trust*.

In more recent cases such as *Bannister v Bannister* (1948) and *Hodgson v Marks* (1971), the courts have preferred to give effect to verbal undertakings to hold land on trust, not as express trusts but as *resulting or constructive trusts*, relying on the fact that s 53(2) LPA provides that the requirement of writing does not extend to these categories of trusts.

Subsisting equitable interests

The owner of an equitable interest in property (whether arising under a trust or by other means) may wish to transfer the benefit of his interest to some other person. This can be done in three ways:

- by declaring himself a trustee of the interest for the benefit of the donee;
- by assigning the interest to some other person to hold on trust for the donee;
- by assigning his interest directly to the intended donee.

In this regard s 53(1)(c) LPA provides that:

a disposition of an equitable interest or trust subsisting at the time of the disposition must be in writing, signed by the person disposing of the same or by agent thereunto lawfully authorised in writing.

The requirement of writing in this context stems from the fact that equitable interests are intangible which means that unless successive transfers are well documented, spurious claims are likely to proliferate and trustees as well as potential purchasers of such interests will find it difficult to ascertain where equitable ownership lies in any given case.

Points of divergence between s 53(1)(b) and s 53(1)(c)

- Under s 53(1)(c) the disposition must itself be in writing. Evidence in writing of an prior oral disposition will not suffice.
- The document disposing of the equitable interest need not be signed by the owner himself but can be signed by his agent.
- Section 53(1)(c) applies with equal force to equitable interests in *personality* (see *Grey v IRC* (1960) and *Vandervell v IRC* (1967)); and in *land* (see *Ivin v Blake* (1993)).
- The inclusion of the word *subsisting* in s 53(1)(c) means that where a person who owns a legal estate or interest in property declares a trust of such property this will not be governed by this provision. Such a declaration will operate to create a new equitable interest rather than to dispose of a subsisting equitable interest. If, however, the property in question is land or an interest in land, such a declaration will be subject to the requirement in s 53(1)(b).

Which dispositions fall within the ambit of s 53(1)(c)?

There has been a certain amount of debate concerning the types of arrangements which can properly be regarded as dispositions for the purpose of s 53(1)(c). Many of the cases in which the courts have had to pronounce on such arrangements have involved disputes over the payment of stamp duty and other taxes. These cases will be dealt with under the following headings.

Assignment of equitable interest to trustee

Where S, the owner of an equitable interest sets out to assign this interest to B, or to T to hold on trust for B, such an assignment will be a disposition within the meaning of s 53(1)(c) and will thus be void if it is not made in writing.

Direction to trustee to hold on trust for another party

Where S transfers property to which he is absolutely entitled to T as his nominee so that the legal title is vested in T but S remains beneficially entitled to the property, and S directs T at a later date to hold the property on trust for B, this direction is a disposition and must therefore be in writing. See *Grey v IRC*.

Transfer of legal title by trustee on the direction of the beneficiary

Where S after transferring property to T to hold as his nominee directs T to transfer the property *outright* to B (rather than to hold it on trust for B) it emerges from *Vandervell v IRC* that this will not be treated as a disposition. In effect, once T acting pursuant to S's instruction, effectively passes the legal title to B, there is no further need for S to divest himself of his equitable interest by means of a written disposition in B's favour.

Declaration of new trust by trustee with consent of beneficial owner

Where T who is holding property on a resulting trust for S declares himself a trustee of the property for B's benefit with S's knowledge and consent, it appears from *Re Vandervell (No 2)* (1974) that this is not treated as a disposition under s 53(1)(c). Instead, it operates to extinguish the resulting trust in favour of S and replace it with a trust in favour of B even where S has executed no document divesting himself of his equitable interest.

Oral contract to assign a subsisting equitable interest

Where S the owner of an equitable interest agrees orally to assign this interest to B for valuable consideration, judicial opinions are divided on the applicability of s 53(1)(c) to such an arrangement. A situation of this nature arose in *Oughtred v IRC* (1960), which involved an oral contract between a mother and her son under which the son agreed to surrender his reversionary interest in a sizeable block of shares in a private company to the mother. The issue at stake here was whether *ad valorem* stamp duty was payable on the transaction. The Court of Appeal considered the oral agreement to be enforceable by specific performance with the result that from the date it was made the son held his equitable interest equitable interest in the shares on trust for his mother without any need to comply with s 53(1)(c). *Ad valorem* duty was assessed on instruments transferring beneficial ownership of shares and was not payable here as beneficial ownership passed to the mother under the oral agreement. The House of Lords by a majority rejected this view, holding on policy grounds that duty was payable in respect of the present transaction, without addressing the crucial issue of whether the son's equitable interest had passed under the oral agreement. Significantly however, the dissenting Law Lords (Lords Cohen and Radcliffe) endorsed the position adopted by the Court of Appeal (See also *Re Holt's Settlement* (1969); *DHN Food Distributors v Tower Hamlets LBC* (1976); *Chinn v Collins* (1981)).

Declaration of self as trustee

Where T holds property on trust for S and S proceeds to declare himself a trustee of his interest for B's benefit will s 53(1)(c) apply? It appears from *Grainge v Wilberforce* (1889) and the judgment of Upjohn J in *Grey v IRC* that the effect of such a declaration with nothing more is that C will be in a position to require S to convey Blackacre according to his directions with B dropping out of the picture. In effect such an arrangement is more in the nature of a disposition as contemplated by s 53(1)(c) than an ordinary declaration.

The position is less clear-cut where S, in declaring the trust, reserves for himself some active responsibilities as a trustee (for example, where the trust in question is a discretionary trust in favour of B and other beneficiaries). It has been suggested on the authority of *Re Lashmar* (1891) that in such an event the trustee does not drop out of the picture which makes the arrangement more akin to a declaration than a disposition. This is disputed by Green (1984) 47 MLR pp 395-399 who contends that it is more appropriate to treat it as a disposition which must therefore be in writing in accordance with s 53(1)(c).

Testamentary trusts

Statutory formalities for testamentary gifts

A person who wishes to dispose of his property on his death is ordinarily required to execute a *will*. Such a will is required to comply with the formalities in s 9 Wills Act 1837 as amended by s 17 Administration of Justice Act 1982. It must be in writing and signed by the testator or some other person by his direction and in his presence. This signature must be made or acknowledged by the testator before two or more witnesses and each witness must sign the will or acknowledge his signature in the testator's presence.

This requirement applies not only where the testator wishes the property to pass outright to the intended beneficiary but also where he wishes it to be held on trust for the beneficiary. The terms of the trust must be set out in the will or in a codicil or in some other document incorporated by reference into the will.

Secret trusts

Occasions have often arisen in which a testator (T) has devised or bequeathed property in his will to a devisee (D) or a legatee (L) and duly notifies D or L that he wishes him to hold the property on trust for the benefit of a third party (B) who is not mentioned in the will. In other instances, T leaves property to D or L, but extracts an undertaking from D or L that when D or L dies he shall in turn leave the property to B, as happened in *Ottaway v Norman* (1972).

In either of these instances any claim by B will fail under the common law, since his interest has not been specifically provided for in T's will. By contrast, equity has shown itself to be less rigid in its approach to situations of this nature and will in appropriate instances compel D or L as the case may be to give effect to T's intention by imposing a *secret trust* on him.

Secret trusts are capable of arising not only where wills are involved, but also where T in our example refrains from making a will because the person to whom the property will devolve if T dies intestate promises to hold it on trust for B once T dies (see *Stickland v Aldridge* (1804)).

Fully secret trusts distinguished from half secret trusts

A *fully secret trust* (FST) arises where no indication is given in the will of the existence of the trust such that on the face of it the person to whom the property is left is to take beneficially; for example, where T's will contains a legacy of £10,000 in favour of L, but before or after executing the will directs L to hold the sum on trust for B when he receives it.

A *half secret trust* (HST) arises where it is clear on the face of the will that the person to whom the property is left is to hold on trust but the beneficiaries are not disclosed in the will; for example, where T leaves £10,000 to L with a directions to hold the sum on trust for objects communicated to him and before executing the will T instructs L to hold the sum on trust for B.

Note It is not in every instance where T specifies that L should apply the property in a manner communicated elsewhere that a HST comes into being. T might for example leave £10,000 to L stating in the will that he does so 'in full confidence' that L will apply this sum towards the objects which I have communicated to him (or employing other words which can be construed as equally *precatory*). It would seem that this will not constitute a HST, since L can argue with justification on the strength of *Lambe v Eames* and similar cases that a trust has not arisen on the face of the will. There might nevertheless be a FST provided the communication referred to in the will was framed in sufficiently imperative terms to impose a trust (see *Re Spencer's Will* (1887)).

Conditions for the enforcement of the FST
As explained by Brightman J in *Ottaway v Norman*, three conditions must be present before a fully secret trust will be upheld, namely: intention, communication and acceptance.

Intention
T must employ words which evince a clear intention on his part to impose a binding obligation on L to hold the property left to him on trust for B. If the words suggest that T intended to leave it open to L to decide whether or not to apply the property for B's benefit there will be no FST. In *Mccormick v Grogan* (1869), T left all his property to L in his will stating in an accompanying letter addressed to L that 'I leave it entirely in your good judgment to do as you think I would if living'. It was held that there was no FST. There was also no trust in *Re Snowden* (1979), where T left her residual estate to her brother stating that he would know what to do and asking that he should 'see to everybody and look after the division for her'.

Communication
The relevant intention must be communicated by T to L during T's lifetime. The communication may be made either before or after executing the will. If T dies without communicating his intention, L will be entitled to take the property beneficially even if evidence later emerges establishing that T in fact intended L to be a trustee (see *Wallgrave v Tebbs* (1855)).

The terms of the trust (especially the nature/identity of the property and the intended beneficiaries) should ordinarily be specified in the communication. This means, for instance, that where T communicates his intention to create the trust to L but does nothing more in his lifetime to communicate its terms and a letter containing the terms comes to light after T's death (as happened in *Re Boyes* (1884)), the FST will fail. At the same time it was emphasised by Kay J in *Re Boyes* that if a letter setting out the terms was handed over by T to L, even if it was contained in a sealed envelope not to be opened by L until T's death, this would be treated as *constructive communication* and L would be bound by the trust (see also *Re Keen* (1937)).

Acceptance
Effect will be given to the FST only where L has accepted that he will carry out the trust. Where there is no such acceptance because T's intention was not communicated L will be entitled to take the property beneficially (*Wallgrave v Tebbs*).

The position is less certain where S has communicated his intention to L who has declined to hold as trustee but T nevertheless leaves the property to him. One possibility is that L will hold on a resulting trust for T's estate on the premise that the communication has negatived any intention to make an outright gift. Another possibility is that L will be entitled to take beneficially, since it is equally arguable that by leaving the property to L, knowing full well that L had declined the trust, T was evincing an intention that L should take beneficially.

Acceptance will in most cases be *express*, but the courts are sometimes prepared to imply acceptance on the basis of tacit acquiescence, where T's intention has been communicated to L and he remains silent (see *Moss v Cooper* (1861) and *Ottaway v Norman*).

Once the details of the intended trust have been communicated to and accepted by L, any additions to the subject-matter or objects will only be enforceable if duly communicated and accepted. In *Re Colin Cooper* (1939), T bequeathed £5,000 to two persons, stating in the will that they were to hold on trust. The terms of the trust had been made known to and accepted by them before the will was executed. T later executed a codicil increasing the legacy to £10,000 without notifying L1 and L2. It was held that the first £5,000 was subject to the secret trust but not the second £5,000. This case was concerned with a HST but the principle enunciated would seem equally applicable to FSTs.

Acceptance where there are two or more legatees/devisees
Where T makes a will which on its face passes property to L1 and L2 but intends that they should hold it as co-trustees for B, both L1 and L2 will be bound by the trust provided the intention has been duly communicated to and accepted by them.

Where the trust is communicated to L1 alone, there is the problem of whether his acceptance is binding on L2 or whether L2 will take a half share of the property beneficially. This problem was addressed in *Re Stead* (1900), by Farwell J who signified that the position would depend on whether it was contemplated in the will that L1 and L2 would hold as *tenants in common* or *joint tenants*.

Tenants in common

Where the property passes under the will to L1 and L2 as tenants in common (eg 'To L1 and L2 in equal shares'), each of them is treated as having a separate and distinct, albeit undivided interest in the property. Accordingly, where L1 alone accepts that he will hold it on trust, *Re Stead* establishes that L2 will not be bound by the trust.

Joint tenants

Where the intention is that L1 and L2 shall hold the property as joint tenants (eg 'To L1 and L2 jointly' or 'To L1 and L2') a questionable distinction has been drawn by Farwell J between communication/acceptance before the execution of the will and communication/acceptance after its execution.

If the gift is to L1 and L2 jointly and *before* the will was executed L1 accepts that he and L2 would hold it on trust, L2 is bound by the trust. By contrast if the communication/acceptance occurred *after* the will was executed, L2 will not be deemed to be bound by the trust. Farwell J was not entirely convinced of the merit of this distinction and it has been criticised by B Perrins in 88 LQR 237 and by textbook writers like Parker and Mellows, and Pettitt. Significantly, however, no later case has overturned the decision in *Re Stead* and it still represents the law.

Conditions for the enforcement of the HST

Whereas FSTs have been judicially enforced for many years, the courts were less forthcoming in according recognition to HSTs until comparatively recently. It was only in *Blackwell v Blackwell* (1929) that it was decisively settled by the House of Lords that it would enforce such trusts. In this case the court upheld a legacy of £12,000 given by T to L1-L5 on trust 'for purposes indicated by me to them'.

Intention, communication and acceptance are as material to HSTs as they are to FSTs.

Intention

A HST is by definition one in which the existence of the trust is manifest in the will. A HST is therefore incapable of arising unless the material intention to impose the trust is proclaimed with sufficient certainty by T in the will itself.

Communication

A HST will fail if it has not been effectively communicated to L. The question of what amounts to effective communication was considered at some length in *Re Keen* where T bequeathed £10,000 to his executors 'to be held on trust and disposed of by them ... as may be notified by me'. Before executing the will, T handed them an envelope listing the objects of the trust, directing them not to open it till he died. It was held:

- that the words 'as may be notified by me' suggested that the objects would be communicated after the will was executed, whereas the handing over of the sealed envelope was in effect communication before execution and that the trust would fail on account of this inconsistency;
- that even if the mode of communication adopted was consistent with the future communication referred to in the will, in the case of HSTs was that the objects must be communicated *before* the trust was executed. The present trust also failed on this ground. This prior communication rule was also accepted in *Blackwell v Blackwell* and was confirmed more recently in *Re Bateman's WT* (1970). This is somewhat surprising given that FSTs are deemed enforceable, whether the communication of the testator's intention was before or after execution. J Mee pointed out in [1992] Conv 202, that this distinction between FSTs and HSTs has been 'almost universally reviled' and this is borne out by the criticisms of the prior acceptance rule by others like Holdsworth (1937) 53 LQR 501; and LA Sheridan (1951) 67 LQR 413.

Acceptance

As far as acceptance is concerned, the applicable rules are similar for both types of secret trust. The only noteworthy points concern the situation under a HST where two or more persons are named in the will as co-trustees. The basic rule here is that they will hold the property as joint tenants so that the aspect of the decision in *Re Stead* dealing with the position of tenants in common is immaterial to HSTs. Moreover because of the requirement that communication must be made before the will is executed it follows that acceptance by any one of the co-trustees will invariably bind the others.

The basis for the enforcement of secret trusts

Fraud

The traditional justification which has long been advanced for upholding secret trusts, even though they do not comply with the formalities laid down by statute is *the prevention of fraud*. In *Mccormick v Grogan* for instance, Lord Westbury observed that 'the jurisdiction which is invoked here is a jurisdiction which is founded altogether on personal fraud'; while in *Blackwell*, Lord Sumner explained that 'for the prevention of fraud, equity fastens on the conscience of the legatee, a trust'.

The difficulty with this approach is that the character of the fraudulent design which warrants the enforcement of secret trusts is not entirely clear.

One view associates fraud with *unjust enrichment*, and proceeds on the premise that giving effect to the trust enables the legatee or devisee to take the property beneficially, thereby unjustly enriching himself. See eg *Drakeford v Wilkes* (1747) and *Mccormick v Grogan*. This explanation is, however, open to question on two grounds.

* It has been argued that if the paramount consideration is to prevent unjust enrichment all that is required would be to direct the property to be held on a resulting trust for the testator.
* Even if unjust enrichment provides a rationale for enforcing a FST, the same is not true of a HST which affords little scope for the legatee/devisee to claim the property beneficially.

An alternative explanation put forward by the courts is that the fraud stems not from the possibility of unjust enrichment but from the very fact that unless the trust is upheld, the *wishes of the testator* will be thwarted and the beneficiaries will be deprived of their entitlement. See eg *Riordan v Bannon* and *Re Fleetwood* (1880) and the judgements of Viscount Sumner and Lord Buckmaster in *Blackwell v Blackwell*.

This explanation is favoured by Dr Hodge, who maintained in [1980] Conv 341 that the prevention of fraud, as thus perceived, is equally material whether one is dealing with a FST or a HST.

By contrast, others such as Oakley (*Constructive Trusts* p 118) consider it impossible to regard this argument as a valid justification for recognising secret trusts. He maintains that it is inappropriate to refer to the terms of the secret trust as the wishes of the testator and to describe those entitled under the secret trust as beneficiaries unless evidence of the terms of the trust are admitted contrary to the Wills Act; and concludes that 'it is not possible to use as justification for admitting evidence contrary to the provisions of the Act, facts which can only be proven if such evidence is admissible'.

The 'Dehors' theory

In the light of the unresolved difficulties inherent in the fraud theory an alternative explanation has gained widespread acceptance among judges and academic commentators. This is that contrary to initial appearances, they are not trusts created by will but arise *dehors* (ie outside and independent of) the will. According to Lord Warrington in *Blackwell*, 'what is enforced is not a trust imposed by will, but one arising from acceptance by the legatee of a trust communicated to him by the testator'. See also statements to the same effect by Dankwerts J in *Re Young* (1951) and Megarry VC in *Re Snowden*.

According to this theory, the declaration of the trust is *inter vivos*, consisting of the communication and acceptance which occur in the testator's lifetime. Accordingly, it need not comply with the formalities of the Wills Act. The relevance of the will in the present connection is that it operates to *vest* the property in the legatee/devisee thereby enabling the beneficiary to enforce it against him.

Two notable cases serve to illustrate how far the courts are prepared to go in their acceptance of the dehors theory, namely:

- *Re Young* which decided that despite s 15 Wills Act (which precludes a witness to a will from taking a benefit under it) a beneficiary under a secret trust would not lose his benefit simply because he witnessed the testator's will.

  Note that if it is the legatee/devisee who attests the will Oakley (p 120) suggests that in the case of a FST, since the legatee/devisee takes beneficially on the face of the will the trust will fail. But where a HST is involved once the will makes it clear that the legatee/devisee is to take as a trustee, it appears from cases like *Cresswell v Cresswell* (1868) that the trust will not fail.

- *Re Gardner (No 2)* which held that where a beneficiary under a secret trust died before the testatrix, this would not extinguish the beneficiary's interest as would happen if the trust arose under the will rather than outside it. This has, however, been roundly criticised in that although the trust had undoubtedly been declared the property had not vested at the time of the beneficiaries death and equity would deem it to have lapsed.

  Note that if a legatee/devisee predeceases the testator, in the case of a FST, the position as stated by Cozens-Hardy LJ in *Re Maddock* (1902) is that the gift will lapse. In the case of a HST, it seems on the authority of such cases as *Re Smirthwaite* that the trust will not lapse because the trustee who has been named in the will dies before it takes effect.

Are secret trusts express trusts or constructive trusts?

There has been considerable debate regarding the status of secret trusts.

Commentators such as Pettitt and Oakley favour the view that secret trusts should be treated as *express* trusts. This accords with the proposition that they are *inter vivos* declarations of trust which arise *dehors* the will.

By contrast, several, judges such as Brightman J in *Ottaway v Norman*, Nourse J in *Re Cleaver* (1981) and Morritt J in *Re Dale* (1993) have expressed the view that secret trusts are *constructive trusts* and this has been echoed by Hodge in [1990] Conv 341. This is consistent with the notion that secret trusts are enforced in order to prevent fraud.

Others like Sheridan (1951) 67 LQR and Hayton and Marshall suggest that HSTs are undoubtedly express trusts, whereas FSTs which have been traditionally associated with the fraud theory can properly be regarded as constructive trusts.

The express-constructive trust debate is especially relevant where the subject-matter of a secret trust is *land*. The issue at stake is whether the communication of the trust must be evidenced in writing in accordance with s 53(1)(c) LPA. Such writing will be needed if the trust is express but not if it is a constructive. The position has not yet been decisively resolved by the courts. However, it has been held in *Re Baillie* (1886) that a HST was unenforceable in the absence of written evidence. By contrast, in the more recent case of *Ottaway v Norman*, the court upheld a FST purely on the strength of oral evidence without paying any heed to the possibility that s 53(1)(c) might be applicable.

Revision Notes

The three certainties

Any declaration of trust must be certain in three material respects: intention, subject-matter and objects.

Intention

This presupposes that the settlor is intent on imposing a legal (as distinct from purely moral) obligation on the party to whom he transfers his property and must be reflected in the words of the declaration, eg to T on trust for B.

Use of the word 'trust' is not absolutely necessary since other words may be construed as equally imperative in substance (*Re Kayford*, eg I hereby direct (instruct, require etc) T to hold for the benefit of B.

Where the words used in making the gift are construed as *precatory* (wish, hope, desire, request, entreat etc) this will not according to the present state of the law operate to create a trust unless there is some other indication that this was the donees intention (*Lambe v Eames*) and allied cases. Contrast with the position before the latter part of the 19th century.

In certain instances, the courts are able to deduce the material intention to create a trust from a combination of words and conduct or by having regard to surrounding circumstances, where words alone would be indecisive (*Paul v Constance*). This liberal approach also manifest in *Re Kayford; Re English & American Ins Co* but contrast with *Re Multi Guarantee Co*.

Subject-matter

The property to be held on trust must be certain, otherwise the trust will fail. Uncertainty regarding the trust property most commonly arises:

* where the terms used to define or describe it are ambiguous or imprecise (*Palmer v Simmonds* – but contrast with the more flexible attitude in *Re Golay's WT*);
* where the property is given to one person with an imprecise gift over of the surplus in favour of another (*Sprange v Barnard*).

Opinion is divided on whether a trust will fail for uncertainty where the property consists of an undifferentiated part of a larger quantity (*Re London Wine Co* (it will); *Hunter v Moss* (it will not)).

Unless the interests to be held by the beneficiaries are certain the trust is also liable to fail (*Boyce v Boyce; Curtis v Ripon*).

Objects

A private trust must be for the benefit of persons and not for abstract impersonal purposes. The trust is judged to be valid only where such persons are certain (*Re Endacott; Re Astor*).

The requirement of certainty is especially problematic with regard to *class gifts*. The difficulties may arise from *conceptual uncertainty; evidential uncertainty;* or from the magnitude of the task involved in *ascertaining* the identity and whereabouts of members.

Where *fixed trusts* are concerned *IRC v Broadway Cottages* prescribes that all members of the class must be ascertainable (the comprehensive list test).The class must therefore be certain in conceptual and evidential terms.

Where *discretionary trusts* are concerned a less stringent test applies which prescribes that it must be possible to say of any given person that he is or is not within the class (the 'is-is not' test): Accordingly, there must be conceptual, but not necessarily evidential certainty (*Mcphail v Doulton; Re Baden*).

Where a trust would otherwise be liable to fail for conceptual uncertainty this may be cured by the settlor providing that the meaning of the terms are to be determined by specified persons (*Re Tuck's ST*).

A trust which is conceptually certain may nevertheless fail on the ground of *administrative unworkability* (*Mcphail v Doulton; R v District Auditor ex p West Yorkshire CC*).

A trust of the type which was enforced in *Burrough v Philcox* will for purposes of the requirement of certainty be treated as a discretionary trust, but in default of selection will be subject to the test for certainty applicable to fixed trust.

Gifts which are expressed to be subject to a *condition precedent* are valid once it can be said of any one person that he satisfies the condition even if the position is unclear with regard to other persons (*Re Allen; Re Barlow*). This represents a less stringent criterion than the test for discretionary trusts.

Formalities for the declaration of trusts

Inter vivos trusts

Declaration of trust of *pure personality* requires no formality.

A *declaration of trust relating to land* must be evidenced in writing (s 53(1)(b)). This requirement may, however, be dispensed with in order to avert fraud (*Rochefoucould v Bousted; Bannister v Bannister; Hogson v Marks*).

Where the subject-matter of the proposed trust is an *equitable interest* (including an equitable interest in *personality*) it must in common with other dispositions of equitable interests be in writing by virtue of s 53(1)(c).

The question of whether a given arrangement constitutes a disposition for the purpose of s 53(1)(c) has arisen in the following contexts:

- a direction by a beneficiary to a trustee to hold his equitable interest on trust for a third party (*Grey v IRC*);
- transfer of the legal title to a third party on beneficiary's instruction (*Vandervell v IRC*);
- declaration of new trust by trustee with beneficiary's consent (*Re Vandervell (No 2)*);
- oral contract by beneficiary to assign subsisting equitable interest (*Oughtred v IRC*);
- declaration by beneficiary that he will hold his equitable interest on trust for a third party (*Grainge v Wilberforce; Grey v IRC; Re Lashmar*).

Testamentary trusts

A trust intended to take effect on the death of the person creating it must ordinarily comply with the requirements of s 9 Wills Act (1837)/ s 17 Administration of Justice Act (1982). Such a trust may nevertheless enforced as a *fully-secret* or *half-secret* trust even where these requirements are not observed.

Fully secret trusts

A FST is one which is not declared on the face of the will but is deemed enforceable on the strength of intention, communicated and acceptance present before or after execution of the will. Note in this connection that:

- the material intention must be to impose an imperative obligation on the legatee or devisee to whom the property is left in the will: (*Mccormick v Grogan; Re Snowden*);

- All the terms of the trust must be communicated, but the communication may be actual or constructive (*Re Rees*). Once such terms have been duly communicated, any subsequent changes in the property or beneficial interests must also be communicated or will not bind the legatee/devisee (*Re Colin Cooper*);
- Acceptance will usually be express, but silence may sometimes be deemed to signify acceptance (*Ottaway v Norman; Moss v Cooper*);
- Where there are two or more legatees/devisees named in the will and once accepts to carry out the trust, the issue of whether the others are also bound by the trust falls to be determined according to the principles in *Re Stead*.

Half secret trusts

A HST arises where the will specifies that property is to be held on trust but does not specify the objects of the trust which are communicated to the trustees named in the will by other means.

The communication rules with regard to the HST differ materially from those applicable to the FST on account of the decision in *Blackwell v Blackwell; Re Keen* and *Re Bateman* that a HST is liable to fail unless the objects have been communicated before execution of the will.

The *dehors* theory

Secret trusts were originally upheld on the footing that they were a necessary mechanism for the prevention of fraud which might be occasioned by a strict insistence on compliance with the formalities of the Wills Act: see eg Lord Westbury in *Mccormick v Grogan*. This rational for the enforcement of the secret trust is no longer regarded as apposite especially with regard to the HST. It has now been superseded by the view that secret trusts arise *dehors* the will and need not comply with the statutory formalities for testamentary dispositions (*Blackwell v Blackwell; Re Young; Re Snowden; Re Gardner (No 2)*).

Express or constructive trusts?

Divergent opinions have been expressed as to whether secret trusts are express trusts or constructive trusts. The fraud theory which originally underpinned the enforcement of FSTs tends to cast them in the role of constructive trusts; whereas the *dehors* theory is predicted on the premise that secret trusts are *inter vivos* express trusts. The matter is not entirely academic especially where land is involved, because

s 53(1)(b) comes into play if they are express but not if they are constructive trusts. In this connection, contrast *Ottaway v Norman* with *Re Baillie*.

3 The constitution of trusts

You should be familiar with the following areas:

- the essential connection between the constitution of trusts and their enforceability
- the significance of the maxim that equity will not perfect an imperfect gift in the context of the constitution of trusts
- the applicable rules where a settlor declares himself a trustee of property already vested in him
- the formal procedures necessary for the constitution of a trust where the settlor seeks to transfer property to other persons to hold on trust
- the various circumstances in which a trust is capable of enforcement in equity or at law, where these procedures have not been fully complied with

Vesting of property as a condition for enforcement of trusts

Once a prospective donor or settlor declares his intention to make an outright gift or create a trust, the enforceability of the gift or trust depends primarily on whether or not it is completely constituted. A gift or trust is deemed to be *completely constituted* from the time the property becomes *vested* in the donee or in the trustee on behalf of the beneficiary.

Where such vesting has occurred, it is no longer open to the donor or settlor to assert any beneficial claim to the property. See *Re Bowden* (1936). For his part the beneficiary/donee acquires a proprietary interest, which the courts will enforce against the donor/settlor as well as the trustee (if any), regardless of whether the beneficiary/donor has furnished any *consideration* in return (see eg *Jeffreys v Jeffreys* (1841); *Paul v Paul* (1882)).

Conversely, where the settlor declares his intention to make a gift or create a trust but the declaration is not accompanied or followed by vesting, the gift/trust is said to be *incompletely constituted*. The declaration may be enforceable against the trustee by a decree of specific performance or the award of damages, if the intended beneficiary furnished consideration. Where no consideration has been furnished the operative principle in this regard, as affirmed in the leading case of *Milroy v Lord* (1862) is that *equity will not assist a volunteer to perfect an imperfect gift*. Here S executed a voluntary deed purporting to transfer shares in L Bank to T to hold on trust for B, the plaintiff. The transfer had to be registered by L Bank before the shares would vest in T. To this end S executed a power of attorney authorising T to take the necessary steps to effect the registration which T failed to do before S died. It was held that B as a volunteer acquired no enforceable interest under this incompletely constituted trust.

Declaration of self as trustee

Where a prospective settlor chooses to declare himself a trustee of his property for the benefit of another, the property will in the ordinary course already be vested in him. Accordingly, the trust is completely constituted immediately the declaration is made. The immediate constitution of the trust in such circumstances will not be affected by the fact that at the material time, the intended beneficiary is unaware of the declaration (see *Middleton v Pollock* (1876); *Standing v Bowring* (1885)).

Before a beneficiary can enforce a trust on this basis, the court must be satisfied, having regard to the settlor's words (or his words and conduct as in *Paul v Constance*) that his intention is to hold the property on trust. Where the material intention is to transfer property to a trustee to hold on trust, but the transfer is ineffective, as in *Milroy v Lord*, it will not be enforced by treating it as a declaration by the settlor of himself as trustee. Similarly, an ineffective outright gift is not enforceable by treating the donor as a trustee (see *Jones v Lock* (1865); *Richards v Delbridge* (1874) and *Hemmens v Wilson Browne* (1993)).

Finally, where there are statutory formalities governing the declaration of the trust, these must be duly observed by the settlor. In particular, where the property concerned is land, effect will be given to the declaration only if it is in writing or evidenced in writing as required by s 53(1)(b) LPA.

Transfer to trustees and outright gifts

Where the settlor opts to create a trust with another person as the trustee (or to make an outright gift), it will be completely constituted when the property has been transferred to the trustee (or donee) in the manner prescribed by the law. The law requires different modes of transfer for various species of property.

Legal estates and interests

Freehold estates in land and leases for three or more years
A deed is required for the conveyance of freehold land as well as the creation or assignment of a lease, where the term involved is three or more years ss 52 and 54 LPA. The transferee's title may also need to be registered under the Land Registration Act (1925).

Chattels
These may be transferred either by a *deed of gift* or *delivery*. See *Cochrane v Moore* (1880); *Thomas v Times Books* (1966); and *Jaffa v Taylor Gallery* (1990). Regarding delivery, the case of *Re Cole* (1964) is noteworthy. Here H said to W when she came to live with him in a house bought and furnished by him that 'Its all yours'. It was held that there was no effective transfer of the contents of the house to W, since H's words and conduct were not sufficiently clear and unequivocal to amount to delivery.

Shares in a company
A transfer of shares requires the execution of an appropriate memorandum of transfer and registration in the company's share register as required by ss 182-183 Companies Act (1985) and s 1 Stock Transfer Act (1963).

Chooses in action
These can only be assigned at law through the procedure in s 136 LPA which provides that the assignment must be (i) absolute; (ii) in writing and (iii) communicated in writing to any party against whom it is to be enforced.

Copyright

Writing is needed for the effective assignment of copyrights (see s 90(3) Copyright Designs and Patents Act (1988)).

Equitable interests

Where the owner of an equitable interest seeks to make an outright gift of his interest or pass it to another person to hold on trust, s 53(1)(c) requires the disposition to be in writing.

The position where every effort is made to vest the property

In the eyes of the common law, property is incapable of vesting in a donee unless the appropriate formalities governing transfer have been complied with in the minutest detail. A less stringent approach has been adopted by equity which now regards a gift or trust as complete and enforceable by the beneficiary, once the settlor or donor has done everything in his power to divest himself of the property, even though the law requires some further task (such as registration) to be performed by a third party.

Thus if S, the owner of shares in a company or registered land seeks to make a gift of the shares or land to B and accordingly executes a transfer form in favour of B (or in favour of T on trust for B) which he hands over with the appropriate certificate, the transfer will be deemed to be effective in equity, even though legal title will not pass until it is duly registered (see *Re Rose* (1952) and *Mascall v Mascall* (1984)).

By contrast, where the court concludes that S has not yet done everything required by law to divest himself of his title (eg if official consent which is needed before he can proceed with the transfer has not yet been received), the gift will remain incomplete in the eyes of equity even if the transfer forms have been duly signed by him (see *Re Fry* (1946)). In effect, this gift will be unenforceable in equity, unless supported by consideration.

The position where vesting occurs by other means

Situation A

Where a property owner expresses an intention to make an immediate gift of the property but dies without having transferred it to the intended donee, the gift will ordinarily fail. However, if the owner's intention persists till his death and the property then becomes vested in the donee as his *personal representative*, this operates to perfect the gift, making it enforceable by the donee under the rule in *Strong v Bird* (1874) as affirmed by such cases as *Re Stewart* (1908), *Re Freeland* (1952) *Re Gonin* (1979) *Simpson v Simpson* (1973) and *Re Burrage* (1993).

Situation B

Where S declares his intention to transfer property to T to hold on trust for B and the property becomes vested in T in a different capacity, it emerges from *Re Ralli's WT* (1964) that *Strong v Bird* applies by analogy so that T will be able to enforce the trust on B's behalf. However, the court in *Re Ralli*, took no account of *Re Brooks' ST* (1939). In this earlier case, S had declared that he would transfer any property he might acquire in future to L Bank as trustee. When S subsequently became entitled to certain funds held by L bank under a different settlement, the court declined to enforce the declaration of trust against the property which had come to the bank in another capacity.

Situation C

Where X agrees with Y for valuable consideration that when Y dies, X will pass some benefit to B, and on Y's death his estate becomes vested in B as his personal representative, it appears on the authority of *Beswick v Beswick* (1968) that this will entitle B to enforce the benefit against X.

Circumstances in which a gift is enforceable without vesting

Marriage settlements

A settlement qualifies as a marriage settlement if three conditions outlined by Lord Goff in *Re Densham* (1975) are satisfied:

* it must have been made in anticipation of a forthcoming marriage or if made after the marriage must be the result of an agreement in anticipation of the marriage;

- in the case of a settlement made in anticipation of marriage it must be expressed to be conditional on the marriage taking place;
- its purpose must be to encourage or facilitate the marriage.

Where a settlor promises to settle property on trustees pursuant to a marriage settlement and the marriage takes place but vesting has not yet occurred, the trust is nevertheless enforceable in equity by the trustees on behalf of the husband and wife and their issue as seen from such cases as *Pullan v Koe* (1913). The reason for equity's willingness to assist in perfecting such gifts is that it regards the husband, wife and issue as having provided notional consideration by virtue of the marriage. The courts will also treat the children of either spouse from an earlier marriage as falling within the marriage consideration, provided they are satisfied that the interest of such children are closely linked with those of the issue of the marriage (see *AG v Jacobs-Smith* (1895)).

Where the marriage settlement provides that the property is to pass to the next-of-kin or some other third party if the husband and wife die without issue, such a third party is not deemed to come within the marriage consideration. Accordingly, the settlor's promise is not enforceable on behalf of the next-of-kin (see *Re D'Angibau* (1880); *Re Plumptre's Settlement* (1910); *Re Pryce* (1917)).

Enforcement of covenants to settle under the common law

Under the common law a covenant (ie *a promise under seal*) is enforceable by the award of *damages* against the covenantor even if the covenantee is a volunteer. By contrast, where no consideration has been furnished, the fact that a promise to transfer property is under seal will not ordinarily render it enforceable in equity by a decree of *specific performance* (see *Jefferys v Jefferys* (1841); *Re D'Angibau* and *Re Ellenborough* (1903)).

The common law attitude to the enforcement of covenants means that where A and B are parties to a voluntary deed under which A covenants to transfer property belonging to him to B, but fails to do so, B may recover damages against him (see *Cannon v Hartley* (1949)).

The position is less certain where a settlor, S, covenants to transfer property to a trustee, T, to hold on trust for B. It has been decided in the cases of *Re Pryce* (1917); *Re Kay's Settlement* (1939) and *Re Cook's ST* (1965), that where such a covenant is not performed, B cannot compel T to bring an action for damages while T for his part will be directed by the court not to do so. In *Re Cook* for instance, FC had upon the resettlement of family property covenanted with the trustees that if certain paintings belonging to him were sold, the proceeds would be paid to them to hold on trust for his children who were volunteers. After the paintings were sold it was held that the trustees were not to take any action to enforce the covenant, at law or in equity.

The position adopted in these cases has received some support from Lee in (1969) 85 LQR 236 but has been widely criticised by such commentators as Elliot (1960) 76 LQR 100; Hornby (1962) 78 LQR 228; Barton (1975) 91 LQR 236 and Meagher and Lehane (1976) 92 LQR 427. Elliot in particular draws attention to the fact that the year before *Re Pryce* was decided, the court had in *Re Cavendish-Browne* (1916) allowed T to claim damages on behalf of B, for the breach of a voluntary covenant by S to settle property left to her under two wills.

It is difficult to reconcile these conflicting authorities, although it is noteworthy that *Re Cavendish-Browne* involved a covenant to settle existing property whereas the other three cases involved covenants to settle after-acquired/future property. This suggests that while it is at least arguable that a trustee may claim damages in the case of a covenant to settle existing property or a definite sum of money, this remedy will not avail him where the covenant relates to future property.

Enforcement in equity where there is a trust of the covenant

Where a voluntary covenant by S to settle property on T on trust for B is breached, B might wish to enforce the covenant without relying on T. Equity provides a means of enforcement by B, if in the court's opinion, S intended that the right to sue on the covenant would be held on trust for B. Where this is the case, the right to sue is treated as a chose in action and the trust of this chose in action becomes completely constituted when the covenant is made, even if the property which S covenanted to settle on trust has not yet been transferred to T.

The leading case in which a covenant was enforced on this basis is *Fletcher v Fletcher* (1844). Here S, by a voluntary deed covenanted with T that within a year of S's death his executors would pay £60,000 to T on trust for B. T who had no wish to accept the trust sought directions from the court on the effect of the covenant. Although the trust of the property was not perfected, since the £60,000 had not yet been paid to T, it was held that from the date of the covenant there was an effective trust of the promise to convey, which B could enforce in equity by suing in his name. This decision is not entirely satisfactory as there was no clear evidence that S intended the right to sue to be held on trust. It is also noteworthy that in *Re Cook's ST*, Buckley J held that even if a trust of a covenant would be enforceable where the promise related to specific property or a specific sum of money (the £60,000 in *Fletcher*), this will not be the case where the promise concerns future property (as in *Re Cook*).

Gifts made in expectation of death (*donationes mortis causa*)

A *donatio mortis causa* (DMC) is a gift made in the donor's lifetime, which is expressed to be conditional upon and intended to take effect on his death. As Buckley J observed in *Re Beaumont* (1902), a DMC is amphibious in nature since it is not a regular *inter vivos* gift taking effect in the donor's lifetime nor is it a full-fledged testamentary gift which must comply with the requirements governing the testamentary disposition of property.

In *Cain v Moon* (1896), Russell CJ laid down three conditions which must exist for a DMC to be valid:

- the gift must have been made in contemplation of the donor's impending death;
- the donor must intend that the property is to revert to him if the contemplated death does not occur;
- the subject-matter of the gift (or the means of gaining control of it) must be delivered to the prospective donee.

Where the subject-matter of the DMC is a chattel and this has been delivered to the donee or trustee or he has been given the means of gaining access to it (eg the key to the place where it is kept), the gift is perfected as soon as the donor dies.

On the other hand, where the nature of the property is such that the steps taken by the donor would not constitute an effective *inter vivos* transfer, title to the property does not vest automatically in the donee/trustee on the donor's death but passes to the personal representatives of the donor. However, as Lindley LJ emphasised in *Re Dillon* (1890), 'The principle of not assisting a volunteer to perfect an incomplete gift does not apply to a DMC'. Equity will therefore intervene to compel the personal representatives to complete the transfer. For instance, if the subject-matter of the gift is a negotiable instrument which was not endorsed by the donor (as in *Re Mead* (1880)); or money in a deposit account (as in *Birch v Treasury Solicitor* (1951)); or a house in respect of which no deed was executed (as in *Sen v Headley* (1991)), the courts may be prepared to enforce it as a valid DMC.

Enforcement under the doctrine of proprietary estoppel

This doctrine contemplates that where a property owner has by his words or conduct represented to another person that the other person is entitled to an interest in the property, thereby inducing that other person to act to his detriment the owner will be *estopped* in equity from denying the truth of the representation. The doctrine has been invoked in cases where a land owner has made an incomplete transfer of an interest in land and the transferee has relied to his detriment on the belief that the transfer is effective. In such circumstances equity will compel the owner to transfer the property or do whatever else is necessary to give effect to the transferees interest as seen from such cases as *Dillwyn v Llewellyn* (1862) and *Pascoe v Turner* (1979).

Revision Notes

Where an intention to create a trust is accompanied by the vesting of the trust property in the proposed trustee, the trust is *completely constituted*. On the one hand, the intended beneficiary acquires a beneficial interest which the courts will enforce whether or not he has furnished any consideration (see *Jeffreys v Jeffreys* and *Paul v Paul*). On the other hand, the settlor becomes incapable of repudiating the trust and reclaiming beneficial ownership of the property (see *Re Bowden*).

Where a settlor expresses an intention to create a trust but the property involved has not become effectively vested in the proposed trustee, such an *incompletely constituted trust* will not ordinarily be enforceable by the beneficiary if he is a *volunteer* (see *Milroy v Lord*).

The settlor as trustee

Where a settlor declares himself a trustee, the trust will be constituted and therefore enforceable from the date of the declaration provided the trust property is vested in him (see *Middleton v Pollock*). But note that the settlor's initial intention must have been to declare himself a trustee and not to make an outright gift or transfer the property to other persons as trustees (see *Jones v Lock; Richards v Delbridge* etc).

Other persons as trustees

Where a settlor promises to create a trust with others as trustees, for the trust to be completely constituted, it has to be shown that the proper procedure for transfer has duly been adopted. Thus where the subject matter of the trust is:

- Freehold/leasehold for three or more years: by deed;
- Chattels: by deed or delivery (but note in particular the *Re Cole* scenario which is often favoured in examinations);
- shares: by memorandum of transfer and registration of transferee in company's books;
- a chose in action: copyright or subsisting equitable interest: by writing.

The insistence of the law that the formal procedures transfer must be strictly complied with before a transfer will be effective has been qualified by equity which treats an outright gift or trust as completely constituted where the settlor has done all that is required of him to transfer the property as in *Re Rose* and *Mascall v Mascall*.

Vesting by other means

Where a property owner promises to make an outright gift or transfer the property to trustees on trust without effectively transferring the property pursuant to this promise, it is clear from the rule in *Strong v Bird* as extended in *Re Ralli's WT* that if the property becomes vested in the trustee or donee by other means equity is prepared to treat the gift or trust as completely constituted and therefore enforceable.

Scope for enforcement where vesting has not occurred

Where the settlor has promised to transfer property to trustees but the property has not become vested in the trustees under any of the above headings, the trust may nevertheless be enforceable either at law or in equity in the following circumstances:

* Where the promise to transfer the property is made in the context of a *marriage settlement*, the spouses and issue of the marriage are notionally deemed to have furnished consideration and the trust is enforceable in their favour (see *Pullan v Koe*). But not in favour of others named as beneficiaries in the settlement (see *Re Plumptre's Settlement, Re Pryce* etc).
* Where the promise is in the form of a *covenant under seal* and the prospective beneficiary is a party to the covenant, he may enforce it at common law by obtaining damages (see *Cannon v Hartley*). If the covenant is made between the settlor and the trustee and the beneficiary is not a party, it has been held in *Re Cavendish-Browne* that the trustees may enforce it on behalf of the beneficiary, by seeking damages. Contrast, however, with *Re Pryce, Re Kay* and *Re Cook*, where the courts were not prepared to allow trustees to claim damages.
* Where there is a promise to transfer existing property or a sum of money to trustees on trust for a beneficiary and the property/money has not been transferred, the beneficiary may enforce the trust if the court is satisfied that the settlor intended *the benefit of the promise* (as well as the property itself) *to be held on trust* for the beneficiary (see *Fletcher v Fletcher*; note, however, *Re Cook*).

- Where a donor makes a gift in expectation of death (a *donatio mortic causa*) and in so doing does not comply with the procedure for a valid *inter vivos* transfer of the property concerned, equity will on the donor's death compel his personal representative to hold the property on trust for the donor donee (see eg *Re Mead*; *Birch v Treasury Solicitor* and in particular *Sen v Headley*).
- Under the doctrine of *proprietary estoppel* an imperfect gift may be enforced by whatever means is considered most appropriate as happened in such cases as *Dillwyn v Llewellyn* and *Pascoe v Turner*.

4 Resulting and constructive trusts

ESSENTIALS

You should be familiar with the following areas: ✓

- the operation of the presumptions of resulting trust and advancement and the rules governing their rebuttal

- the circumstances in which resulting trusts arise automatically

- the general nature of the constructive trust

- the rise and decline of the new model constructive trusts

- the main headings under which constructive trusts are traditionally enforced

- the relevance of resulting and constructive trusts in the context of disputes over the family home

- Lon Fuller's concept of the morality of law

- the main criticisms of natural law theory

Resulting trusts

Every express trust derives its force from a conscious declaration of trust by the settlor. There are, however, many situations in which trusts are capable of arising where no such declaration was made or where a trust has been declared but its terms do not cover the situation in question. A trust which arises in such circumstances may be either a *resulting trust* or a *constructive trust*. The enforceability of both types of trust is re-inforced by s 53(2) LPA which provides that they need not comply with the formalities which govern the creation of express trusts.

The general nature of resulting trusts

Where one person (A), transfers or directs the transfer of property to which he is beneficially entitled to another person (B) without expressly declaring B a trustee of the property, equity will in certain circumstances compel B to hold it on trust for A. A trust of this nature is known as a *resulting trust.*

The traditional premise upon which resulting trusts were imposed in the absence of any formal declaration of trust by A, was that A in transferring or directing the transfer of the property was *presumed* to have intended that B would hold it on trust for him.

In more recent times, it has come to be accepted that while some categories of resulting trust are enforced on the basis of the transferor's presumed or implied intention, others are capable of arising even where it is evident that he had no such intention. In effect, as Megarry VC explained in *Re Vandervell's Trusts (No 2)* (1974) there are two species of resulting trusts namely:

- *presumed (or implied) resulting trusts* which arise either where one person transfers property to or purchases property in the name of another without intending to make an outright gift; and
- *automatic resulting trusts* which are imposed where a settlor creates a trust that fails to dispose of his entire beneficial interest in the settled property. According to Megarry VC, this type of resulting trust 'does not depend on any intentions or presumptions but is the automatic consequence of [the settlor's] failure to dispose of what is vested in him'.

Presumed resulting trusts

Voluntary transfer of property

Personal property
Where A transfers personal property owned by him to B for no consideration, a resulting trust is presumed under which B must hold the property for A's benefit unless he can prove that A intended an outright gift to him (see *Standing v Bowring* (1885); *Re Howes* (1905); *Re Vinogradoff* (1935); *Re Muller* (1953) and *Thavorn v BCCI* (1985)).

Real property
Before 1925, a voluntary conveyance of real property by its owner also gave rise to a presumption of resulting trust in his favour. The position is no longer as clear-cut in the light of s 60(3) LPA (1925) which provides that:

in a voluntary conveyance, a resulting trust for the grantor shall not be implied, merely by reason that the property is not expressed to be conveyed for the use or benefit of the grantee.

Opinions differ regarding the true import of s 60(3). Some leading works such as Snell and Pettitt suggest that the effect of the provision is that on a voluntary conveyance of land, a resulting trust will no longer be presumed but will only be imposed if there is evidence that this was the grantor's intention. Others like Hanbury & Martin and Parker & Mellows favour the view that the provision 'does not preclude the implication of a resulting trust on general equitable principles'.

In the judicial sphere, the position seems to be equally uncertain. In *Hodgson v Marks* (1971) Russell LJ acknowledged that it was 'debatable' whether a resulting trust would be presumed on the voluntary conveyance of land, while in *Tinsley v Milligan* (1993) Lord Browne-Wilkinson stated that it was 'arguable' that the position regarding the presumption of resulting trust upon a voluntary conveyance of land had been altered by the 1925 legislation. Unhelpfully, however, neither judge took the opportunity to clarify the position and the law therefore remains unsettled.

Purchase in the name of another

Where A provides the money for the purchase of *real property* (whether freehold or leasehold) and directs that it should be conveyed or assigned to B or registered in B's name, a resulting trust will be presumed. B will be deemed to hold the legal title on trust for A, unless there are indications that A intended to make an outright gift to him. Note in this connection the dictum of Eyre CB in *Dyer v Dyer* (1788) as affirmed in more recent cases such as *Pettitt v Pettitt* (1970) and *Gross v French* (1975).

By the same token, where A pays for the purchase of *personal property* in the name of B, a resulting trust will also come into being, unless there is evidence of a contrary intention (see eg *Fowkes v Pascoe* (1875); *Shepherd v Cartwright* (1955); *Crane v Davis* (1981)).

Contributions

A resulting trust is capable of arising, not only where A provides the entire purchase money, but also where the money is contributed by A and B. This means in effect that:

- If A and B contribute towards the purchase of property and the conveyance is in B's name, the legal title will be vested in B but A and B will be entitled to equitable interests proportionate to their respective contributions (see *Bull v Bull* (1955); *Dewar v Dewar* (1975); *Sekhon v Alissa* (1989); *Harwood v Harwood* (1991); *Tinsley v Milligan* (1993) and *Garvin-Mack v Garvin-Mack* (1993)).

- If A and B contribute the purchase money and the property is conveyed to both, unless there is evidence to the contrary, a resulting trust will be presumed under which their respective beneficial interests will be determined by their contributions (see *Springette v Defoe* (1992) and *Tagoe v Layea* (1993)). It also emerges from *Springette* that if the property purchased is council property and A as a sitting tenant, is eligible for a discount under a 'right to buy' scheme, the discount will be treated as part of her contribution for the present purpose.

- If the property is purchased by means of a mortgage taken out by A and the property is conveyed in A's name, but B contributes substantially towards paying off the mortgage, a resulting trust will be presumed in B's favour (see *Moate v Moate* (1948); *Cowcher v Cowcher* (1972) and *Winkworth v Edward Baron Development Co* (1987)).

The presumption of advancement

The presumption of resulting trust which arises where A voluntarily transfers property to B or purchases property in B's name is reversed if A happens to be B's *husband* or *father* or stands *in loco parentis* to B. Traditionally, equity has taken the view that in such cases A has an obligation to provide for B, with the result that A will be presumed to have intended to make an outright gift to B of the property so transferred or purchased. The presumption which arises in this connection is known as the *presumption of advancement*.

Husband and wife

The presumption of advancement has long been recognised where a husband transfers property to his wife or purchases property in their joint names or in her name alone. The operation of this presumption was declared to be 'perfectly settled' by Malins VC in *Re Eykin's WT* (1877), and has been affirmed in a long line of cases such as *Thornley v Thornley* (1893); *Gascoigne v Gascoigne* (1918); and *Tinker v Tinker* (1970).

In the past few decades, however, wives have increasingly contributed in their own right to the upkeep of the family so that the same weight is no longer attached to the supposition that the husband is under an obligation to provide for his wife as in by-gone years. In response to this trend, the courts, while acknowledging that the presumption continues to operate in favour of wives, are more concerned with discovering the true intention of the spouses in each case and will only fall back on the presumption where there is no evidence of such intention. See the comments of Evershed MR in *Silver v Silver* (1958) and Lord Diplock in *Pettitt v Pettitt* (1970).

Mistresses

The presumption of advancement does not apply where a man transfers property to or purchases property in the name of his mistress (see *Soar v Foster* (1858); *Diwell v Farnes* (1959) and *Garvin-Mack v Garvin-Mack* (1993)).

Husbands

The presumption does not arise in favour of a husband where his wife transfers property to him or purchases property in his name or their joint names (see *Mercier v Mercier* (1903); *Pearson v Pearson* (1965); and *Heseltine v Heseltine* (1975)).

Father and legitimate child

The relationship between a father and his legitimate child is one which for centuries been held to give rise to a presumption of advancement where the father transfers property to the child or purchases property in the child's name (see *Lord Grey v Lady Grey* (1677); *Crabb v Crabb* (1834); *Re Roberts* (1946) and *Shepherd v Cartwright* (1955)).

Mothers

There is no corresponding presumption where mother and child are concerned, the rationale being that the duty to provide for a child ordinarily lay with the father (see *Re Devisme* (1863) and *Bennet v Bennet* (1879)). It was, however, accepted in *Bennett* that 'in the case of a mother it is easier to prove a gift than in the case of a stranger: in the case of a mother, very little evidence beyond the gift is wanted, there being very little motive required to induce a mother to make a gift to her child'.

A person in *loco parentis*

A person *in loco parentis* is one who according to Lord Eldon in *Ex p Pye* (1811) 'puts himself ... in the position of the person described as the lawful father of the child' (see also *Powys v Mansfield* (1837)).

Where A stands *in loco parentis* to B and either transfers property to B or purchases property in B's name, a presumption of advancement will arise in favour of B (see *Ebrand v Dancer* (1680) grandfather-grandchild; *Re Paradise Motor Co* (1968) stepfather-stepson and *Beckford v Beckford* (1774) father-illegitimate child).

Rebutting the presumptions of resulting trust and advancement

Whenever the presumption of advancement is applicable, it operates to rebut the presumption of resulting trust. Even if the relationship between the parties is not one that will give rise to the presumption of advancement, the presumption of resulting trust may be rebutted by other evidence. In *Fowkes v Pascoe* (1875), for example, a woman purchased stock in the joint names of herself and an infant relative of hers. While accepting that their relationship did not raise a presumption of advancement in the infant's favour, the court concluded that the only rational inference to be drawn in the circumstances was that she intended that on her death the infant would take the stock beneficially and not hold it on a resulting trust (see also *Standing v Bowring*).

Where the relationship between the parties is such that the operative presumption is the presumption of advancement this can equally be rebutted where the evidence shows that the material intention was that the property would be held on trust. This was the case for instance in *Scawin v Scawin* (1841) where a father purchased stock in his son's name and the son later admitted that he was aware that his father did not intend that the stock should pass as an outright gift to him. Again in *Warren v Gurney* (1944) where a father purchased a house in his daughter's name, his retention of the title deeds, coupled with his contemporaneous declarations were held to rebut the presumption of advancement operating in her favour. Also in *Marshall v Crutwell* (1875) and *Simpson v Simpson* (1992) where two husbands transferred their bank accounts into the names of their wives, the presumption of advancement was rebutted because there was evidence in each case that this was done purely for convenience since both husbands were seriously ill and could not undertake banking transactions.

The rules in *Shepherd v Cartwright*

Where the evidence relied on to rebut the presumption of resulting trust or advancement consists of *acts or statements*, the admissibility of such evidence is governed by the decision in *Shepherd v Cartwright* (1955). In this case a man purchased shares in the names of his wife and children and then proceeded to act as if he was beneficially entitled to the shares. In deciding whether evidence of the man's conduct was admissible to rebut the initial presumption of advancement the House of Lords formulated two rules:

- acts or declarations made *before* or *at the time of* the transfer or purchase are admissible either *for* or *against* the maker;
- acts and declarations made *after* the transfer or purchase has been concluded are admissible in evidence only *against* the maker.

On the strength of Rule 2, it was held that the husband's conduct after the purchase of the shares would not be admissible in his favour to rebut the presumption of advancement.

Evidence of illegal conduct

Where in furtherance of some illegal purpose A purchases property in B's name or transfers property to B who happens to be his wife or child, it has been decided in such cases as *Gascoigne v Gascoigne* (1918); *Re Emery's Investment Trusts* (1959); *Chettair v Chettair* (1962) and *Tinker v Tinker* (1970) that A will not be allowed to adduce evidence of this illegal purpose with a view to rebutting the presumption of advancement in B's favour. This refusal to allow evidence of A's illegal purpose has been justified primarily by invoking the maxim that 'He who comes into equity must come with clean hands'.

The House of Lords has recently held in *Tinsley v Milligan* (1993) that the position is different where A transfers property to B or purchases property in B's name and the operative presumption is of resulting trust. In such instances, even if the property was put in B's name for an unlawful purpose, A will not be deprived of his beneficial interest, since the presumption in his favour means that he need not adduce any evidence and is therefore not obliged to rely on the illegality in asserting his entitlement. Although this decision was followed in *Garvin-Mack v Garvin-Mack* (1993), it has forcefully been argued by Stowe in his review of *Tinsley v Milligan* in (1994) MLR 441, that it is unsatisfactory from the practical standpoint as well as in policy terms.

Automatic resulting trusts

As Lord Diplock observed in *Vandervell v IRC* (1966), 'equity abhors a beneficial vacuum'. Accordingly, where S transfers property to T under a trust which leaves some or all of the beneficial interest undisposed of, equity will automatically fill this vacuum by requiring T to hold the outstanding equitable interest on a resulting trust for S. Such automatic resulting trusts are capable of arising in a variety of contexts.

Where S has not effectively declared the intended trust but the property has become vested in T

Where S intends to create a trust and accordingly transfers the trust property to T but the trust cannot take effect because it has not been properly declared, T will hold the property on a resulting trust for S or, if S is dead, for his estate. Thus, in *Re Keen* (1937) where the court declined to enforce a half-secret trust declared by a testator because it had not been properly communicated, a resulting trust arose in favour of the testator's estate. Again in *Re Vandervell (No 2)* (1974), S arranged to transfer shares owned by him to the Royal College of Surgeons but retained an option to re-purchase them for £5,000. S empowered the trustees of his children's settlement to exercise this option without stating the persons for whose benefit they were to hold the re-purchased shares. It was decided that the option to purchase was subject to a resulting trust in favour of S.

Where a validly declared express trust fails because conditions attached to the trust are not fulfilled

Where for instance S transfers money to T, directing T to accumulate the capital and income and pay it to S's infant son B, if B attains the age of 21, the trust will fail if B dies at the age of 17 and the fund will be held on a resulting trust for S.

By the same token where property is transferred to trustees under a marriage settlement, the trust is conditional on there being a valid marriage, so that if the marriage is void *ab initio*, the trust will fail and a resulting trust will arise in the settlor's favour (see *Re Ames Settlement* (1946) and *Essery v Cowlard* (1884)).

Where the trust duly takes effect but fails to dispose of the entire beneficial interest

Where for instance S transfers property to T, directing T to hold it on trust for B for B's life but omits to state the person who is to take beneficially on B's death, T will be compelled to hold the property on trust for S. Cases in which resulting trusts are imposed on account of failure to dispose of the entire beneficial interest often stem from bad drafting. As Harman LJ aptly put it in *Re Cochrane* (1955) 'a resulting trust is the last resort to which the law has recourse when the draftsman has made a blunder or failed to dispose of that which he sets out to dispose'.

Where a surplus is left after a trust has been carried out

Where a trust is created which specifies that the trust fund is to be applied towards a particular purpose and the purpose is achieved without exhausting the fund it has been decided in some cases that the surplus will be held on a resulting trust for the settlor or contributors. In *Re Trusts Of The Abbott Fund* (1900), a trust was set up for the upkeep of two deaf and dumb old ladies. When the two ladies died, the court held that the balance of the trust fund went on a resulting trust to the contributors. In *Re Gillingham Bus Disaster Fund* (1958) a sizeable sum of money had been raised by the mayors of three towns through a public appeal launched in response to a serious accident involving a squad of marine cadets. Only a part of this money was needed to meet the funeral expenses of the cadets who had died and to take care of those who had been injured as other financial arrangements existed for these purposes. The court held that the rest of the money was subject to a resulting trust for the contributors.

These cases must be contrasted with *Re Andrew's Trust* (1907) and *Re Osoba* (1979). In *Re Andrew's* several persons had subscribed to a fund set up for the stated purpose of educating the infant children of a deceased clergyman. After the children had all been educated, it was held that the balance of the fund would not result to the subscribers but would pass to the children. In *Re Osoba*, O directed in his will that his residuary estate was to be applied towards educating his daughter up to university level. It was held that there would be no resulting trust of the property to O's estate after she completed her university education. The court in each case took the view that the material intention was to make absolute gifts to the beneficiaries and that the references to the provision of education merely indicated the motive uppermost in the minds of the respective donors.

Where an unincorporated association has ceased to exist leaving surplus funds

Where several persons come together to form an unincorporated association it is common for them to generate funds by subscriptions, fines, donations, fund-raising activities etc. If the association is subsequently dissolved or otherwise becomes defunct the courts are often called upon to determine what should happen to the association's surplus funds and other assets. As signified by Gardner in a review of the decided cases in (1992) Conv 41, two distinct judicial approaches have emerged.

The resulting trust approach

While an unincorporated association is still in existence, its funds/assets are commonly held on trust by the treasurer, the Committee or specifically designated trustees. In the light of this the courts have held in several cases that if the association ceases to exist these funds or assets will be held on a resulting trust. In *Re Printers' And Transferrers' Society* (1899) for instance a society had been formed to raise funds by weekly contributions to fight for improved working conditions for members and support them if they took industrial action. When the society was dissolved, it had 201 members and funds of over £1,000. The court held that the sum would be subject to a resulting trust for those who were members at the time of dissolution in proportion to their contributions. In *Re Hobourn Aero Components [Etc] Fund* (1946) a fund had been set up during the Second World War with contributions from the employees of a company to assist those employees on war service or who were the victims of air raids. At the end of the war, the fund had a cash surplus, which Cohen J decided was to be held on a resulting trust. However, unlike in the *Printers' and Transferrer's* case, Cohen J concluded that the resulting trust arose in favour of contributors past and present relative to their contributions. More recently in *Davies v Richards & Wallington Industries* (1990) an occupational pension scheme was wound up and after making provision for outstanding entitlements of employees there was a surplus. It was held that the part of the surplus representing the employer's contribution would go on a resulting trust to the employer.

The contractual approach

An unincorporated association will usually have a constitution or some other set of rules which define a member's rights and obligations in relation to the association as well as other members. The constitution represents the contract that binds the members together and disputes between them fall to be determined primarily by reference to its terms. Accordingly, the courts have increasingly preferred to determine who is entitled to the assets of a defunct association, not on the basis of a resulting trust but in the light of this contract.

This approach was initially adopted in *Cunnack v Edwards* (1892). Here a friendly society was formed in 1810 to raise funds through subscriptions, fines etc for the payment of annuities to widows of its members. By 1892, when the last of these widows died, the society had a surplus of £1,250 in its coffers. The personal representatives of some members claimed that this sum would pass under a resulting trust to the estates of the members. The court held that each member contracted with the society that on paying his contribution he thereby divested himself of all interest in the money, in return for the benefit his widow would receive on his death. There was therefore no basis for a resulting trust and the money would pass to the Crown as *bona vacantia*.

This decision was followed in *Re West Sussex Constabulary [etc] Fund Trusts* (1971) which held that on the dissolution of a benevolent fund the monthly subscriptions of members would not revert to them under a resulting trust, since they had contracted to receive benefits for themselves and their families in return for relinquishing their claims to any money subscribed to the fund.

In the case of *Re Bucks Constabulary Friendly Society (No 2)* (1979) it was again affirmed that where an unincorporated association ceases to exist its surplus assets will be dealt with in accordance with the contract between the members rather than on the basis of a resulting trust. However, Walton J noted that when *Cunnack v Edwards* was decided the legislation governing friendly societies forbade distribution of surplus funds but the modern legislation did not. He concluded from this that on the dissolution of the Bucks Constabulary Fund, the money in the fund fell to be distributed among the members for the time in accordance with the contract between them (see also *Re GKN Bolts and Nuts Ltd Sports and Social Club* (1982)).

Where the contract dictates that the surplus should be distributed among the members in the event of dissolution, they will be entitled to equal shares, unless the contract provides for a different mode of distribution as was the case in *Re Sick And Funeral Society Of St John's Sunday School Golcar* (1973).

Where money has been paid with a stipulation that the money should be applied for a particular purpose

Where A pays money to B, on the basis that it should only be applied towards a specified purpose, it has been established in *Barclays Bank v Quistclose Investments* (1970) that if the purpose cannot be carried out a resulting trust will arise. In this case, R Company was unable to pay dividends it had declared on its shares and borrowed money from Q to enable it pay the dividends. The money was put in a special account at B bank which was notified that it could only be used for this purpose. R Company went into liquidation before paying the dividends and the bank sought to retain the money to cover debts owed to it by R Company. The House of Lords rejected the bank's claim and held that as the dividends could no longer be paid the money was subject to a resulting trust in Q's favour (see also *Carreras Rothmans Ltd v Freeman Mathews Treasure Ltd* and *Re EVTR* (1987)).

Note however that where two parties enter into a business transaction under which one party makes a payment to the other without requiring it to be kept and applied for a particular purpose, the money paid will not be subject to a Quistclose-type trust (see *Guardian Ocean Cargoes Ltd v Banco Do Brasil* (1994)).

Constructive trusts

The general nature of constructive trusts

The problem of definition
A number of definitions of the constructive trust have been proffered in the leading textbooks. For instance *Hanbury & Martin* define it as 'one which arises by *operation of the law* and not by reason of the intention of the parties, express or implied'; Snell defines it as 'one *imposed by equity* in order to satisfy the demands of justice and good conscience without reference to any express or implied intention of the parties'; while *Pettitt*, in much the same vein, defines it as 'one *imposed by equity* regardless of the intention of the owner of property.' None of these definitions is wholly satisfactory. In the first place to categorise constructive trusts as trusts imposed by equity is somewhat misleading since the essence of every trust is that it is enforced by equity. Again, the assertion that they arise by operation of law is not conclusive as a defining characteristic because as Gardner points out, in *An Introduction to The Law of Trusts*, all trusts arise by operation of the law

in the sense that 'trusts are legal obligations and only the law can place legal obligations on people'.

It has accordingly been observed by Edmund-Davies LJ in *Carl Zeiss Stiftung v Smith & Co (No 2)* (1969) that 'English law has no clear-cut all embracing definition of the constructive trust'. This is due in large measure to the fact that the constructive trust is the residual category which according to Hanbury and Martin 'is called into play where the court desires to impose a trust and no other suitable category exists'. Consequently, as Edmund-Davies J remarked 'its boundaries have been left perhaps deliberately vague so as not to restrict the court by technicalities in deciding what the justice of a particular case may demand'. Being the residual category, the constructive trust has been invoked in a disparate range of situations which cannot easily be encompassed within a single definition. It is thus less problematic, and probably more instructive, to focus attention instead on the main situations in which the courts have been prepared to impose constructive trusts.

Traditional and new model constructive trusts

The traditional approach

In English law, the traditional view of the constructive trust is that it is a *substantive institution* in much the same way as an express or resulting trust. As thus conceived, the constructive trust like other trusts is designed to vindicate pre-existing proprietary rights by drawing upon a body of precisely formulated and generally applicable principles which over the years have been well assimilated into the general law of property.

An important feature of the traditional approach is that the courts have been largely content to give effect to constructive trusts in a limited number of well-defined situations, such as:

- where a trustee or other fiduciary misappropriates property entrusted to him or made unauthorised profits from his office;
- where a third party knowingly receives or assists in disposing of trust property in breach of trust;
- where mutual wills have been executed by two testators;
- where one person seeks to take undue advantage of statutory provisions designed to prevent fraud at the expense of another;
- where a specifically enforceable contract of sale has arisen;
- where legal title is obtained by unlawful killing.

(Misappropriation by fiduciaries; knowing receipt/assistance and mutual will are examined in greater detail below.)

Another important feature of the traditional approach is that a distinction is drawn between the situations in which constructive trusts will be imposed and the remedies available for enforcing such trusts. Such remedies include:

- a personal action against the constructive trustee;
- recovery of the trust property; and
- tracing into the proceeds of sale of such property.

The 'new model' approach

In the US, the constructive trust is widely regarded not as a substantive institution but as a *remedial device* to be invoked against any person who acquires or retains property at the expense of another, thereby unjustly enriching himself at the expense of another. The chief attribute of the remedial constructive trust is its flexibility. Instead of being confined in its operation to a limited range of well-established situations like the institutional constructive trust, it has a wider remit as 'the formula through which the conscience of equity finds expression' – *per* Cardozo J in *Beatty v Guggenheim Exploration Co* (1919).

In *Re Sharpe* (1980), the notion of the constructive trust as a remedy in the American mould was seen as a novel concept and on the whole has not been much favoured by English judges (though the possibility of imposing such a trust was recently raised by Slade LJ in *Metall Und Rohstoff AG v Donaldson Lufkin & Jenrette Inc* (1990)).

Significantly however, the flexibility of the American approach provided the impetus for the emergence of the *new model constructive trust* as a vehicle for extending the operation of the constructive trust beyond its traditional frontiers. In practice this meant that where in a dispute relating to property, reliance on established principles would work unfairly against either party, the court by invoking a constructive trust of the new model, could adjust their respective entitlements with a view to redressing the balance. Lord Denning, who the most powerful advocate of the new model, declared in *Hussey v Hussey* (1972), that it was 'a trust imposed by law whenever justice and good conscience require it'.

Main spheres of application

- The influence of the new model constructive trust was most perceptible in *disputes between spouses or co-habitees with regard to family property*. Its earliest manifestation was in *Heseltine v Heseltine* (1971), where it was employed to prevent a husband from claiming beneficially, two sums of money that had been paid to him by his wife. A strict application of the prevailing law would have supported his claim, but Lord Denning felt that it would be inequitable as between the parties to allow this to happen. Also relevant are the cases of *Cooke v Head* (1972) and *Eves v Eves* (1975). In each case the family home had been acquired in the name of the male partner but his mistress had done a great deal of physical work in improving the home. Lord Denning concluded that this was a sufficient reason for awarding a fair share of the beneficial interest the home to the mistress (1/3 in *Cooke* and 1/4 in *Eves*) and warranted the imposition of a constructive trust against the male partner.
- Lord Denning was also actively instrumental to the introduction of the new model constructive trust into the *sphere of contractual licenses* on equitable grounds. As seen from *Binions v Evans* (1972), this was intended to strengthen the licensee's position by treating his personal right as an equitable proprietary interest enforceable against a third party assignee of the licensor who has notice of the licence. See also *DHN Food Distributors v Tower Hamlets LBC* (1976) and *Re Sharpe* (1980).
- A constructive trust was similarly imposed in accordance with general equitable principles in *Peffer v Rigg* (1977) in favour of the owner of an unregistered equitable interest against a purchaser of the legal title with notice of the equitable interest.

Criticisms of the new model constructive trust

Notwithstanding the eminent stature of Lord Denning, the new model approach has generated considerable disquiet among various commentators. In particular, RH Mausley in (1977) 28 NILQ 123 calls into question 'the rule that in cases where the plaintiff ought to win but has no legal doctrine or authority to support him a constructive trust will do the trick'.

Oakley in his work on *Constructive Trusts* and Hayton in his contribution to Jowell & McAuslan's work on *Lord Denning: The Judge and the Law* maintain that such a subjective approach is especially undesirable in disputes about property rights. Both commentators echo the

view of Bagnall J in *Cowcher v Cowcher* (1973) that in determining property rights 'the only justice that can be attained by mortals is ... the justice which flows from the application of sure and settled principles'. A
further criticism voiced by Oakley is that the new model by concen-
trating on the need to do justice between the parties to the dispute
might well prejudice rights of third parties not involved in the dispute.

The unease which has been voiced by these commentators has been
echoed by several Antipodean judges who have called into question
the legitimacy of the new model constructive trust in such cases as
Carly v Farrelly (1975) *Allen v Snyder* (1977) and *Muschinski v Dodds*
(1986).

The current situation

As the shortcomings of the new model have become increasingly evident, English courts have been reluctant to follow Lord Denning's lead.
Since the 1980s the courts have not sought to extend the new model into
other areas of the law. Even in those areas in which it was invoked in
the past, they have been anxious to rein in the new model constructive
trust by insisting that it will not be imposed arbitrarily but within well-
defined limits and in accordance with settled principles.

In the first place, in disputes over the family home, the courts have
now established in cases such as *Burns v Burns* (1984); *Grant v Edwards*
(1986); and decisively in *Lloyds Bank v Rosset* (1991) that a constructive
trust will no longer be imposed where the home is in the name of one
partner simply because the judge deems it to be fair to the other partner. There must be a common intention that both partners should have
an interest in the property and detrimental reliance on this intention
by the partner in whose favour the trust is imposed.

Secondly, in connection with contractual licences, the courts are
now considerably more circumspect than they once were, about
imposing constructive trusts. In *Ashburn Anstalt v Arnold* (1989), the
Court of Appeal acknowledged that the imposition of a constructive
trust in *Binions v Evans* was justified because the assignee of the licensor not only had notice of the licence but was able to purchase the
property which was the subject of the licence at reduced price. At the
same time, the court did not accept that a constructive trust ought to
be upheld in favour of a licensee in every case where a licensor assigns
his interest to a purchaser with notice, declaring that 'We do not think
it desirable that constructive trusts of land should be imposed on infer-
ences from slender material'.

Finally, the decision in *Peffer v Rigg* that a constructive trust will be imposed on equitable grounds to protect the holder of an unregistered equitable interest against a purchaser with notice has now been thrown into doubt by *Williams & Glyn's Bank v Boland* (1981). In this case, the House of Lords affirmed that where registered land was concerned, the concept of notice had no relevance so that a purchaser would only be bound by a registrable interest if it appeared on the register. It is only where the purchaser makes it expressly clear that he is purchasing the property subject to that specific equitable interest (as happened in *Lyus v Prowsa Developments Ltd* (1988)) that the court will now protect the interest by imposing a constructive trust.

In the light of these developments, Pettitt has been able to detect 'a movement away from a revolutionary new model constructive trust towards an evolutionary extension of the traditional constructive trust'.

The main categories of traditional constructive trusts

Trustees and other fiduciaries as constructive trustees

Equity has long insisted that a person in a fiduciary position must not allow his interests to conflict with his duty and in particular must not, unless authorised, profit from his position (see *Bray v Ford* (1896)).

Who is a fiduciary?

It has been observed by Fletcher-Moulton J in *Re Coomber* (1911) that 'fiduciary relations are of many different types'; and by Slade J in *English v Dedham Vale Properties* (1978) that 'categories of fiduciary relations which give rise to constructive trusteeship should [not] be regarded as falling into a limited number of strait-jackets or as being necessarily closed'.

The key feature of the fiduciary relationship is that one party (the principal) reposes confidence on another (the fiduciary). Common examples of such relationships are those between trustee-beneficiary, company director/promoter-shareholder; agent-principal and solicitor-client. Indeed the court went as far as to suggesting *Reading v AG* (1951) that a fiduciary relationship arises whenever one party entrusts another with a job to perform. In this case a British soldier stationed in Egypt had escorted several consignments of contraband through Cairo dressed in his uniform thereby enabling lorries carrying the contraband to cross checkpoints without being searched. It was held that there was a fiduciary relationship between him and the Crown which entitled the Crown to recover the money he had made in the process.

Situations in which constructive trusts have been imposed

The types of factual situations in which the courts have imposed constructive trusts on fiduciaries are many and varied. They include:

Where a fiduciary has received remuneration to which he is not entitled
A trustee or other fiduciary is under a duty not to make unauthorised payments to himself or accept unauthorised payments out of funds belonging to his principal, or otherwise appropriate to himself payments received from third parties to which his principal is properly entitled. Where he does so he is liable to account as a constructive trustee for the sums received as seen from such cases as *Sugden v Crossland* (1856): £75 paid to trustee from his successor as consideration for retiring from trust; *Erlanger v New Sombrero Phosphate Co* (1898): unauthorised sale at a profit of company promoter's property to the company; *Williams v Barton* (1927): commission received by trustee for bringing trust business to his employers, a firm of stockbrokers; *Re Macadam* (1946): directors' fees received by trustees who were appointed to the board on the strength of power to appoint exercisable by the trust; and *Guinness PLC v Saunders* (1990): payment to company director under a contract not approved by the board for negotiating proposed take-over of another company.

Where a fiduciary enters into a transaction on his own behalf which he should have pursued for his principal's benefit
In such an event, the fiduciary will be obliged to hold any benefits accruing from the transaction on a constructive trust for his principal. The position in this regard is exemplified by:

The rule In Keech v Sanford (1726)
According to this rule, where trust property includes a leasehold interest, the trustee is bound on the expiry of the term to seek a renewal on behalf of the trust and if he renews the lease on his own behalf he will be obliged to hold the new lease on constructive trust for the beneficiaries even if it was the lessor who had declined to renew.

The rule has subsequently been extended to other persons in a fiduciary position such as personal representatives, agents and partners (see eg *Re Biss* (1902)). It has also been applied in a situation where a husband who held the lease of a matrimonial home on trust for himself and his wife, purchased the *leasehold reversion* from the lessor (see *Protheroe v Protheroe* (1968)).

Regal (Hastings) Ltd v Gulliver (1942)

The principle underpinning the decision in *Keech v Sanford* was reaffirmed in a different context in this case. Here R Ltd formed a subsidiary company, A Ltd to secure the leases of two cinemas. A Ltd had a share capital of £5,000 but R Ltd only had the resources to pay for 2,000 worth of shares. The cinema owner would not grant the leases unless all the shares were fully paid up. The directors and company solicitor of R Ltd subscribed for the balance. This arrangement was never formally authorised or ratified by the shareholders as a body. R Ltd was later sold and in the process the directors made substantial profits from their share holding in A Ltd The new owners of R Ltd sued in the company's name to recover the profits and the directors were held to be accountable as constructive trustees for these profits. See also *Industrial Development Consultants Ltd v Cooley* (1972).

Regal (Hastings) must, however, be contrasted with Commonwealth cases such as *Peso Silver Mines Ltd v Cropper* (1966) (Canada) and *Queensland Mines Ltd v Hudson* (1978) (Australia) in which the courts displayed more sympathy towards directors who profited from commercial opportunities not taken up by their companies.

Use of confidential information by fiduciary for his own ends

Where a fiduciary exploits confidential information or knowledge acquired in his fiduciary capacity for his own benefit he is placed in the position of a constructive trustee with regard to such benefit. In the leading case of *Boardman v Phipps* (1967), B a solicitor to a trust and TP, one of the beneficiaries were able to take over and profitably manage a company in which the trust had a substantial share holding by utilising information and opportunities which came their way purely as a result of their connection with the trust. It was held by the House of Lords that even though B and TP had acted honestly in their dealings with the trust they were liable to account as constructive trusts for the profits accruing to them from the venture.

Receipt of bribes

Whereas in the situations outlined above, the fiduciary's liability to account is enforced by means of a constructive trust, the position has long been different with regard to the receipt of bribes by fiduciaries. In this connection it was established by the Court of Appeal in *Lister &*

Co v Stubbs (1890) that where a fiduciary accepts a bribe, his principal will have a personal claim against him for the amount, but not a proprietary claim, as the fiduciary will not be regarded as a constructive trustee of it. Although this decision has been followed in cases such as *Powell And Thomas v Evans Jones & Co* (1905); and *Iran Shipping Lines v Denby* (1987), it has been criticised by the likes of Oakley in his *Constructive Trusts* and Hayton and Marshall. It is also significant that the decision was recently called into question in the New Zealand case of *Reid v AG For Hong Kong* (1993) where the Privy Council decided that a public servant who bought real property with bribes received in the course of his employment held the property on a constructive trust for the government. However, the decision in *Reid* has itself been vigorously criticised by Watts in (1994) 110 LQR 179 and in any case is no more than a persuasive authority in the English courts. It remains to be seen whether the House of Lords will reach the same conclusion as the Privy Council when the opportunity presents itself.

Strangers as constructive trustees

Where a trustee (or other fiduciary) improperly allows property or funds entrusted to him to fall into the hands of strangers he will be liable for any loss occasioned to the beneficiaries. Where the trustee is not in a position to make good the loss, considerable scope exists for imposing a constructive trust on the stranger. This may be done on the ground that the stranger:

- has wrongly assumed responsibility for administering the trust as a trustee *de son tort*;
- has knowingly received trust property or funds; or
- has knowingly assisted the trustee in fraudulently disposing of trust property or funds.

Strangers who will not be liable as constructive trustees

There are three situations a stranger will not be affixed with liability as a constructive trustee.

Where the stranger acquires trust property as a bona fide purchaser for value without notice
See *Pilcher v Rawlins* (1872).

Where the stranger has received trust property or funds as an innocent volunteer
In such instances, the beneficiary can trace the property into the hands of the volunteer if it still exists in some traceable form. However, the

volunteer is not deemed to stand in a fiduciary position with regard to the beneficiaries. Consequently, he will not incur the liability of a constructive trustee if the property has passed out of his hands without his being aware of the trust (see *Re Diplock* (1948); *Re Montagu's ST* (1987) and *Agip (Africa) Ltd v Jackson* (1992)).

Where the stranger is an agent acting on the trustee's behalf
It is commonplace for trustees to delegate certain aspects of their responsibilities to agents like solicitors, stockbrokers or valuers and to entrust such agents with trust funds or property. In such an event, the position as outlined by Bacon VC in *Lee v Sankey* (1872), is that 'a mere agent of trustees is answerable only to his principal and not to the *cestui que trust* in respect of trust monies coming into his hands merely in his character as an agent'. Subsequent cases such as *Barnes v Addy* (1874); *Mara v Browne* (1896) and *Williams-Ashman v Price And Williams* (1942) have also confirmed that an agent acting on behalf of a trust will not ordinarily be liable as a constructive trustee for any loss to the trust estate once he has acted honestly in the performance of his agency.

At the same time, it is clear from these cases that where the agent goes beyond his duties and proceeds to intermeddle in the administration of the trust by doing acts which are characteristic of a trustee, this may render him liable as a trustee *de son tort*. Furthermore, where an agent is adjudged to have acted in a manner which shows dishonesty or want of probity he may be liable as a constructive trustee either for knowing receipt or knowing assistance (see *Carl-Zeiss Stiftung v Herbert Smith* (1969)).

Imposition of a constructive trust on a trustee *de son tort*

Under the law relating to administration of estates, a stranger who without obtaining a grant of probate or letters of administration proceeds to administer a deceased person's estate is an *executor de son tort* and will be answerable for any impropriety in administering the estate. By the same token, cases such as *Mara v Browne* establish that where a person who is not a trustee and who has no authority from the trustee becomes involved in administering the trust estate, he is a *trustee de son tort* and will be liable under a constructive trust to the beneficiaries for the trust assets as well as any loss occasioned by him.

Knowing assistance

A stranger will be liable as a constructive trustee where he has 'assisted with knowledge in a dishonest or fraudulent design on the part of the trustees': *per* Lord Selborne in *Barnes v Addy;* or 'knowingly assisted in a fraudulent and dishonest disposition of the trust property': *per* Esher MR in *Soar v Ashwell.*

Where misappropriated property or funds have been disposed of by a stranger on the instructions of a dishonest trustee or other fiduciary this will be treated as a case of knowing assistance rather than knowing receipt (see *Agip (Africa) Ltd v Jackson).*

There will also be knowing assistance, where a stranger has been an accessory to a fraudulent design, without ever being in receipt of trust property or funds as in *Eaves v Hickson* (1861). As Pettitt points out however, imposing a constructive trust on a stranger who has never received trust property is somewhat anomalous for on general principles a person becomes a trustee only if he has property vested in him. Even if it is accepted that a stranger who assists in disposing of property without ever receiving it is a constructive trustee, his liability is personal rather than proprietary and the remedy of tracing cannot be purued against him in respect of such property.

In *Baden Delvaux & Lecuit v Societe Generale etc* (1983), Peter Gibson J identified four elements which must be present for a stranger to be affixed with liability on the basis of knowing assistance. These according to him are:

- the existence of a trust or other fiduciary relationship;
- the existence of a dishonest and fraudulent design on the part of the trustee or other fiduciary (and not merely some misfeasance or breach of trust falling short of dishonesty);
- assistance by the stranger in the design; and
- guilty knowledge on the part of the stranger.

Actual knowledge

As far as knowledge is concerned there is little difficulty where the stranger has (i) actual knowledge that the trustee is engaged in a fraudulent breach of trust. Equally, where it is evident that the stranger has (ii) wilfully shut his eyes to the obvious or (iii) wilfully and recklessly failed to make such enquiries as a reasonable and honest person would make, it is generally accepted that he will be treated as if he possesses actual knowledge and will accordingly be liable for knowing assistance once the other three elements are present.

Constructive knowledge

The position is not as clear-cut where the stranger has neither been wilful nor reckless, but nevertheless had knowledge of (iv) circumstances which would indicate the facts to an honest or reasonable man or (v) circumstances which would put an honest and reasonable man on enquiry.

Judging from cases like *Selangor United Rubber Estates Ltd v Cradock (No 3)* (1968) and *Karak Rubber Co Ltd v Burden (No 2)* (1972) liability for knowing assistance may be imposed on the basis of knowledge within categories (iv) and (v). Peter Gibson J endorses this in the *Baden Delvaux* case, although he opines that in the commercial context at least, a stranger should not be liable for knowing assistance on the strength of category (iv) or (v) knowledge, save in exceptional circumstances.

The view in most cases, however, is that a stranger will be liable for knowing assistance only if there is dishonesty or want of probity on his part. If this is so, constructive knowledge of the type envisaged by categories (iv) and (v) which entail lack of care rather than dishonesty will not suffice. See *Carl-Zeiss Stiftung v Herbert Smith; Belmont Finance Corp v Williams Furniture Ltd (No 1)* (1979); *Re Montagu's ST* (1987); *Lipkin Gorman v Karpnale Ltd* (1989); *Eagle Trust PLC v SBC Securities* (1991); and *Polly Peck International v Nadir (No 2)* (1992).

Knowing receipt or dealing

Cases in which a constructive trust will be imposed on a stranger on the basis of knowing receipt fall into three broad contexts:

- Where the stranger who receives property from a trustee or other fiduciary is aware at the outset that it has been transferred to him in breach of the trust or the fiduciaries duties. For example:
  (a) where a beneficiary under a trust knows that he has received more than his share of the trust property, he will be obliged to hold the surplus on a constructive trust;
  (b) where a creditor is aware that the debt due to him has been paid not from the debtor's personal resources but from funds held by him as a trustee or other fiduciary (see *Nelson v Larholt* (1948) and *International Sales And Agencies Ltd v Marcus* (1982)).
- Where the stranger receives trust property without notice of the trust, but having become aware of the trust deals with the property in a manner that is inconsistent with the rights of the beneficiaries. For example, where a trustee transfers trust funds to an innocent volunteer and the latter uses the money to buy property in his own name after he learns of the trust, he will hold the property on a constructive trust (see *Re Diplock*).

- Where the stranger receives the property which he knows is subject to a trust without being in breach of trust and later deals with it in a manner which is inconsistent with the trust.

On the issue of *knowledge*, the weight of judicial authority has long favoured the view that in knowing receipt cases, a stranger may become a constructive trustee whether his knowledge is actual or constructive (see *Karak v Burden; Belmont Finance v Williams* and *International Sales v Marcus*). Accordingly, a stranger who had no actual knowledge (category i) and was not wilful or reckless in disregarding the obvious or failing to make proper enquiries (categories ii and iii) may still be liable as a constructive trustee on the basis of knowledge within categories iv and v.

This must, however, be set against the position taken by Megarry VC in *Re Montagu's ST* (1987), where the Vice Chancellor insisted that in order to establish personal liability for knowing receipt actual knowledge is required.

Although some support has been expressed for this position by Vinelott J in *Eagle Trust v SBC Securities*, it has been called into question by Harpum (1987) 50 MLR 217 and extra-judicially by Millet J (1991) in 107 LQR 71. It was also rejected by Millet J in *Agip v Jackson*, where he re-iterated that constructive knowledge is sufficient to found a claim for knowing receipt (see also *Polly Peck International v Nadir*).

Constructive trusts in the context of mutual (and joint) wills

Where two parties agree that on the death of each, his or her property shall devolve in a particular manner and both parties execute wills intended to give effect to this agreement, such wills are called *mutual wills*. Where the agreement is embodied in one will executed by both parties, this is known as a *joint will*.

Mutual wills are usually framed in terms which are identical or substantially the same, with each party leaving property in the first instance to the other party and thereafter to the same ultimate beneficiaries.

Any two persons may choose to execute mutual or joint wills. For example, two elderly sisters who are childless may agree (as in *Re Wilford's Estate* (1879)) that whichever one dies first her property will go to the survivor for life and thereafter pass to their nieces. In most cases, however, such wills are principally employed by spouses to give effect to agreements between them that when they die, they shall each leave their property to the children of the marriage. The wills of the spouses may provide:

- that property belonging to each spouse shall pass to the other for life remainder to their children or other named beneficiaries as in *Gray v Perpetual Trustee Co Ltd* (1928) and *Re Hagger* (1930);
- that property belonging to each spouse shall pass to the other spouse absolutely with a substitutionary provision to the effect that if the other spouse dies first, the property shall devolve on their children as in *Re Cleaver* (1981);
- that on the death of each spouse his or her property will pass to the children with no provision for any interest therein to go in the first instance to the other spouse as in *Re Dale* (1993).

As long as both spouses adhere to their initial agreement and neither attempts to revoke his or her will, their issue will become entitled to the property of both on the survivor's death. Where the problem arises is if either spouse has a change of mind after the execution of the wills and no longer wishes his or her property to devolve in the agreed manner.

Where the other spouse is still alive

It is a long-standing probate principle that a testator is free to revoke his will whenever he wishes. If for instance, the wife (W), decides during the lifetime of her husband (H) that she no longer wants to go along with the agreement she may avail herself of the freedom to revoke but must notify H (see *Dufour v Pereira* (1769) and *Stone v Hoskins* (1905)). Neither H nor their children as the ultimate beneficiaries can compel her not to revoke her will, though H may conceivably be able to claim damages for breach of contract.

Where the other spouse is dead

If W does not revoke her will in H's life-time and H for his part dies without revoking his will, W may then revoke her will or may remarry, thereby automatically revoking all her earlier wills. In either event, the children of the marriage, not being parties to the agreement cannot sue her for breach of contract. It has also been doubted in *Re Dale* that H's personal representatives can pursue such a claim (contrary to the decision in *Beswick v Beswick* (1968) that where two parties contract to confer a benefit on a third party, this is enforceable by the personal representative of either contracting party).

Equity is, however, prepared to intervene on the premise that it would be fraudulent for W to revoke her will, given that H who made his will pursuant to the agreement with W can no longer revoke his as he is dead. In this connection rather than compel W not to revoke her will, equity prefers instead to give effect to the agreement in favour of the children of the marriage by imposing a *constructive trust* on W's personal representative. The willingness of the courts to impose trusts in such circumstances dates back to the decision of Lord Camden LC in *Dufour v Pereira* and is evident in recent cases such as *Re Cleaver* and *Re Dale*.

In *Re Cleaver*, after H married W they executed mutual wills in which each left their property to the other with a substitutionary gift in favour of H's children by a previous marriage. H and W later amended their wills reducing the share of one child, M, to a life interest. W made several wills after H died. In the last of these W left all her property to M and her husband and nothing to H's other children. Nourse J held that W's executors were bound to hold her estate on trust for the benefit of all H's children as provided in the mutual wills. In *Re Dale*, H and W in 1988 executed wills in which they each left all their property to their son and daughter equally. In 1990, after H's death, W made another will, leaving £300 to her daughter and all her other property to her son. Morritt J, having carefully reviewed most of the earlier decisions, including *Re Cleaver*, concluded that the doctrine of mutual wills was applicable to the present case, even though W had received no benefit under H's will.

Note, however, that the fact that H and W have executed wills that are nearly identical will not warrant the imposition of a constructive trust, where there is no evidence to show that they had agreed that the wills would be irrevocable (see *Re Oldham* (1925)).

When does the constructive trust come into being?

Where H and W execute mutual and either of them dies without revoking his or her will and the surviving spouse executes a new will in different terms before eventually dying, an issue arises as to whether the constructive trust imposed in such circumstances takes effect on the first death or after the survivor's death.

This issue was addressed by Mitchell in (1951) MLR 136. Relying on the authority of *Re Hagger*, he concluded that the trust takes effect on the first death. In this case, H and W executed a joint will in 1902, under which the survivor was to have a life interest in certain property with remainders over to certain named beneficiaries including EP. W died in 1904, and in 1921 H executed a new will which was inconsistent with the joint will. EP died in 1923 while H died in 1928. The court held that a constructive trust had arisen under the joint will from the time W died in 1904. As EP was still alive at that time, her interest did not lapse (as it would have done if the trust came into force on H's death) but passed to her personal representative.

To what property does the trust attach?

It is not always easy to determine which property is subject to the constructive trust.

Where the parties executing mutual wills specify in their agreement or the wills, the exact property covered by the arrangement, as happened in *Re Green* (1951) the courts will rely on this.

Quite often, however, parties who wish to execute mutual wills do not specifically define the property which will be covered by the arrangement. In such instances, it has been suggested by commentators like Mitchell and more recently Hanbury and Martin that the trust will at the very least affect whatever property has passed from the first testator to die to the survivor. In the *Re Hagger* type of mutual will which confers only a life interest, the survivor, will be entitled to the income derived from the property of the first testator but will hold the capital on trust for the ultimate beneficiaries. Even where the wills provide that the first testator's property is to pass the survivor absolutely, the Australian case of *Birmingham v Renfrew* (1937) as well as *Re Cleaver* establish that the survivor will be entitled to full enjoyment of the property in his lifetime but will be obliged to ensure that on his death the residue will pass in accordance with the mutual wills. In effect, as Dixon J explained in the *Renfrew* case, the survivor takes the property subject to a *floating obligation* which crystallises into a trust when he eventually dies.

It also appears that in the absence of anything to the contrary, the trust extends to the survivor's own property. There are, however, conflicting views on the matter. On the one hand, in *Re Hagger*, Clauson J accepted that property owned by the survivor *at the first testator's death* will be held on trust. On the other hand, Astbury J suggested in *Re Oldham* that the trust applies to whatever property belongs to the survivor at his own death.

In his article, Mitchell goes further than either judge contending that the trust should cover everything owned by the survivor at the first testator's death as well as all his subsequently acquired property. As indicated by Hanbury and Martin, if this view is correct, the effect of mutual wills is to reduce the survivor to the position of a life tenant in respect of all his property so that he will be entitled to the income, while holding the capital on trust for the ultimate beneficiaries.

Trusts of the family home

Where a couple (whether married or unmarried) have set up home together, subsequent events such as the breakdown of the relationship or the bankruptcy or death of either party often give rise to disputes concerning their respective interests in the family home. Where the relationship has broken down, the dispute will usually be between the couple, but where the material event is bankruptcy, death etc, the opponent is often a third party such as a trustee in bankruptcy, mortgagee or personal representative.

Depending on the circumstances, the courts may find it appropriate to settle the dispute: (i) by exercising its jurisdiction under the Matrimonial Causes Act (MCA); (ii) by giving effect to any *express declarations* the couple may have made regarding their beneficial interests in the property; (iii) by imposing a *resulting trust* or (iv) by imposing a *constructive trust*.

Sections 24 and 25 MCA

Where a dispute about the matrimonial home arises in the context of proceedings for divorce, judicial separation or nullity, the MCA empowers the court to make whatever order is just and practicable in the circumstances, without being bound by the strict rules of property law. To this end it may order either spouse to transfer or settle property for the benefit of the other spouse or their children; and may vary any subsisting agreements or settlements they have made regarding property.

This wide discretionary cannot be invoked in disputes between:

- one spouse and a third party eg *Re Densham* (1975): (wife v husband's trustee in bankruptcy); *Lloyd's Bank v Rosset* (1991): (wife v husband's mortgagee);
- unmarried partners eg *Cooke v Head; Eves v Eves; Burns v Burns* (1984); *Grant v Edwards* (1986) and *Hammond v Mitchell* (1991) (man-mistress); *Tinsley v Milligan* (1992) (homosexual lovers).

Where disputes about the family home do not come within the ambit of the MCA, the beneficial interests of spouses or co-habitees are determined according to the general rules of property law. As Lord Diplock pointed out in *Gissing v Gissing* (1971) this means that the applicable principles are those of the law of trusts.

Express declarations regarding beneficial interests of partners

In most instances a party who claims a beneficial interest in the family home will base his or her claim on a resulting trust or constructive trust. However, there is no need to fall back on a resulting or constructive trust if, at the time the property was acquired, the relevant conveyance expressly declared what beneficial interests that party would have in the property as happened in *Goodman v Gallant* (1986). Here a man contributed one-quarter and his mistress three-quarters to the purchase price of a house which was conveyed to both of them as *beneficial joint tenants*. It was held on the strength of this that each was beneficially entitled to a half-share of the house even though the contributions of the mistress would have entitled her to a three-quarter share under a resulting trust.

Resulting trusts of the family home

Where legal title to the family home is vested in one partner alone, having been purchased in the name of that partner (usually the man), the other partner (whether a wife or mistress) may be entitled to a beneficial interest in the property under a resulting trust. According to Dixon (1988) Denning LJ 27, this resulting trust may be *immediate or cumulative*.

Immediate resulting trust

Where at the time of purchase, the wife or mistress made a direct financial contribution towards the purchase price, a resulting trust will be presumed in her favour and takes effect immediately the property becomes vested in the man. Where in similar circumstances, property is purchased in the name of a mistress with contributions from her partner, a resulting trust will also be presumed in his favour. By virtue of this resulting trust the contributing partner becomes entitled to a beneficial interest proportionate to the amount contributed.

On the other hand, where property is purchased in the wife's name, with the husband having contributed to the purchase price, the operative presumption is of advancement. However, it appears from *Silver v Silver* (1958) and *Pettitt v Pettitt* (1970) that less weight will now be attached to this presumption than in the past.

Cumulative resulting trust

Where the legal title to the family home is in one partner's name, but the other partner contributes substantially towards paying off the mortgage on the property, the courts are willing to infer from such cumulative contributions that the intention of the couple is that the contributor will acquire an equitable interest in the property (see *Burns v Burns; Winkworth v Edward Baron* (1986) and *Lloyds Bank v Rosset*). Even though in *Rosset*, Lord Bridge described the trust arising in these circumstances as a constructive trust it is widely accepted that it is more in the nature of a resulting trust (see Hanbury & Martin p 265 and Dixon p 31).

Moreover, the courts have come to accept that where a partner has not contributed to the purchase price or payment of the mortgage, account can be taken of that partner's financial contributions towards household expenses which enable the other partner in whom the legal title is vested to pay off the mortgage. A trust will be imposed in favour of the contributor if the contributions were made pursuant to a common intention and were referable to the acquisition of the property. According to Fox LJ in *Burns v Burns*, the term resulting trust is probably not inappropriate, where indirect contributions of this kind are concerned. Such a trust, as Dixon explains would be a cumulative resulting trust.

Constructive trusts of the family home

Constructive trusts have featured prominently in disputes relating to the family home since the early 1970s. The two landmark cases which set out the principles upon which constructive trusts will be imposed in this sphere are *Pettitt v Pettitt* and *Gissing v Gissing*. These cases established that where the legal title to the home is in the name of one partner, a claim by the other partner to a beneficial share under a constructive trust will succeed if a common intention that the claimant will acquire an interest in the home has been expressed or can be inferred and the claimant has relied on this to his or her detriment. See S Gardner (1993) 109 LQR 263.

In a line of cases which included *Cooke v Head, Eves v Eves* and most recently *Hall v Hall*, Lord Denning while accepting whole-heartedly that the constructive trust could be invoked in determining entitlement to the family home chose to treat it as a discretionary formula for adjusting the property rights of spouses and co-habitees in order to achieve a fair and just solution between them (*the new model approach*).

Although Lord Denning's approach is not dissimilar to that favoured in Canada where constructive trusts have been imposed in family disputes to prevent *unjust enrichment* (*Pettkus v Becker*) (1980) and in Australia where they have been imposed on grounds of *unconscionability* (*Baumgartner v Baumgartner* (1987)), English courts have preferred to adhere to the more orthodox principles set out in *Gissing* and *Pettitt*. This has been especially noticeable since Lord Denning relinquished judicial office as seen from such cases as *Burns v Burns, Midland Bank v Dobson, Grant v Edwards, Lloyds Bank v Rosset* and *Hammond v Mitchell*.

The effect of the reversion to orthodoxy is that a constructive trust will no longer be imposed in favour of a co-habitee or spouse simply because the judge perceives it to be fair and just, but can only be imposed where the requisite common intention and detrimental reliance are established.

Common intention

It is now clear from the judgment of Lord Bridge in the *Rosset* case that in order to establish common intention there must be evidence of some express agreement, arrangement or understanding, however imperfectly remembered and however imprecise its terms. The common intention cannot be inferred from the conduct of the parties, unless the claimant has contributed directly towards purchasing the property or paying the mortgage.

Detrimental reliance

Once the common intention is present, the detrimental reliance may assume a variety of forms. These include (i) contributions to the purchase price or mortgage repayments (*Lloyds Bank v Rosset*); (ii) financial contributions towards household expenses (*Grant v Edwards*); (iii) supporting the speculative business ventures of the other partner where these are financed by loans secured by the family home (*Hammond v Mitchell*); and (iv) contributions in kind towards improving the property (*Eves v Eves*). See also recent cases like *Ivin v Blake* (1994) and *Halifax Building Society v Brown* (1995).

It however emerges from such cases as *Burns v Burns* and *Midland Bank v Dobson* that the performance of routine domestic chores such as cooking, child-raising, weekend do-it-yourself activities etc, will not constitute a sufficient detriment to warrant the imposition of a constructive trust. (But note in this connection the criticisms voiced by Sufrin (1987) 50 MLR 94, 98-100.)

Revision Notes

Resulting trusts

There are two types of resulting trust: *presumed* and *automatic*. See Megarry VC's judgment in *Re Vandervells Trust (No 2)*.

Presumed resulting trusts

Presumed resulting trusts rise under two headings, namely:

- where there has been a voluntary transfer of property; and
- where property is purchased by one person in another's name.

Voluntary transfer

Where an owner of *personal property* transfers it to a *stranger* (ie someone other than his wife, child or person to whom he stands in *loco parentis*), the stranger is presumed to hold under a resulting trust (see *Standing v Bowring; Re Howes; Re Vinogradoff; Re Muller;* and *Thavorn v BCCI*).

Where the property which has been transferred to the stranger is *real property*, the effect s 60(3) LPA is that it is no longer certain whether a resulting trust will be presumed in favour of the transferor: 'debatable' (*Hodgson v Marks*); 'arguable' (*Tinsley v Milligan*).

Purchase in the name of another

Where one person provides money for the purchase of property (*real* or *personal*) and arranges for the property to be put in the name of another, the nominal owner is presumed to hold it on a resulting trust for the person providing the money (see *Dyer v Dyer; Pettitt v Pettitt; Gross v French; Fowkes v Pascoe; Shepherd v Cartwright* and *Crane v Davies*).

A resulting trust will also be presumed, where for example:

- two persons contribute towards the purchase price of property, which is put in the name of one of them (see eg *Bull v Bull; Dewar v Dewar; Sekhon v Alissa; Harwood v Harwood; Tinsley v Milligan* and *Garvin-Mack v Garvin-Mack*).
- two persons contribute 75% and 25% respectively towards the purchase price and the property is conveyed to them jointly or in equal shares (see *Springette v Defoe* and *Tagoe v Layea*).

- the property is purchased in the name of one person by means of a mortgage taken out by him and another person contributes significantly towards paying off the mortgage (see eg *Winkworth v Edward Baron Development Co Ltd*).

The presumption of advancement

This displaces the presumption of resulting trust where the person transferring or paying the purchase price is the *husband* of the person to whom the property has been transferred (see *Re Eykyn's Trusts; Thornley v Thornley; Gascoigne v Gascoigne;* and *Tinker v Tinker* but note the reservations expressed about the continued applicability of the presumption in cases such as *Silver v Silver* and *Pettitt v Pettitt*).

This presumption also applies where a *father* transfers property to or purchases property in the name of a *legitimate child* (see *Re Roberts; Shepherd v Cartwright;* and *Re Crabb*); but not where a mother does the same (see *Re De Visme* and *Bennet v Bennet*).

The presumption can also be invoked where the person transferring property or paying the purchase price is *in loco parentis* (see *Ebrand v Dancer; Beckford v Beckford* and *Re Paradise Motor Co*).

Rebuttal

Both presumptions are capable of rebuttal. Thus, the presumption of *resulting trust* was deemed to have been rebutted in *Fowkes v Pascoe* and *Standing v Bowring;* while the presumption of advancement was rebutted in cases like *Scawin v Scawin; Warren v Gurney; Marshall v Crutwell* and most recently *Simson v Simpson*.

In *Shepherd v Cartwright*, the House of Lords laid down the basic rules governing the admissibility of evidence in rebuttal:

- acts/declarations made before or at the time of transfer are admissible in favour of the maker as well as against him;
- acts/declarations after transfer are admissible against the maker but inadmissible in his favour.

Evidence will also be inadmissible to rebut the *presumption of advancement*, where such evidence discloses that a husband or father has transferred or purchased property in the name of his wife or child to achieve an *illegal purpose* (see *Gascoigne v Gascoigne, Re Emery's Investments Trusts, Chettair v Chettair,* and *Tinker v Tinker*).

But where a person transfers property to a stranger or purchases or contributes to the purchase of property in a stranger's name, so that

the operative presumption is of *resulting trust*, the fact that the transaction was intended to achieve an illegal purpose, will not of itself render the presumption of resulting trust inapplicable (see *Tinsley v
Milligan; Garvin-Mack v Garvin-Mack*).

Automatic resulting trusts

Automatic resulting trusts commonly arise in these situations:

- where an express trust is not validly declared but property has
  passed to a trustee (see *Re Keen* and *Re Vandervell (No 2)*);
- where a validly declared express trust fails, because of an unful-
  filled condition as in *Re Ames' Settlement*;
- where the trust fails to dispose of the entire beneficial interest as in
  Re Cochrane;
- where a surplus is left after the purpose of the trust has been fully
  carried out as happened in *Re The Trusts Of The Abbott Fund* and *Re
  Gillingham Bus Disaster Fund*. Note however the refusal to impose
  resulting trusts in other cases such as *Re Andrew's Trust* and *Re
  Osoba*;
- where an unincorporated association has ceased to exist, its surplus
  funds have sometimes been dealt with on the footing that a result-
  ing trust arises in favour of the contributors. See eg *Re Printers &
  Transferrers [etc] Society*, *Re Hobourn Aero Components [etc] Fund* and
  Davis v Richards & Wallington Industries.
  In other cases, however, the courts have favoured a contractual
  approach with varying results see as *Cunnack v Edwards, Re West
  Sussex Constabulary [etc] Fund Trusts, Re Bucks Constabulary Friendly
  Society, Re GKN Bolts and Nuts [etc] Club* and *Re Sick & Funeral
  Society Of St Johns Sunday School, Golcar*;
- where money is made available for a stated purpose but can no
  longer be applied for that purpose, a Quistclose-type resulting trust
  will arise (see *Barclays Bank v Quistclose Investments Ltd, Carreras
  Rothmans Ltd v Freeman Mathews Treasure Ltd* and *Re EVTR Ltd*, but
  note *Guardian Ocean Cargoes v Banco Do Brasil*.

Constructive trusts

General
The constructive trust has usually been defined in terms which signify that it arises by operation of law rather than by reason of the intention of the parties. Neither this nor any other definitions are

93

considered entirely satisfactory, not least because the residual character of the constructive trust means that it is capable of arising in a wide range of situations which bear little relation to one another and which are not amenable to a single, all-embracing definition.

New model constructive trusts

In English law, the constructive trust has evolved as a substantive institution and English judges have traditionally imposed constructive trusts not on an *ad hoc* case-by-case basis in response to the dictates of conscience, but only within certain well-defined factual situations.

A more flexible approach is evident in America, where the constructive trust is employed as a remedial device designed to prevent unjust enrichment. The American approach provided the impetus for the emergence of the new model constructive trust in English law, with Lord Denning, as its main proponent.

In its heyday, reliance was placed on the new model trust:

- in determining the entitlement of spouses and co-habitees in disputes over the family home (eg *Cooke v Head* and *Eves v Eves*);
- in protecting a contractual licensee against a third party to whom the licensor had assigned the property (eg *Binions v Evans*);
- in protecting the holder of an unregistered equitable interest against a purchaser of the legal estate (eg *Peffer v Rigg*).

A number of criticisms have been levelled against the new model approach by judges and academic commentators alike, who feel that entitlement to property should be determined by reference to sure and settled principles rather than subjective notions of justice. It is therefore not entirely surprising that in recent years, the influence of the new model has waned considerably even in those areas with which it is most commonly associated. The decline of the new model is evident from such cases as *Burns v Burns*, *Grant v Edwards*, *Lloyds Bank v Rosset* and *Ashburn Anstalt v Arnold*.

Fiduciaries as constructive trustees

The essence of a fiduciary relationship is that one person reposes confidence on another by entrusting him with a job or task to perform (see *Reading v AG*). Where a fiduciary (eg a trustee, agent, employee, company director/promoter, partner, etc) seeks to profit from his position he will be liable to account as a constructive trustee.

The main situations in which constructive trusts have been imposed on fiduciaries are:

- where a fiduciary has received remuneration to which he is not properly entitled as in *Sugden v Crosland, Williams v Barton Erlanger v New Sombrero Phosphate Co, Re Macadam* and *Guinness Plc v Saunders;*
- where a fiduciary enters into a transaction on his own behalf which he should have pursued on his principal's behalf. See eg the rule in *Keech v Sanford* (renewal of leases/reversions) and cases like *Regal (Hastings) Ltd v Gulliver* and *IDC v Cooley;*
- where a fiduciary employs confidential information to his advantage as in *Boardman v Phipps.*

Where the enrichment of the fiduciary involves the receipt of a bribe *Lister v Stubbs* has decided that he will be liable personally but not as a constructive trustee. Recently, however, the Privy Council rejected this in *Reid v AG For Hong Kong.*

Strangers as constructive trustees

A constructive trust will not be imposed against a stranger who has received, disposed of or otherwise dealt with trust property where the stranger is:

- a bona fide purchaser for value without notice (*Pilcher v Rawlins*); or an innocent volunteer (*Re Diplock; Re Montagu's ST* and *Agip (Africa) Ltd v Jackson*);
- an agent who has neither been fraudulent, nor gone beyond his duties as an agent in dealing with trust property (*Lee v Sankey; Barnes v Addy; Mara v Browne*; and *Williams-Ashman v Price and Williams*).

On the other hand, a constructive trust is capable of being imposed against a stranger in the following circumstances:

- where the stranger is a *trustee de son tort* who has wrongfully assumed responsibility for administering the trust (see eg *Mara v Browne*);
- where the stranger *knowingly assists in a fraudulent and dishonest disposition of trust property* (*Barnes v Addy; Soar v Ashwell*). Liability may be imposed under this heading not only where the trust property has actually been transferred to the stranger to dispose of according to the trustee's directions (see *Agip Ltd v Jackson*),

but also where he has never been in receipt of such property (as in *Eaves v Hickson*).

There has been some debate concerning the degree of knowledge required in order for a stranger to be liable as a constructive trustee. Five possible categories of knowledge were identified by Peter Gibson J in the *Baden Delvaux case*. Categories (i)-(iii) are equated with *actual knowledge* and categories (iv) and (v) with *constructive knowledge*. The weight of judicial opinion appears to favour the view that before a constructive trust will be imposed for knowing assistance, there must be actual knowledge (such as would signify dishonesty or want of probity) and not just constructive knowledge (such as would signify negligence).

- where the stranger has *knowingly received trust property* for his own benefit (rather than having received it merely with a view to assisting the trustee in a breach of trust).

In this context there have also been differences of opinion regarding the degree of knowledge which a stranger must possess. In a number of cases, the courts accepted that a stranger would be liable whether he had actual knowledge (categories (i)-(iii)) or constructive knowledge (categories (iv)-(v)). However, in *Re Montagu's ST*, Megarry VC insisted that actual knowledge will be required. See also the recent judgement of Vinelott J in *Eagle Trust Plc v SBC Securities Ltd*. The view taken by Megarry VC has not completely prevailed, however, since there are indications in other recent cases that constructive knowledge will suffice in knowing receipt cases. See eg Millett J in *Agip Ltd v Jackson* and the Court of Appeal in *Polly Peck International Plc v Nadir*.

Mutual wills

Where two persons have reached an agreement concerning the manner in which their property shall devolve when they die, and embody this in their wills, if one party thereafter dies without revoking his will, equity will seek to prevent the survivor from going back on the agreement, by imposing a constructive trust. Accordingly, even if the survivor purports to revoke the will made pursuant to the agreement and execute a fresh will, his or her personal representative will be obliged to give effect to the terms of the agreement in preference to any inconsistent terms contained in the new will (see *Dufour v Pereira*; *Re Hagger*; *Re Cleaver* and *Re Dale*).

Trusts in the context of the family home

Disputes between a husband and wife regarding their respective enti-tlements to the family home will generally be determined on the basis of ss 24-25 MCA where they arise in the context of matrimonial pro-ceedings. But where the dispute is between the spouse and a third party or between an unmarried couple, the wide discretion conferred by the MCA will not avail the court.

In such circumstances, if the parties have in the process of acquiring the family home made formal declarations regarding their beneficial interests (eg in the conveyance), the court will give effect to this on the same basis as it would give effect to any *expressly declared trust* (see *Goodman v Gallant*).

Where both parties have contributed towards the purchase price and the property is in the name of one (commonly the man), an *imme-diate resulting trust* will be imposed in favour of the woman, where there is no express declaration regarding their beneficial interests.

Where the property is purchased by means of a mortgage taken out in the man's name and the property is conveyed in his name, a *cumu-lative resulting trust* will arise in favour of the woman:

- if she contributes substantially towards paying the mortgage (see *Burns v Burns; Winkworth v Edward Baron Developments* and *Lloyds Bank v Rosset*); or
- if she has enabled the man to pay off the mortgage by making sub-stantial financial contributions towards household expenses on the strength of a common intention that she would thereby acquire an interest in the property (see eg *Burns v Burns*).

Where the partner claiming a beneficial interest in the family home has not contributed directly towards the purchase price or paying off the mortgage, but relies on financial contributions to household expenses or contributions in kind, it is more common for such a claim to be founded on a constructive trust.

The House of Lords in *Pettitt v Pettitt* and *Gissing v Gissing*, laid down the basis on which the courts would impose a constructive trust in such circumstances. In particular, their Lordships specified that there must be *common intention* and *detrimental reliance*.

Significantly in such cases as *Cooke v Head, Eves v Eves* and *Hall v Hall*, where Lord Denning chose to resolve disputes about the family home by imposing *new model constructive trusts* he attached little weight to these requirements, being pre-occupied instead with the need to achieve a just solution. However, in subsequent cases culminating in the House of Lords decision in *Lloyd's Bank v Rosset*, the courts have re-affirmed the applicability of the orthodox principles enunciated in *Pettitt and Gissing*.

5 Charitable trusts

For centuries, public-spirited persons have sought to promote the general good of their society and the well-being of their fellow citizens by donating part of their wealth to charity. Some donors have been content to make gifts to voluntary bodies established for charitable purposes to assist in carrying out these purposes. Others have preferred to appoint trustees of their own choice to hold property on trust for purposes which are charitable.

The significance of charitable status

Responsibility for deciding whether a trust or voluntary body is charitable lies with the courts and the Charity Commissioners in their respective spheres of operation. Where a trust or voluntary body is adjudged to be charitable this is an acknowledgment that it is of such benefit to the public that it merits special treatment under the law. Charitable trusts therefore enjoy several advantages not available to trusts within the private domain.

- A private trust will generally fail unless the intended beneficiaries are identified with sufficient certainty. By contrast, a charitable trust is capable of being enforced by the Attorney General where the settlor merely outlines a purpose without referring either directly or indirectly to human beneficiaries. For example, if a testator leaves £10,000 'to A and B on trust for charitable purposes' without anything more this will be valid.

- A private trust will ordinarily fail where it is impossible to carry out the settlor's intention whereas the operation of the cy-pres doctrine means that a charitable trust is much less likely to fail on this account.
- Charitable trusts are capable of enduring for much longer periods than private trusts and there are currently many charities funded by endowments which are several centuries old. Such trusts are valid because the rule against perpetual duration which seeks to ensure that trust capital is not preserved for an excessively long period does not apply to charities.
- Charities enjoy tax advantages that are unavailable to private trusts or non-charitable bodies, eg exemptions from income tax, capital gains tax, corporation tax, value added tax, stamp duties and relief from non-domestic rates. This, above other reasons, is why charitable status is considered especially desirable and explains the involvement of the Revenue in many charity cases.

The requirements of a valid charitable trust

A charitable trust must satisfy three requirements, namely:

- the purposes or objects of the trust must be charitable;
- the trust must promote some public benefit;
- the trust must be wholly and exclusively charitable

Charitable purposes

In ordinary usage, the words charity/charitable connote the idea of goodwill or benevolence towards one's fellow men. As Lord Macnaghten emphasised in *Commissioners Of Special Income Tax v Pemsel* (1891) the popular meaning of these words are not identical with their legal meaning. Accordingly, it is not all purposes which may be regarded as charitable in the popular sense that will be charitable in the legal sense. By the same token, the fact that a donor considers the purpose of his gift to be charitable does not invariably make it charitable in the eyes of the law. See *Re Hummeltenberg* (1923) and *Re Pinion* (1965).

Viscount Simonds stated in *IRC v Baddely* (1955) that there is no limit to the number and diversity of ways in which a man may seek to benefit his fellow man. It is thus not surprising that Parliament and the courts have been unable to provide a single all-embracing definition of charity in the legal sense. The nearest we have to a statutory definition is s 96(1) Charities Act (1993) which defines charity to mean 'any institution, corporate or not, [including any trust] ... established for charitable purposes'.

This definition is not entirely helpful as it does not elaborate on the types of purposes which are charitable. Accordingly, in order to determine whether a purpose is charitable, it is still necessary to refer to the preamble to the Charitable Uses Act (CUA) 1601 as the courts have done for centuries. The approach adopted by the Courts has been:

* to recognise as charitable any trust whose purpose fits into any of the categories of purposes that were specifically declared to be charitable by the CUA; and
* to extend, by analogy, the range of recognised charitable purposes to include those which come within the spirit and intendment of the CUA. As Lord Wilberforce observed in *Scottish Burial Reform Society v Glasgow City Corporation* (1968), this pragmatic approach has enabled the courts over the centuries to develop the law in this field in a manner which has kept pace with changing social trends, needs and attitudes.

The purposes enumerated in the CUA and those falling within its spirit and intendment have been classified into four headings by Lord Macnaghten in the *Pemsel* case; namely:

* the relief of poverty;
* the advancement of education;
* the advancement of religion; and
* other purposes beneficial to the community.

The relief of poverty

The preamble to the CUA refers to 'the relief of aged, impotent and poor people'. This has been construed disjunctively so that a trust will be charitable if its beneficiaries are poor but not aged or sick (see *Rowntrees Housing Association v AG* (1983).

In seeking to ascertain whether a trust is for the relief of poverty, an initial difficulty stems from the fact that poverty, as Evershed MR remarked in *Re Coulthurst* (1951) 'is a word of wide and somewhat indefinite import'. He suggested as a general proposition that persons can fairly be regarded as poor if they have to go short in the ordinary acceptation of the term regard being had to their status in life and so on. What amounts to poverty may thus range from utter destitution to the relative deprivation felt by those who have known better times.

The most obvious way of creating trusts for the relief of poverty is for prospective settlors to employ the words 'poor/poverty' as in *AG v Peacock* (1676) and *Re Darling* (1896); or similar terms such as 'needy': *Re Reed* (1893) and *Re Scarisbrick* (1951); 'indigent': *Weir v Crum-Brown* (1908); 'limited means': *Re Gardom* (1914); or 'fall[en] on evil days': *Re Young's WT* (1953) etc.

Even where the word 'poor' or a similar expression has not been used it may still be possible to deduce from the nature and context of a gift that it is to relieve poverty. In *Biscoe v Jackson* (1877) a legacy for the foundation of a cottage hospital and soup kitchen was held to have been intended by the testator to benefit the poor. Also in *Re Lucas* (1922) a fund, out of which modest payments were to be made to the oldest respectable inhabitants of Gunville was held to have been intended for the benefit of the aged poor in the locality, because of the small amounts involved.

However, a trust will not charitable under this heading, where it is not exclusively for the benefit of the poor in general or a particular class of poor persons. In *Re Gwyon* (1930), a fund to provide clothing for boys in Farnham was held not to be for the relief of poverty since there was nothing to indicate that only the children of the poor could receive such clothing. Again in *Re Sander's WT* (1954) a scheme intended to provide houses for the working classes in a given locality was held not to be for the relief of poverty since not all those belonging to 'the working classes' were poor persons. Contrast with *Re Niyazi's WT* (1978).

Finally, as Peter Gibson J emphasised in the *Rowntree* case, a gift will only be valid under the present heading where the application of the trust fund is intended to relieve needs which are associated with the condition of poverty in so far as the persons in such a condition cannot alleviate such needs from their own resources or can only do so with difficulty.

The advancement of education

The preamble to the CUA specifically refers to 'maintenance of schools of learning, free schools and scholars in universities' and 'the education and preferment of orphans'. In line with this, the ancient universities and public schools have for centuries been recognised as charitable foundations and the same status has been been accorded to newer universities, colleges and schools. Purposes falling within the terms of the preamble which the courts have upheld as charitable include the endowment of professorships and lectureships (*AG v Margaret & Regius Professors In Cambridge* (1682)); the provision of stipends for fellows and scholars of a College (*The Case Of Christ's College Cambridge* (1757) and the award of prizes in schools (*Re Mariette* (1915)).

Since the CUA was enacted, it has come to be recognised that the advancement of education encompasses much more than the process of learning in a classroom environment. As Wilberforce J observed in *Re Hopkins' WT* (1964) 'the word education must be used in a wide sense, certainly extending beyond teaching'. In *Incorporated Council Of Law Reporting v AG* (1972) Buckley LJ described education in this extended sense as 'the improvement of a useful branch of human knowledge and its public dissemination'.

Examples of purposes that have been upheld as charitable in the educational sphere include the following:

Research

There is no difficulty in recognising as charitable, the conduct of research in such fields as medicine, science or technology since advances in these fields are likely to be of demonstrable practical benefit to the community.

The position is less clear-cut where the research is into areas of knowledge which are unlikely to have far-reaching practical applications as seen from cases like *Re Shaw's WT* (1952) and *Re Hopkins' WT*. In *Re Shaw's WT*, the proposed research was into the advantages of replacing the existing 26 letter alphabet with a 40 letter alphabet. Harman J considered that the object of such research was 'merely the increase of knowledge' and held that it was not charitable. A more liberal view was taken in *Re Hopkin's WT* where research by the Francis Bacon Society with a view to locating the Bacon-Shakespeare papers was held to be charitable. In reaching this conclusion Wilberforce J signified that research would be considered charitable if it was of educational value to the researcher or so directed as to lead to something that would pass into the store of educational material or improve the sum of communicable knowledge in a particular area.

The position with regard to research was reviewed in *McGovern v AG* (1981) where Slade J outlined conditions which must be satisfied in order for research to qualify as charitable, namely:

- the subject-matter of the proposed research should be a useful area of study;
- the end-product of the research should be for the benefit of the public or an appreciable section thereof; and
- it must be within the contemplation of the researchers and the donor who is funding the research that the knowledge acquired from the research would be disseminated to others.

Publication of educational material

In *Incorporated Council Of Law Reporting v AG* a non-profit making body engaged in publishing law reports was held to be charitable (see also *Re Stanford* (1924) (publication of a new English dictionary).

Museums etc

The courts regard the foundation and maintenance of such amenities as museums, libraries, zoological gardens etc to be of sufficient educational value to be charitable (see *British Museum Trustees v White* (1826) and *Re Lopes* (1931)).

Learned/professional bodies

It is clear from a host of cases that various learned societies and professional bodies are deemed to be engaged in activities which contribute to the advancement of education and are therefore to be accorded charitable status (see *Royal College Of Surgeons v National Provincial Bank* (1952); *Royal College Of Nursing v St Marylebone BC* (1959); *Institute Of Civil Engineers v IRC* (1932) and *CITB v AG* (1973).

Artistic activities

Cases like *Re Shakespeare Memorial Trust* (1923), *Royal Choral Society v IRC* (1943) and *Re Delius* (1957) show that advancement of education includes promoting various art forms. As Greene MR put it in *Royal Choral Society v IRC*:

A body of persons established for the purpose of raising the artistic taste of the country is established for educational purposes because the education of artistic taste is one of the most important things in the development of a civilised human being.

By contrast, in *Re Pinion* (1965), a gift of an art studio and its contents with directions for it to be converted into a museum open to the public was held not to be charitable. Experts testified that the collection was no more than a haphazard assembly of objects with little artistic or aesthetic merit and the court decided that no useful educational purpose could conceivably be served by foisting such a pile of junk on an unsuspecting public.

Sports and pastimes

A trust to promote sports or leisure among a group of persons is not generally treated as charitable. The courts have, however, accepted that the provision of sporting facilities or the promotion of various games either in a particular school or among students or pupils generally is charitable in the educational sphere since recreation is widely regarded as an important facet of a child's education.

Thus in *Re Mariette*, a gift to a school, to enable it to build Squash and Eton Fives courts for its pupils was upheld as charitable. Also in *IRC v Mcmullen* (1981) a trust to provide facilities for pupils at schools and universities for football or other games or sports was held to be charitable.

An issue raised in *Re Dupree's DT* (1945) that remains unresolved is where the line is to be drawn between sports and pastimes that are educational and those that are not. Vaisey J held in this case that an annual youth chess competition was charitable but in so doing declared:

One feels, perhaps, that one is on a rather slippery slope. If chess, why not draughts? If draughts, why not bezique and so on to bridge and whist and by another route, to stamp collecting and the acquisition of bird's eggs?

Students Unions

Almost every university or college has a students union which exists primarily to promote the welfare of its student body. As seen from *Baldry v Feintuck* (1972), *London Hospital Medical College v IRC* (1976), *AG v Ross* (1986) and *Webb v O'Doherty* (1991), such unions have been recognised as charitable on the footing that their activities serve to advance the main educational purpose of their parent university/college.

One point that emerges clearly from the decisions in *Baldry v Feintuck, AG v Ross and Webb v O'Doherty* is that insofar as unions are accorded charitable status on the premise that their purposes are educational, they can be restrained from devoting their funds to overtly political causes. This accords with the well-established principle:

Political propaganda masquerading ... as education is not education within the [preamble to the CUA] ... In otherwords it is not charitable (per Vaisey J in Re Hopkinson (1949)).

See also *Bonar Law Memorial Trust v IRC* (1933), *Re Bushnell* (1975) and *McGovern v AG*.

The advancement of religion

The repair of churches is the only religious purpose expressly set out in the CUA. However, within a few years after the Act came into force the courts began to accept other religious purposes as charitable. For example, in *Pember v Inhabitants of Kington* (1639) a gift to maintain a preaching minister was pronounced to be charitable. Today, a wide range of purposes and organisations are recognised as charitable within the religious sphere.

Advancement of religion in the context of Christianity

When the CUA was enacted, Christianity was the only religion known to the vast majority of the population. Consequently, the advancement of religion has been overwhelmingly associated with Christianity and the courts have recognised as charitable a host of Christian denominations including:

- The Church of England (*Re Barnes* (1930) and *Re Tonbridge School Chapel (No 2)* (1993));
- The Roman Catholic Church (*Re Hetherington* (1989); *Re Flynn* (1948) and *Re Schoales* (1930));
- The Baptist Church (*Re Stricklands WT* (1936));
- The Unitarians (*Re Nesbitt's WT* (1953)); and
- The Exclusive (Plymouth) Brethren (*Holmes v AG* (1981)).

Within the realm of Christianity, gifts for a wide range of purposes have been held to be charitable. These include:

- the upkeep of the clergy (*Middleton v Clitheroe* (1798); *Re Williams* (1927) and *Re Forster* (1939));

- the promotion of the missionary work of bodies like the Church Missionary Society (*Re Clergy Society* (1856) and the Society for the Propagation of the Gospel in Foreign Parts (*Re Maguire* (1870));
- the support of religious communities which undertake spiritual, pastoral or social work involving contact with the outside world (see *Re Banfield* (1968). But contrast with *Gilmour v Coats* (1949));
- the saying of masses for the dead (*Re Hetherington* (1989)) and the preaching of sermons (*Re Parker's Charity*) (1863));
- the erection and maintenance of a churches, chapels etc or parts thereof such as a stained glass window (*Re King* (1923)); a chancel (*Hoare v Osborne* (1866)); church bells (*Re Pardoe* (1906)); the gallery (*AG v Day* (1900)); the church organ (*AG v Oakover* (1736)) or the maintenance of graveyards and monuments attached to the church (*Re Vaughan* (1886); *Re Douglas* (1905) and *Re Eighmie* (1935).

Even where a gift is not expressed to be for a specific purpose of a religious nature, the courts have often been able to deduce from the language that the gift is intended to further the cause of Christianity and is therefore charitable as in *Re Darling* (1896) where the material words were 'to the service of God' and (*Re Barker's WT*) where the gift was 'for God's work'.

In the same manner, where a donor makes a gift to an official such as a bishop or vicar, who by virtue of his office performs religious functions without specifying any purposes, the courts have held in such cases as *Re Garrard* (1907); *Re Flinn* (1948) and *Re Rumball* (1956) that this will be a valid charitable gift for the advancement of religion.

Finally, the courts have displayed a high degree of tolerance even to obscure sects on the fringes of Christianity. In *Thornton v Howe* (1862), Romilly MR upheld as charitable, a trust for the publication of the writings of Joanna Southcott whose followers believed that she was with child by the Holy Spirit and would give birth to a new messiah, even though he, apparently regarded this belief as foolish and devoid of foundation. Also in *Re Watson* (1973), Plowman J upheld as charitable a trust to propagate the Scriptures as expounded in the works of a certain Hobbs who was the leader of a small group of undenominational fundamentalist Christians despite evidence that the works had no intrinsic merit. It even emerges from *Orme and Durst v Associated Newspapers Ltd* (1980) that trusts set up by the Unification Church (the 'Moonies') had been registered as charities.

The charitable status of non-Christian faiths

In *Thornton v Howe*, Romilly MR observed that 'the Court of Chancery makes no distinction between one sort of religion and another'. This view was echoed a century later in *Neville Estates v Madden* (1962) by Cross J who affirmed that 'as between religions the law stands neutral, but it assumes that any religion is better than no religion at all'. In line with this he held that a trust created to build and run a synagogue was a valid religious trust.

As British society has grown increasingly multi-cultural, this liberal approach has also been adopted in dealing with other faiths. Thus for instance, a host of organisations which promote religions such as Islam, Hinduism and Sikhism have now registered as charities by the Charity Commission (see for example *Birmingham Mosque Trust Ltd v Alavi* (1992)).

The position of non-religious bodies which promote ethical standards and principles

While most religions seek to regulate the conduct of adherents by imposing strict moral codes, the essence of religion is a belief in and devotion to a higher unseen power which is deemed to be worthy of worship and reverence. Accordingly, an ethical or moral society which is not concerned with the worship of a supernatural being will not be charitable in the religious sense (see *Re South Place Ethical Society* (1980) and *United Grand Lodge v Holborn BC* (1957)).

Other purposes beneficial to the community

Some of the purposes set out in the CUA (notably the relief of the aged and impotent and the repair of bridges, causeways, havens, seabanks and highways) are not concerned with promoting education or religion or relieving poverty and have thus been categorised as other purposes beneficial to the community.

In addition, over the years, the courts have responded to changing social conditions by treating as charitable under this residual category, gifts for a wide range of other purposes not expressly provided for in the preamble. Even where no purpose is specified but a trust is declared for the inhabitants of a named locality it qualifies as a charitable trust under this heading as seen from *Goodman v Saltash Corp* (1882) and *Peggs v Lamb* (1993).

In determining which purposes are charitable under the fourth heading, various judges have favoured different approaches. On the one hand, in *Williams Trustees v IRC* (1947), Lord Simmonds opined that when a new purpose is being considered, the courts must be satisfied not merely that it is beneficial to the community but that it is beneficial in a manner adjudged to be within the spirit and intendment of the CUA. On the other hand in *ICLR v AG* Russell LJ advocated a more flexible approach arguing that where the purpose in question is one that appears to be demonstrably beneficial to the community or of general public utility, effect should be given to it under the fourth heading unless there is some good ground for otherwise excluding it.

The categories of purposes which the courts have had to deal with under the fourth heading include the following:

The welfare of the aged and the impotent

A trust for the benefit of the elderly is charitable, whether its purpose is to provide them with direct financial aid (as in *Re Lucas* (1922) and *Re Robinson* (1951)) or to provide them with facilities and services such as accommodation (as in *Re Cottam's WT* (1955) and *Joseph Rowntree Memorial Trust Housing Assn Ltd v AG* (1983)).

Such a trust will be valid, whether it is expressly stated to be for the elderly or for persons over a specified age (60 in *Re Glyn's WT* (1950) and 65 in *Re Robinson/Re Cottam's WT*); or for persons in an establishment such as a nursing home for the elderly (as in *Re Bradbury* (1950)).

As Dankwerts J emphasised in *Re Glyn's WT* it is not necessary that the intended beneficiaries must be poor as well as elderly for the trust to be charitable. Note however, the problem posed by Megarry (1951) 67 LQR 164 and (1955) 71 LQR 16 on whether there can be a charitable trust for elderly millionaires.

The relief of the impotent

Where a trust is intended to alleviate the condition of persons afflicted by sickness, injury, disease, or other physical or mental ailments this will render it charitable. Purposes that have been upheld as charitable include:

* the funding of hospitals which do not operate for private profit (see *Re Smith's WT* (1962) and *Re Resch's WT* (1969)).
* establishing a home for the nurses in a hospital (see *Re White's WT* (1951));

- promoting the well-being of patients by providing accommodation for their relatives (see *Re Dean's WT* (1950));
- providing assistance to persons with particular disabilities such as blindness (see *Re Lewis* (1955));
- caring for persons addicted to alcohol, drugs etc (see *Re Banfield* (1968)); or persons in need of recuperation from stress-induced conditions (see *Re Chaplin* (1933));
- the training of medical and nursing personnel (see *Royal College Of Nursing v St Marylebone Corpn* (1959)); and
- the conduct of medical research (see *Steel v Wellcome Custodian Trustees Ltd* (1988)).

The provision and maintenance of public works and amenities

The courts have upheld as charitable, trusts for the building or maintaining bridges and highways (*AG v Governors Of Harrow School* (1754) and *Forbes v Forbes* (1854)); the supply of water to a town (*Jones v Williams* (1767)); the provision of a hall for the public (*Re Spence* (1938)) and the erection of public statues or other memorials to honour nationally or internationally renowned persons (see the Report of the Charity Commissioners for 1981).

The relief of human suffering or distress

Disasters

Where an appeal fund is set up in response to a particular accident or disaster such a fund may be accorded charitable status. This was the case, for instance, with the appeal fund launched in 1966 in the wake of the Aberfan Disaster in which a huge coal tip collapsed, killing 116 children and 28 adults.

Where the stated object of the appeal is to alleviate suffering and deprivation caused to disaster victims or their families, those administering the fund may claim charitable status on the basis that it is for the relief of poverty, even where the class of potential beneficiaries is small.

Even if the appeal is not framed in such specific terms, the fund may still be deemed charitable if the class of potential beneficiaries is sufficiently large to constitute an appreciable section of the community. In *Re North Devon And West Somerset Relief Fund Trusts* (1953) an appeal fund was launched in response to the Lynmouth flood disaster of 1952 inviting the public to contribute to the relief of those affected by the disaster. After examining the terms of the appeal Wynn-Parry J declared that he was unable to discover 'any intention to benefit this part of the community in any way which the law did not regard as charitable' and therefore concluded that the fund was charitable.

The position is different where an appeal is made in terms which are not exclusively charitable. In *Re Gillingam Bus Disaster Fund* (1958) an appeal which was launched after an accident in which some Marine cadets were killed and others injured stated that the fund was to be applied towards the funeral expenses of the dead and the care of the injured and that any surplus was to be used for worthy causes. Harman J refused to hold that the fund was charitable on the ground that while charitable purposes were undoubtedly worthy causes, not every worthy cause was charitable in nature.

Emergency/rescue services

Gifts to bodies involved in relieving human suffering by dealing with life-threatening emergencies are treated as charitable under this heading (see *Thomas v Howell* (1874) and *Re Wokingham Fire Brigade Trusts* (1951)).

The improvement of national security

One of the purposes specified in the preamble to the CUA is the 'setting out of soldiers'. This has been enlarged by the courts to cover other purposes which serve to enhance the efficiency or morale of the armed forces, such as improving the shooting ability of soldiers (*Re Stephens* (1892)); or protecting the UK from attack by hostile aircraft (*Re Driffil* (1949)).

Gifts to various units of the army have also been recognised as charitable in cases like *Re Lord Stratheden And Campbell* (1894), *Re Good* (1905) and *Re Gray* (1925). In *Re Gray* for instance, the gift in question was to the 6th Dragoon Guards to promote shooting, fishing, cricket, football, polo etc. Contrast, however, with *IRC v Glasgow (City) Police Athletics Association* (1953). Here an association to promote sports and general pastimes within a police force was refused charitable status.

The encouragement of good citizenship or moral welfare

Where a gift is for a purpose designed to encourage good citizenship or uplift the moral tone of the society it will be charitable under the fourth heading. Thus for instance, in *Re South Place Ethical Society,*

111

Dillon J, decided that although a body engaged in the study and dissemination of ethical principles was not charitable in the religious sphere it was charitable under this heading.

Gifts for a wide range of purposes have also been held to be charitable in the present context. These include:

- the discouragement of the traffic in drink (*Re Hood* (1931));
- the institution of prizes for the best kept gardens in a parish (*Re Pleasants* (1923));
- the purchase of camp sites for Boy Scouts (*Re Webber* (1954)).

The well-being of animals

Gifts and bodies which are intended to promote the welfare of animals have been upheld as charitable in cases like *University Of London v Yarrow* (1857), *Re Wedgewood* (1915) and *Re Moss* (1949). The rationale for this is that kindness to animals tends to check any inborn human tendency to cruelty and is therefore beneficial to society.

It is, however, clear from *Re Grove-Grady* (1929) and *National Anti-Vivisection Society v IRC* (1948) that not all purposes connected with animal welfare qualify as charitable. In the first case, a gift to a society whose objects included establishing a refuge for animals against molestatation or destruction by man was held not to be charitable. In the court's view, it conferred no benefits on mankind by offering advantages to animals that were useful to man or by allowing observation or research; nor did it neccesarily offer protection to animals generally. In the latter case, the Anti-Vivisection Society whose primary goal was the banning of experiments using animals was denied charitable status on the ground that the benefits yielded by such experiments outweighed any interest to be served by discontinuing them.

Recreation and sports

It was decided in *Re Hadden* (1932) and *Re Morgan* (1955) and reaffirmed in *IRC v Guild* (1992) and *Oldham Borough Council v AG* (1993) that the provision of playing fields, parks and other recreational facilities for the general public or those living in a particular locality is charitable.

In addition, sporting activities or facilities which are not open to the public may qualify as charitable because they are linked with the education of the young (*IRC v Mcmullin; Re Mariette*); or promote the efficiency of the armed services (*Re Gray*).

Except in the situations outlined above, the courts have decided in such cases as *Re Nottage* (1895), *Re Clifford* (1911) and *Re Patten* (1929) that the promotion of sport or the provision of recreational amenities are not charitable purposes.

In another line of cases including *IRC v City of Glasgow Police Athletics Assn, Williams Trustees v IRC* and *IRC v Baddely*, bodies which were set up for purposes that might otherwise have been upheld as charitable, were denied charitable status on the ground that their purposes were framed in terms which included a purely social or recreational dimension. In *Baddeley*, land was conveyed to a Methodist mission to establish a community centre. The centre was to provide facilities for religious services and for the social and physical training and recreation of Methodists and those likely to become Methodists who were living in West Ham and Leyton. Whereas the gift would clearly have been charitable had the proposed centre been exclusively for religion the inclusion of the social-recreational element and the fact that the recreational amenities would not be open to the public led the House of Lords to conclude that it was not charitable.

This decision placed in doubt the status of civic amenities such as village halls and community centres as well as Womens Institutes and miners' welfare associations which were hitherto deemed to be charitable. The Recreational Charities Act 1958 was enacted to clear these doubts. In summary, the Act states that it is charitable to provide or assist in the provision of facilities for recreation or other leisure-time activities if these facilities are provided in the interests of social welfare.

In order to fulfil the social welfare requirement, two conditions must be satisfied. These facilities must:

- have been provided with the object of improving the condition of life of persons for whom they are primarily intended;
- must be available either
  (a) for the use of the public at large or the female members of the public; or
  (b) on a more restricted basis for persons who by reason of infirmity, disability, youth, age, social/economic circumstances have need for such facilities.

The Act fell to be considered in *IRC v Mcmullin* in relation to a trust sponsored by the Football Association to promote soccer among pupils and university students. The trial judge and the majority of the Court of Appeal concluded that facilities would be charitable under the Act, only if they would benefit those who were considered to be deprived or in some form of need. Not all pupils or students who might benefit from the present trust were in such need and the trust was thus held not to be charitable under the Act. Bridge LJ however dissented, arguing that it was not a strict requirement for the conferment of charitable status under the Act, that use of the facilities must be confined to the deprived. His position has subsequently been endorsed in *IRC v Guild* where the House of Lords accepted that a council-owned Leisure Centre was charitable within the meaning of the Act, even though access to it was not restricted to the deprived or needy.

The requirement of public benefit

As a general rule, a trust is not charitable if it is for the benefit of persons belonging to the benefactor's private circle, who he would naturally feel obliged to provide for; but is charitable only if it is intended to benefit the wider community or the public at large in some way. The issue of public benefit has assumed immense importance since World War II when great increases in personal and corporate taxes have made the fiscal advantages enjoyed by charities particularly attractive. Remarking on this trend Lord Cross in *Dingle v Turner* (1972), spoke of the temptation 'to enlist the assistance of the law of charity in private endeavours in order to gain tax benefits'. While the law does not object to legitimate activities in the private domain, policy considerations dictate that only those which are of wider public benefit deserve to be subsidised in this manner by the taxpayer.

The degree of strictness with which the courts approach the issue of public benefit depends on which of Lord McNaghten's headings they are dealing with in any particular case and we must therefore examine the public benefit requirement under each heading.

Trusts for the relief of poverty

A gift to specified persons who happen to be poor will not be deemed to be charitable however numerous they may be. On the other hand, as pointed out by Jenkins LJ in *Re Scarisbrick* (1951) and Templeman J in *Re Cohen* (1973) a gift is to the poor members of a class to relieve their poverty will be charitable, even if the class is small and personally connected to the donor.

To begin with, it has long been established in such cases as *Isaac v Defriez* (1754) that where the object of a trust is to relieve poverty among the donor's relatives, notwithstanding the narrowness of the class and the personal nexus, the gift will be regarded as charitable. Although the charitable status of gifts to poor relations was questioned in *Re Compton* (1945), it has since been re-affirmed in cases like *Re Scarisbrick* and *Re Cohen*.

As with gifts to poor relations, the courts have also recognised as charitable, gifts for the relief of poverty among:

- members of a friendly society (*Re Buck* (1896));
- fellow members of the donor's club (*Re Young* (1951));
- the employees of a given firm or company (*Re Gosling* (1900); *Gibson v South American Stores Ltd* (1950) and *Dingle v Turner*).

This recognition that gifts to the poor members of what is essentially a private class are charitable has led Hanbury and Martin to conclude that 'the requirement of public benefit has been reduced in the field of poverty almost to vanishing point'.

Trusts for the advancement of education

Where a trust is for a purpose other than the relief of poverty, the public benefit requirement is applied more stringently. In order for such a trust to be charitable, it must, in the words of Lord Westbury in *Verge v Somervell* be for the benefit of the community or an appreciably important class of the community.

The effect of the public benefit requirement in the educational sphere is illustrated by *Re Compton* (1945) which involved a trust for educating the descendants of three named persons. In deciding whether it was charitable, the Court of Appeal had to determine whether the intended beneficiaries were an appreciable section of the community. According to the court a designated group would form an appreciable section of the community if (i) they were not numerically negligible and (ii) the quality that distinguished them from the community at large was not one which depended on their relationship to a particular individual. Applying this test, the Court held that the present trust was not charitable.

The Compton test was adopted in *Oppenheim v Tobacco Securities Trust* (1951) where the House of Lords had to decide whether a trust for the education of the children of employees and former employees of a tobacco company was charitable. The class was not numerically negligible as there were over 110,000 employees. This was not conclusive, however, for as Lord Simonds emphasised in the lead judgment 'a group of persons may be numerous, but if the nexus between them is their personal relationship to a single propositus or to several propositus they are neither the community nor a section of the community for charitable purposes'. The nexus between the potential beneficiaries in this case was their relationship to a single employer. In the court's view this was sufficiently personal to prevent the trust from being charitable.

Lord Macdermott, however, dissented, arguing that the *Compton* test ought not to be treated as being of general applicability and conclusiveness. In his view, the issue of whether a group constituted a section of the community, was one of degree to be dealt with on the facts of each case rather than on the basis of any hard and fast rule inherent in the test. His judgment vividly highlights the contradictions and difficulties flowing from a strict application of the test and similar views were expressed *per obiter* by Lord Cross in *Dingle v Turner*.

Following the *Oppenheim* decision, those seeking to create trusts to educate the children of employees have sometimes set up educational trusts ostensibly for the public while arranging for the trustees to use most of the trust fund to educate the employees' children. Thus in *Re Koettgen* (1954) a trust was set up to offer commercial education to members of the public unable to afford it but the trustees were directed to accord preference to families of the employees of a named company in respect of up to 75% of the trust fund. The trust was held to be charitable. By contrast in *IRC v Educational Grants Assn Ltd* (1967) an association was set up for the advancement of education in general terms but derived its funds from the Metal Box Co Ltd. The association claimed a tax rebate for a particular period on the basis that it was a charitable body. The court found that during the period in question, between 76% and 85% of its income had been paid towards educating the children of persons connected with the company and therefore held that it was not entitled to the rebate (see also *Caffor v Income Tax Commissioner Colombo* (1961)).

Trusts for the advancement of religion

In the sphere of religion as in the sphere of education, the courts are prepared to uphold a gift as charitable only if it is deemed to be of benefit to the public or a section thereof. However, whereas the *Compton* test prescribes that in the realm of education the recipients of the benefit must not be numerically negligible, the law appears to be more liberal in the religious sphere since charitable status has been accorded to obscure sects with a minimal following in cases such as *Thornton v Howe* and *Re Watson*. In this connection, the material consideration is whether the essential purpose is to make available a religious service or activity to those members of the public who wish to avail themselves of it, even though very few choose to do so.

By contrast, where the material purpose is to encourage religious pursuits in an environment completely insulated from the public, the courts are less inclined to regard the purpose as charitable. This is vividly illustrated by the case of *Gilmour v Coats* (1949) which involved a gift of £500 to a Carmelite convent run by a community of cloistered nuns who devoted themselves entirely to prayer and contemplation and did not engage in any activities whatsoever outside their community. The House of Lords held that the community's activities did not satisfy the requirement of public benefit and the gift was therefore not charitable.

The decision in *Gilmour v Coats* cast doubt on the correctness of cases such as *Re Caus* (1934), which had held that gifts for the saying of masses were charitable. Significantly however, in the recent case of *Re Hetherington* (1989), where a testatrix left £2,000 for the saying of masses for the repose of her soul and the souls of her husband, parents and sisters, it was held that the gift satisfied the public benefit requirement on two grounds:

• The gift could properly be construed as requiring the masses to be said in public. Such a public celebration of a religious rite would have such an edifying effect on those attending that this would be a sufficient public benefit.

• The sum dedicated to saying masses would help provide stipends for priests thereby assisting in the endowment of the priesthood.

Trusts for other purposes beneficial to the community

The public benefit requirement is central to the validity of trusts coming within the fourth heading since the common denominator by which they are defined is that they must be for purposes that are of benefit to the community. This means that whatever advantages or entitlements are conferred by a trust under this heading must, as stated in *Verge v Somervill*, be available to the community or an appreciable section of the community.

The operation of the requirement under this heading was considered in *IRC v Williams Trustees*. In this case, one reason why a trust for the benefit of Welsh people in London failed was that the Welsh in London did not form an appreciable section of the community. Also instructive is *IRC v Baddeley* where the intended beneficiaries were

117

members/would-be members of the Methodist Church in an area of London. The House of Lords held that the requirement was not satisfied since the benefit was intended not for the whole community or the inhabitants of a given geographical area, but for what was essentially a class within a class.

A difficulty that arises in this connection is that opinions will sometimes differ on whether a designated group of persons in a given geographical area constitutes a section of the community or a private class. Thus for instance, as Lord Cross indicated in *Dingle v Turner* a trust for the benefit of the ratepayers of the Royal Borough of Kensington and Chelsea may be construed by some as a charitable trust for a section of the community and by others as a trust for a fluctuating body of private individuals.

Finally, once it is clear that the purpose of a trust is to confer some benefit on the public or an appreciable section thereof, the fact that only a limited number of people may wish to take advantage of it will not be a basis for holding that it is not charitable. As Lord Simonds observed in this connection in *Baddely*, A bridge which is available for all the public may undoubtedly be a charity and it is indifferent how many people use it. But confine it to a selected number of persons, however numerous and important, it is then not clearly a charity'.

The requirement that the trust must be exclusively charitable

The general rule is that if a trust is framed in terms which enable the trustees without being in breach of trust to apply any part of the trust fund to a non-charitable purpose, it will fail.

Thus in *Williams Trustees v IRC*, a trust that was predominantly for charitable purposes in the educational sphere nevertheless failed because one of its purposes was the promotion of sport and recreation among Welsh people living in London which was not charitable. This was also the case in *IRC v City Of Glasgow Police Athletics Association* where the association had a charitable dimension (improving the efficiency of the police) and a non-charitable dimension (catering for the recreational and social needs of its members).

Substitution of the word 'charitable' with words of wider import

Quite often the failure of an intended charitable gift on the ground that it is not exclusively charitable is caused by poor drafting. The most common pitfall for unwary draftsmen is the use of words which in ordinary parlance carry the same general connotation as the term charity but which have been held to be of wider import than the notion of charity in the legal sense. In *Morice v Bishop of Durham* (1805) a gift to the Bishop of Durham to be applied by him 'to such objects of benevolence and liberality' as he should most approve failed because its objects were not exclusively charitable. And in *Re Gillingham Bus Disaster Fund*, it was held that a disaster appeal made on the basis that part of the fund would be applied to 'worthy causes' was not exclusively charitable since certain causes might conceivably be worthy without being charitable.

Combination of the word 'charitable' with words of wider import

The courts sometimes have to pronounce on the validity of a trust where the draftsman has employed words which in themselves would be construed as charitable together with words of wider import.

The 'or' cases

If the word 'or' appears between multiple purposes one of which is charitable and the other of wider import, the courts will ordinarily construe the 'or' as disjunctive and hold that the gift is not exclusively charitable. See *Blair v Duncan* (1902): charitable or public; *Re Diplock* (1951): charitable or benevolent; *AG v NPB* (1924): charitable or patriotic; and *Houston v Burns* (1918): public, benevolent or charitable.

These may however be contrasted with *Re Bennett* (1920) which held that a gift 'for charity or other public purpose' was charitable. In the court's view, the use of the word 'other' in the present context signified that the type of public purpose contemplated by the donor was one *ejusdem generis* with charity. Also in *Guild v IRC* a gift for establishing a public leisure centre 'or some similar purpose connected with sport was held to be charitable.

The 'and' cases

Where the word 'and' appears between two expressed purposes, the first of which is charitable and the second non-charitable, the words will generally be construed in a conjunctive manner. Consequently, any word of wider import which if employed in isolation would encompass non-charitable purposes will be qualified by the accompanying charitable purpose, such that the trust will be regarded as exclusively charitable. Thus in *Blair v Duncan*, the court remarked that if the material phrase had been 'charitable and public', rather than 'charitable or public', effect might have been given to the trust because the words could have been read as charitable gifts of a public character or vice-versa (see also *Re Sutton* (1885): charitable and deserving and *Re Best* (1904): charitable and benevolent).

On the other hand, where a trust is expressed to be for more than two purposes and the word 'and' is inserted between the last two purposes, such a trust is not regarded as exclusively charitable (see *Re Eades* (1835): religious, charitable and philanthropic; and *Williams v Kershaw* (1920): benevolent, charitable and religious).

Situations in which inclusion of non-charitable purposes will not invalidate a charitable trust

Where the charitable object of the trust is facilitated by non-charitable purposes

A gift or organisation may be regarded as charitable even where its objects permit a certain amount of expenditure of a non-charitable nature if such expenditure facilitates the carrying out its charitable purposes. In *Re Coxen* (1948), a sum of over 200,000 was left on trust for the Court of Aldermen of the City of London for the following purposes:

* £100 pa for a dinner at their annual meeting to discuss the affairs of the trust and 1:1s to each alderman for attendance;
* the balance to be applied by them for them in support of a specified medical charity. The trust was held to be charitable.

Where the non-charitable dimensions of the trust are incidental to its main charitable object

* As Lord Cohen explained in *IRC v Glasgow Police Athletics Assn* a trust will be recognised as charitable where its 'main purpose ... is

charitable and the only elements in its constitution and operation which are non-charitable are merely incidental'. This reasoning was adopted in *Incorporated Council Of Law Reporting v AG* where it was contended that the publication of law reports by the Council was not exclusively charitable since legal practitioners often benefitted from fees earned by using such reports. The court held that the monetary benefit to legal practitioners was incidental to the main purpose of the reports which was to provide material for the academic study of law and the trust was thus charitable.

Where there is the possibility of severance or apportionment

If it can be deduced from the terms of a trust that a specific part of the property or funds is intended to be applied towards a charitable purpose and the balance towards a non-charitable purpose, the gift will not neccesarily fail in its entirety. As far as possible the courts will be prepared to sever and give effect to the charitable purpose to the exclusion of the non-charitable purpose. This was the case in *Salusbury v Denton* (1857), where a testatrix directed that part of a legacy should be applied towards the foundation of a charity school and the remainder for the benefit of her relations.

Where the Charitable Trusts (Validation) Act 1954 applies

This Act is specifically concerned with trusts created by instruments coming into effect before 16 December 1952. Where provision is made in such a trust instrument for purposes which are partly charitable and partly non-charitable but the entire property can, consistently with the terms of the instrument, be applied towards the charitable purposes, such an 'imperfect trust provision' is validated by the Act which prescribes that the trust will take effect as if it were exclusively for the charitable purposes.

The operation of the Act is well illustrated by *Re Wykes* (1961) where a trust for 'benevolent or welfare purposes, was held to be valid on the ground that consistently with the terms of the trust the whole fund could be applied towards such established charitable purposes as the relief of poverty. Other relevant cases include *Re Mead* (1961) and *Leahy v AG New South Wales*.

The cy-pres doctrine

Where a charitable trust has been validly declared, a variety of circumstances may render it impossible, impracticable or inappropriate to carry out the donor's charitable purpose. The cy-pres doctrine was evolved to deal with such situations. Where it applies, effect will be given to the donor's charitable intention by means of a scheme under which the property will be devoted to a purpose which as nearly as possible resembles his original charitable purpose.

On the other hand, where all the requirements for the creation of a charitable trust have not been satisfied, the cy-pres doctrine cannot be invoked. Thus in *Re Gillingham Bus Disaster Fund* where the court held that a disaster appeal which referred *inter alia* to worthy causes was not exclusively charitable, the doctrine could not be relied on to render the appeal fund charitable. Also in *Re Jenkins WT* (1966) where a testatrix left property to be shared equally among seven named organisations, six of which were charitable while the seventh was not, the court declined to apply the doctrine to the share of the non-charitable organisation.

Where the doctrine applies, responsibility for devising a suitable scheme lies with the Charity Commission or the courts. Section 13(5) Charities Act 1993 imposes a duty on the trustees of the relevant charity to implement the scheme so devised. The trustees cannot on their own determine the manner in which property should be applied cypres (apart from trustees of some small charities who may do so within limits imposed by s 43 Charities Act 1993).

The scope of the doctrine

In discussing the scope of the doctrine, it is necessary to distinguish between the position before 1960 and the position since the enactment of the Charity Act 1960.

The position before 1960

Before the enactment of the Charities Act in 1960 the doctrine was applicable in two situations:

- Where there was a surplus after a specified charitable purpose had been duly accomplished. This is exemplified by *Re King* (1923) where a testator left 1,500 to install a stained glass window in a church. As the cost of a suitable window was about £800, it was held that the balance should be spent on a second window.

• Where it was impossible or impracticable to carry out the purpose of the trust. The application of the doctrine on this ground is well illustrated by *Biscoe v Jackson* (1887). A testator left £10,000 to charity directing his trustees to use £4,000 out of it to provide a soup kitchen and cottage hospital for the parish of Shoreditch. As the law then stood, this was impossible since it required land already held in mortmain. No such land was available in the area. The court held that the money should be used for other purposes beneficial to the people of Shoreditch.

Also in *Re Burtons Charity* (1938) trustees were required to pay trust income to the vicar of a parish to enable him to appoint three or more curates for the parish. Rises in stipends payable to curates made it impossible for the income to support three curates and the court approved a scheme modifying the terms of the gift to enable the income to be used to pay only two curates.

By contrast the doctrine was inapplicable where the intended charitable purpose was neither impossible nor impracticable but had become manifestly outdated, was adequately catered for by the welfare services or no longer represented an efficient use of resources. In *Re Weir Hospital* (1910) premises which a testator left for use as a hospital were unsuited to this purpose and the Charity Commissioners approved a scheme to use them as a nurses home. The court declared the scheme *ultra vires* on the ground that the stated purpose was neither impossible nor impracticable.

To get round this constraint, the courts took a liberal view of what amounted to impossibility in such cases as *Re Dominion Students' Hall Trust* (1947). Here, a trust set up to promote a spirit of common citizenship and closer ties among the peoples of the British Empire ran a hostel which was restricted to students of European origin. The court acknowledged that the operation of the trust as it stood was not entirely impracticable but granted a cy-pres order removing this restriction on the ground its retention would defeat its main object.

The position since 1960

The Charities Act 1960 extended the operation of the doctrine to a variety of circumstances which do not neccesarily involve impossibility or impracticability. Under s 13 (now superseded by s 13 Charities Act

1993) the original purposes of a charitable gift can be altered to allow the trust property to be applied cy-pres in the following circumstances:

- where the original purpose has as far as possible been fulfilled;
- where the original purpose cannot be carried out at all or cannot be carried out according to the directions given or the spirit of the gift;
- where the original purpose provides a use for only part of the property;
- where the property and other property applicable for similar purposes can be more effectively pooled together and suitably applied towards common purposes;
- where the gift was made by reference to a class of persons or geographical area that has since ceased to be a unit or otherwise ceased to be practicable or suitable. A case in point is *Peggs v Lamb* (1993) which concerned two charities for the benefit of the freemen of Huntingdon. The court held that in view of the decline in their numbers and having regard to the spirit of the gift, the freemen had ceased to be a suitable class by reference to which the charitable purposes could be carried out. Consequently, a cy-pres scheme was needed to enlarge the class to cover all the inhabitants of Huntingdon;
- where the original purpose has since it was laid down been adequately provided for by other means; or ceased to be charitable in law; or ceased to provide a suitable and effective method of using the property. In *Re Lepton's Charity* (1972) for example trustees of land were directed in 1715 to pay £3 out of the annual income of the land to the Protestant minister of a town and apply the remainder, amounting to £2 per annum to the poor of the town. By 1967 the annual income of the trust was nearly £800. The court held that paying a pittance of £3 to the minister out of the greatly increased annual income did not represent a suitable and effective method of using the property and approved a cy-pres scheme whereby the minister would receive £100 a year.

Initial and subsequent failure

An important factor in determining whether a cy-pres order can be made is whether the charitable purpose was incapable of fulfilment when the gift was made or the trust created (initial failure); or only became incapable of fulfilment after the gift or trust had come into effect (subsequent failure).

Initial failure

Where there has been initial failure of the charitable purpose, the crucial issue is whether the donor wished the property to be applied exclusively for the specified purpose or had an 'overridding intention to devote [the property] to charity in general' (*per* Harman J in *Re Sanders' WT* (1954)).

The cy-pres doctrine has no place where the donor intended the property to be applied for the specified purpose and no other one. In *Re White's Trust* (1886) a testator bequeathed stock worth £1,000 to officers of the Tinplate Workers Company to purchase land on which to build almshouses for poor tinplate workers. The company could not obtain a suitable site and did not in any case have the funds to maintain an almshouse. The court found that the testator did not contemplate that the legacy could be used for any other purpose. In view of this, the gift could not be saved by applying the cy-pres doctrine and therefore failed. See also *Re Rymer* (1895); *Re Wilson* (1913) and *Re Good's WT* (1950).

By contrast, if the court can discern a general (or paramount) charitable intent underlying the gift, the cy-pres doctrine will apply if the stated purpose fails at the outset. For instance, in *Biscoe v Jackson*, the testator's original purpose could not be fulfilled because suitable land was unavailable for the proposed soup kitchen and cottage hospital. However, the fact that the money to be used for this purpose was to be taken from £10,000 left to charity by the testator led the court to conclude that he had a general charitable intent and to make a cy-pres order (see also *Re Lysaght* (1966) and *Re Woodham's (Deceased)* (1981)).

Gifts to non-existent charities

The question of whether there has been initial failure and the presence of a general charitable intent has been especially problematic in the context of gifts to non-existent charitable bodies. In this connection, the following principles have emerged from the decided cases.

• Where there is a gift in favour of a charitable body which went out of existence before the gift took effect, there will be no initial failure if in the court's view the institution has continued in some other form. It follows that the gift is valid without any need to prove a general charitable intent as required by the cy-pres doctrine. This is seen from *Re Faraker* (1912). Here £200 was left to Mrs Bailey's Charity, Rotherhite. A charity called Hannah Bayley's Charity had been founded in 1765 to assist poor widows in the town. This and several other local charities had in 1905 been consolidated under a scheme by the Charity Commission for the benefit of the poor in Rotherhithe. The court held that the scheme did not operate to destroy the Bayley trust but simply meant that its activities were being carried out through a different machinery. Consequently, there was no initial failure and the legacy would pass to the new scheme.

However, if the gift is to an incorporated charity which according to its constitution can be dissolved and its assets distributed, it has been held in *Re Stemson's WT* (1970) that the charity will be incapable of continuing in another form after dissolution. This means that a gift to it after dissolution will fail unless the donor is shown to have had a general charitable intent.

- Where a gift is made to a charitable body that no longer exists and the gift was made for its purposes, there will be no initial failure if such purposes can be fulfilled by other means.

In determining whether a gift to a charitable body is for its purposes *Re Vernon's WT* (1972) is instructive. Buckley J decided in this case, that a gift to an unincorporated charity by name without more takes effect as a gift for its purposes and so will not fail if the charity no longer exists at the date of the gift. Conversely, a gift to an incorporated charity will ordinarily take effect as a gift to it beneficially and will thus fail if has gone out of existence. This decision was followed in *Re Finger's WT* (1972) where a testatrix made gifts to the National Radium Commission (an unincorporated charity) and the National Council for Maternity and Child Welfare (an incorporated charity) both of which had ceased to exist at the time of her death. The court held that the first gift would not fail as it was for purposes that could be carried out by other bodies, whereas the second gift would fail unless it was saved by the cy-pres doctrine.

- Where a gift is for a charity which never existed it will fail from the outset but the courts are inclined to ascribe to the donor a general charitable intent and having done so to apply the gift cy-pres. This is evident from *Re Harwood* (1956) where a testator who died in 1934, left £300 to the Peace Society in Belfast and £200 to the Wisbech Peace Society. There had been a Wisbech Peace Society but it had ceased to exist by 1934 whereas the Peace Society of Belfast had never existed. Farwell J held that the gift to the Wisbech Peace Society would fail since he could not discover a general charitable intent. At the same time, he held that the gift to the Peace Society in Belfast was applicable cy-pres since he could discern it a general intention to benefit societies whose object was the promotion of peace.

• Where a gift is made to several bodies and all but one of these bodies is charitable, opinion is divided on whether the cy-pres doctrine applies to the share of the non-charitable body.

In *Re Satterthwaite's WT* (1966) a testatrix directed that her residuary estate should be shared among a number of institutions concerned with animal welfare all of which were charitable except the London Animal Hospital. No charity of this name had ever existed but the plaintiff who was a vet had before the testatrix made her will run a practice under that name and now claimed that he was entitled to a share of the fund. The court held that the gift was essentially one for a non-existent charitable institution and that since all the other institutions nominated by T were existing charitable bodies, there was a paramount charitable intention and the share due to the London Animal Hospital would be applied cy-pres for other animal welfare purposes.

By contrast, in *Re Jenkins WT* (1966) a legacy was directed to be shared equally between six charitable bodies and a non-charitable body and Buckley J refused to allow the one-seventh share in favour of the non-charitable body to be applied cy-pres.

The position with regard to funds raised by public collections

Section 14 Charities Act 1993 covers situations where funds have been donated by the public for a charitable purpose that fails. It provides that any such donation will be applied cy-pres, if the donor either fails to reclaim it or disclaims any entitlement to it after prescribed advertisements and inquiries have been made by the collecting charity.

Where the contributions are made by means not adapted to distinguishing one gift from another (eg collecting boxes) or are the proceeds of lotteries and other such fund raising activities, the money may be applied cy-pres without any need for advertisements or enquiries. In effect, it is conclusively presumed that each contributor intended to make an out and out gift to charity.

Subsequent failure

Where a gift is made for a charitable purpose which the trustees have begun to carry out or for the benefit of a charitable body which was undoubtedly in existence at the time it was made, the property in question will remain in the charitable domain notwithstanding that the purpose in question is no longer possible, practicable, suitable (etc); or that the charitable body has ceased to exist. In such instances, the case will be one of subsequent failure and the position of the law is that in determining the destination of the property, the cy-pres doctrine will apply regardless of whether the donor had a general charitable intent.

Thus in *Re King* T's residuary estate was bequeathed for the installation of one stained glass window in a church. The window was installed for £800 and Romer LJ held that the balance should be applied cy-pres towards installing a second window. (But note with *Re Stanford* where in similar circumstances the court surprisingly held that the surplus would go on a resulting trust to the estate of the donor.)

An equally instructive case is *Re Slevin* (1891). Here T left a legacy for an orphanage. This orphanage was in existence at the time of T's death but was closed soon thereafter before T's will was administered. It was held that the gift would be applied cy-pres without regard to T's charitable intent since this was a case of subsequent failure in that the orphanage was still in existence at the time the gift took effect.

In instances such as the foregoing where a testamentary gift has been made to a charitable body which has become defunct, the material date in determining whether the case is one of subsequent impossibility is the date on which the will took effect, not the date on which the intended benefit comes into possession. The significance of this is evident from such cases as *Re Wright* (1954). Here T died in 1933 leaving property in her will for B for life and directing that on B's death, this property was to be used to found a convalescent home for impecunious gentlewomen. The scheme was practicable in 1933, but by the time B died in 1942, the balance of probability was against it. It was held that this was not a case of initial failure since the property had been effectively dedicated to charity in 1933 and thus the property would be applicable cy-pres without reference to whether T had manifested a general charitable intent (see also *Re Moon* (1948) where a similar conclusion was reached).

Revision Notes

Charitable and private trusts compared

Charitable trusts enjoy several advantages over private trusts:

- they are not subject to the same strict requirements governing certainty of objects as private trusts;
- they are much less likely to fail than private trust on account of the cy-pres doctrine;
- the perpetuity rules do not apply with the same strictness to charitable trusts as they do to private trusts;
- most importantly, they enjoy a wide range of tax concessions not available to private trusts.

Requirements of a valid charitable trust

The requirement that the purposes must be charitable
In the legal sense a trust is deemed to be charitable if it is for a purpose which is either expressly provided for in the preamble to the CUA or a purpose sufficiently analogous to one of those provided for in the preamble that it is deemed to come within its spirit and intendment (*Morice v Bishop Of Durham, Scottish Burial Reform Society v Glasgow City Corporation*).

The range of activities which are directly covered by the preamble or fall within its spirit and intendment fall into the four broad categories set out by Lord Macnaghten in *Cit v Pemsel*.

Category 1: relief of poverty

The CUA expressly refers to 'the relief of aged, impotent and poor people'. This is construed disjunctively so that a trust will be charitable if its intended beneficiaries are poor but not old or in bad health (*Rowntrees Housing Association v AG*).

Although the notion of poverty is relative, Evershed MR affords a useful judicial insight into its meaning in *Re Coulthurst*.

A person who intends to create a trust to relieve poverty usually employs the word poverty/poor or words of similar import (needy, indigent, reduced circumstances, limited means, fallen on evil days etc). Where such words are not used, the intention to benefit the poor may still be deduced from the nature and context of a gift (*Biscoe v Jackson; Re Lucas*).

Where the nature of the benefits provided by a trust is such that those who may be expected to seek such benefits will be predominantly poor, but the benefits are not exclusively reserved for the poor, it will not qualify as a trust for the relief of poverty (*Re Gwyon; Re Sander's WT*).

Category 2: advancement of education

Educational purposes specifically mentioned in the CUA include the maintenance of schools and scholars and the education and preferment of orphans. On the strength of this the charitable status of various educational establishments has been recognised (*AG v Margaret & Regius Professors; The Case Of Christ's College Cambridge; Re Marriette*).

Other valid educational activities, projects and bodies include:

- research (*Re Shaw; Re Hopkin's WT; Mcgovern v AG*);
- publication of educational material (*ICLR v AG; Re Stanford*).
- museums, libraries, zoological gardens etc (*British Museum Trustees v White; Re Lopes*);
- learned/professional bodies (*Royal College of Surgeons v NPB; Royal College Of Nursing v St Marylebone BC; Institute of Civil Engineers v IRC and CITB v AG*);
- artistic activities (*Re Delius; Re Shakespeare Memorial Trust; Royal Choral Society v IRC*, but note *Re Pinion*);
- sports and leisure pastimes in schools or among persons of school age (*Re Mariette; IRC v Mcmillan; Re Dupree's DT*);
- students' unions (*Baldry v Feintuck; London Hospital Medical College v IRC; AG v Ross; Webb v O'Doherty*). Note in several of these cases, the underlying tension between the educational status of the Unions and political objectives and campaigns which they often espouse.

Category 3: advancement of religion

One of the charitable objects set out in the CUA is the repair of churches. A wide range of other religious bodies and activities have also been recognised as charitable.

Different Christian denominations and various activities associated with such denominations have been recognised as charitable (as seen from the cases cited on pp 108-109).

Even obscure sects on the fringes of Christianity have been accorded charitable status (*Thornton v Howe; Re Watson*).

In addition to bodies or purposes associated with Christianity, recognition has also been given to non-Christian faiths in the charitable sphere eg *Neville Estate v Madden* (Judaism); *Birmingham Mosque Trust Ltd v Alavi* (Islam).

Category 4: other purposes beneficial to the community

Purposes of this nature referred to in the CUA include the relief of the aged and impotent and the repair of bridges etc. Over the years, numerous other purposes have been treated as charitable under this heading.

Two distinct judicial approaches have emerged on the issue of whether a trust is charitable under this heading, namely: Lord Simmond's stricter approach in *Williams Trustees v IRC* and Russel LJ's more flexible approach in *ICLR v AG*.

Examples of charitable trusts under the fourth heading include:

* locality trusts (*Goodman v Saltash Corp; Peggs v Lamb*);
* trusts for the welfare of the aged (*Re Lucas; Re Robinson; Re Cottam's WT; Rowntree Memorial Trust v AG; Re Glyn's WT; Re Bradbury*);
* trusts for the relief of the sick, through such measures as funding hospitals; establishing nurses homes; providing accommodation for patient's relatives; sponsoring medical research; assisting persons with disabilities etc. See the cases on pp 111-112;
* trusts for public works, amenities and monuments (*AG v Governors Of Harrow School; Forbes v Forbes; Jones v Williams; Re Spence*);
* trusts to relieve human suffering and distress including disaster appeal funds (*Re North Devon [Etc] Relief Fund Trusts; Re Gillingham Bus Disaster Fund*); and trusts which support the activities of the emergency services (*Thomas v Howell; Re Wokingham Fire Brigade Trusts*);
* trusts to improve national security by improving the efficiency of the armed services (*Re Lord Stratheden and Campbell; Re Gray*) or otherwise promoting the defence of the realm (*Re Driffil*);

- animal welfare trusts (*University Of London v Yarrow; Re Wedgewood, Re Moss*). Note, however, *National Anti-Vivisection Society v IRC, Re Grove-Grady*;
- recreational trusts are recognised as charitable if they:
  (a) benefit school children (*Re Mariette; IRC v Mcmullin*);
  (b) promote the efficiency of the armed services (*Re Gray*); or
  (c) provide facilities or amenities available to the general public or a more restricted class in the interests of social welfare as defined by the Recreational Charities Act 1958 (*Re Hadden; Re Morgan IRC v Guild*);

Outside these contexts, purposes connected with sport or recreation are not generally regarded as charitable (*Re Nottage; Re Clifford; IRC v City Of Glasgow Police Athletics Association; William's Trustees v IRC; IRC v Baddely*).

The requirement of public benefit

Where the object of a trust is to relieve poverty, it will be regarded as charitable even if it is for the benefit of a small group of persons who are personally connected with the benefactor such as his relations (*Isaac v Defriez; Re Scarisbrick; Re Cohen*); or his employees (*Re Gosling; Gibson v South American Stores Ltd, Dingle v Turner*), or members of his club (*Re Young*).

By contrast, in the field of education, the public benefit requirement is more stringently applied. See *Re Compton And Oppenheim v Tobacco Securities Trust* where the courts formulated the 'personal nexus test'. But note the criticisms of this test by Lord Mcdermott in *Oppenheim* and Lord Cross in *Dingle v Turner*.

In *Re Koettgen*, decided a few years after *Oppenheim*, it was held that a trust to promote commercial education among members of the public with a preference for employees of a named company was charitable. It is, however, doubtful in the light of the decision in *IRC v Educational Grants Association* whether a trust of this nature which is expressed to be for the education of the public but which provides for the use of trust funds principally for the education of members of a preferred private class will now be regarded as charitable.

The public benefit test also applies in respect of trusts for religious purposes as seen from *Gilmour v Coats*. However, the aspect of the *Compton* test which states that the class of beneficiaries must not be numerically negligible is not strictly observed in the religious sphere (*Thornton v Howe; Re Watson*).

The public benefit requirement is applied as strictly where a trust is for other purposes beneficial to the community as it is in the context of educational trusts. Under this heading, the benefits of the trust must according to *Verge v Somervell* be available to the community or an appreciable section thereof. The requirement is not satisfied if the trust is framed in terms which suggest that the intended beneficiaries are not a section of the community but a class within a class (*IRC v William's Trustees; IRC v Baddely*).

Finally, once the benefit is available to the public at large or an appreciable section of the community, the relevant trust or gift will be charitable even if only a limited number of people are willing to take advantage of it (*IRC v Baddely*).

The requirement that the trust must be exclusively charitable

Where a trust is framed in such terms that the trust property or fund can be applied towards non-charitable as well as charitable purposes, it will not qualify as a charitable trust (*William's Trustees v IRC; IRC v City Of Glasgow Police Athletics Assn*).

Often a trust fails on this account because the words used in declaring it are words of wider import than the word charitable in its legal sense (eg benevolent, worthy, philanthropic etc) (*Morice v Bishop Of Durham; Re Gillingham Bus Disaster Fund*).

Where the word charitable is employed together with a word of wider import and they are connected by the word 'or', the courts have construed this to mean that the gift is not exclusively charitable and will therefore fail (*Blair v Duncan; Re Diplock; Re Myers; AG v NPB; Houston v Burns; Re Macduff*).

By contrast, where the connecting word is 'and', the courts will as a general rule construe the trust as one which is exclusively charitable (*Blair v Duncan; Re Sutton; Re Best*).

In certain situations, the inclusion of non-charitable purposes will not invalidate a charitable trust:

- where the object of the trust is charitable but the carrying out of the object is facilitated by the inclusion of a non-charitable purpose (*Re Coxen*);
- where the non-charitable elements in the trust are incidental to its main charitable object (*IRC v City Of Glasgow Police Athletic Assn*);

- where the charitable purpose can be severed from the non-charitable one and given effect on its own (*Salisbury v Denton*);
- where the Charitable Trusts (Validation) Act 1954 applies (*Re Wykes, Re Mead, Leahy v AG*).

The cy-pres doctrine

Where it becomes impossible, impracticable or inappropriate to perform a validly declared charitable trust in the manner originally prescribed, the cy-pres doctrine may enable the donor's intention to be carried into effect in some other way. The doctrine cannot, however, be invoked in cases where the requirements of a charitable trust are not fulfilled (*Re Gillingham Bus Disaster Fund; Re Jenkin's WT*).

For many years the doctrine applied only where a charitable purpose had been fulfilled leaving a surplus (as in *Re King*) or where it was impossible or impracticable (as in *Biscoe v Jackson; Re Burton's Charity; Re Weir Hospital*).

Since the enactment of the Charities Act 1960, the application of the doctrine is no longer restricted to cases of impossibility or impracticability but now extends to other situations where the original purpose, though not impossible or impracticable is no longer entirely appropriate or suitable (eg *Re Lepton's Charity; Peggs v Lamb*).

Where there has been an initial failure of the original charitable purpose, the application of the cy-pres doctrine will depend on whether the donor had a general charitable intention.

If no such intention was present, the court will not apply the trust fund cy-pres and there will be a resulting trust in favour of the donor (*Re White's Trust; Re Rymer; Re Wilson; Re Good's WT*). On the other hand, where such an intention can be discerned, the cy-pres doctrine will apply if the stated purpose fails at the outset (*Biscoe v Jackson; Re Lysaght; Re Woodham*).

Particular problems have been encountered regarding initial failure and the cy-pres doctrine where gifts are made to non-existent charities. Where the charity ceased to exist before the gift was made but effectively continued in another form, it has been decided in *Re Faraker* that this will not be a case of initial failure and the charity in its new manifestation will be entitled to the gift without proving a general charitable intent.

Again, if the charity has gone out of existence but the gift is construed not as one to the charity *per se* but as a gift for its purposes, the courts will not treat this as a case of initial failure but will allow the gift to be applied by other means towards fulfilling that purpose without requiring proof of a general charitable intent (*Re Vernon's WT; Re Finger's WT*).

Where the gift is for a charity which never existed at all rather than one which has gone out of existence, the courts will treat this as a case of initial failure. However, as seen from *Re Harwood*, the courts are quick to discover a general charitable interest and thus apply the cy-pres doctrine in such cases.

The need to prove that a gift is accompanied by a general charitable intent is alleviated by s 14 Charities Act 1993 in situations where funds have been raised for a charitable purpose through public contributions.

Finally, in cases of subsequent failure of a charitable gift or trust, the cy-pres doctrine applies automatically to the gift or trust fund without any need to prove a general charitable intent (*Re King; Re Slevin; Re Wright; Re Moon*).

6 The administration of trusts

The appointment, retirement and removal of trustees

The appointment of trustees

Capacity

As a general rule any legal person with the capacity to own property may be appointed a trustee. Note in particular that:

- aliens are incapable of owning an interest in a British ship and cannot hold such property on trust (s 17 Status of Aliens Act of 1914 as amended by the British Nationality Act 1948);
- infants are incapable of holding legal estates in land by s 1(6) Law of Property Act (LPA) 1925. In addition s 20 LPA provides that 'The appointment of an infant to be a trustee in relation to any settlement or trust shall be void'. It was, however, held in *Re Vinogradoff* (1935) and *Re Muller* (1953) that an infant may be a trustee under a resulting trust.

In addition to human beings, certain corporate entities including the Public Trustee and a host of trust corporations run by various financial institutions are often appointed either as ordinary trustees or custodian trustees.

How many trustees may be appointed? As far as trusts of personalty are concerned there is no restriction on the number of initial trustees. However, a sole trustee is not to be recommended for reasons of accountability. Equally, it may be cumbersome to have too many trustees and it is rare to appoint more than four. Moreover, where a subsisting trust has less than four trustees, there is scope for appointing additional trustees under s 36(6) Trustee Act (TA) 1925 provided the number of additional and existing trustees does not exceed four.

With regard to real property, the appointment of a sole trustee is not prohibited. It is, however, usual to appoint two or more trustees since s 14(2) TA provides that a sole trustee of land held under a settlement or on trust for sale (other than a trust corporation) cannot give a valid receipt if the trust property is sold. Under s 34(2) TA a maximum number of four trustees is prescribed This, however, is subject to several exceptions, the most important being where the trust relates to land held for charitable, ecclesiastical or public purposes.

The initial trustees

It is the prerogative of the settlor to appoint the first trustees. This is usually done in a will or other trust instrument. In the case of an *inter vivos* trust (but not a testamentary one) the settlor may be one of these trustees.

In the years after assuming office, the initial trustees may begin to die off. In order to ensure that a trustee's death does not disrupt the continuity of the trust, it is the practice to vest the trust property in the trustees as *joint tenants* instead of *tenants in common*. The effect of this is that if one trustee dies the trust property will vest in the survivors by virtue of the right of survivorship (*jus accrescendi*). If no new trustees are appointed the property will ultimately vest in the last survivor and on his death will vest in his personal representatives under s 1 Administration of Estates Act 1925 and s 18(2) TA.

Where there are no initial trustees to administer the trust

A longstanding maxim of equity proclaims that a trust will not fail for want of trustees. On the strength of this maxim, the courts have been able to give effect to testamentary trusts not only where all the trustees appointed by the will have died before the testator as seen from *Re Smirththwaite* (1871) but also where no trustees have in fact been named in the will as seen from *Dodkin v Brunt* (1868).

In the case of *inter vivos* trusts, where the settlor has executed a conveyance or transfer to named trustees who were alive at the date of the conveyance or transfer, the trust will not fail even if all the trustees thereafter disclaim the trust or die without having taken any steps to administer it (see eg *Jones v Jones* (1874) and *Mallott v Wilson* (1903)). On the other hand, where the material conveyance or transfer *inter vivos* has not named any trustees or the trustees named in it died before it was executed, Pettitt suggests that the trust will be incompletely constituted and as such equity will not intervene to prevent its failure.

Subsequent trustees

The process of administering a trust may stretch out over many years and the need may arise from time to time to appoint new trustees in place of or in addition to the serving trustees. A settlor who anticipates this possibility may insert into the trust instrument an express power to appoint new trustees. In most instances, however, the settlor is content to rely on the statutory formula set out in s 36 TA.

Appointment under s 36

The statutory powers conferred by s 36 encompass the appointment of replacement trustees and additional trustees.

Replacement trustees

Section 36(1) and (2) states that one or more persons may be appointed to fill a vacancy which has arisen or is liable to arise among existing trustees in any of the following circumstances, namely where a trustee:

- is dead;
- has remained outside the UK for a continuous period of 12 months;
- desires to be discharged from the trust;
- either refuses to act, is unfit to act (eg due to bankruptcy, conviction for criminal dishonesty etc), or is incapable of acting (eg by reason of old age or mental disorder etc);

- is an infant;
- or has been removed from the trust in the exercise of a power contained in the trust instrument.

In any of these circumstances, the power of appointing new trustees is exercisable in order of preference by:

- the person(s) nominated in the trust instrument to exercise the statutory power;
- the surviving or continuing trustee(s) for the time being;
- the personal representatives of the last surviving or continuing trustee.

Where those who are entitled to exercise this statutory power are the surviving or continuing trustees, an issue has arisen as to whether a trustee who is being replaced is entitled to participate in choosing his successor. The difficulty in this connection stems from the fact that s 36(8) states that the provisions in s 36 pertaining to a continuing trustee include a refusing or retiring trustee if he is willing to act. This provision is especially useful where a sole trustee seeks to retire or relinquish office or where all the existing trustees seek to do so at the same time but its effect is less certain where apart from the trustee being replaced, there are others who will continue in office. It appears from *Re Coates To Parsons* (1886) that an appointment by the trustees who will continue in office, without involving the outgoing trustee will not be void and support for this is to be found in *Re Stoneham's ST* (1952) where it was held that the concurrence of a trustee who had remained abroad for 12 months was not necessary for the appointment of his replacement. Nevertheless, if the trustee being replaced is competent and willing to act it is prudent for the avoidance of doubt, that his involvement should be sought in selecting his replacement.

Additional trustees

Section 36(1) is primarily concerned with the appointment of new trustees to replace existing ones but also makes some allowance for appointment of additional trustees since it empowers the appointment of one or more trustees in place of an outgoing trustee in the circumstances outlined above.

Additional trustees may also be appointed under s 36(6) where no outgoing trustee is being replaced. This can only be done if at the time of the appointment there are no more than three trustees and the number of trustees after appointment must not exceed four. Responsibility for appointing additional trustees lies with the persons empowered to do so in the trust instrument or if there are no such persons, with the existing trustees.

Formalities for appointment

Any appointment of new trustees under s 36(1) or (6) must be in writing. The common practice is to execute a deed which serves the dual purpose of satisfying the requirement of writing and ensuring that the property is duly vested in the existing and new trustees as joint tenants.

Appointment by the Court

The courts possess substantial powers under s 41 TA to order the appointment of new trustees. This may be done in place of or in addition to existing trustees or where there are no trustees. Even before the Act was passed, the court was competent to order the appointment of new trustees where necessary, in the exercise of its inherent jurisdiction.

An appointment will be made by the courts under s 41 only where it is expedient to make such an appointment but it is found to be inexpedient, difficult or impracticable to do so either under the terms of the trust instrument or under s 36.

Situations in which judicial intervention in the appointment of new trustees would be justified include the following:

- where the last surviving trustee dies intestate and no one applies to administer his estate;
- where all the trustees named in a will pre-decease the testator and difficulties are encountered in administering his estate (see *Re Smirthwaite*);
- where a person empowered to appoint new trustees by the trust instrument or s 36 is incapable of doing so for reasons such as infancy (see *Re Parsons* (1940); old age or infirmity see *Re Lemann's WT* (1883) and *Re Phelps' ST* (1885); or because he is trapped behind enemy lines: see *Re May's WT* (1941));
- where friction between the persons empowered to appoint new trustees delays an appointment unduly (see *Re Tempest* (1866)).

At the same time the courts have declined to appoint new trustees where the persons with the power to make such appointments are in a position to do so. In particular, the mere fact that the beneficiaries do not regard as suitable the persons put forward by those with the power to appoint new trustees and wish to appoint their own trustees is not seen as a good enough reason for the courts to intervene. In *Re Brockbank* (1948) the beneficiaries wished to appoint a trust corporation to replace an outgoing trustee. The continuing trustee opposed this insisting that it would be unduly expensive. The beneficiaries contended that as they were all *sui juris* and absolutely entitled to the trust property, their wishes must prevail. It was held that the beneficiaries had the right to terminate the trust if they so wished, but while it subsisted they were not entitled to control the exercise of the trustee's statutory power to appoint. See also *Re Higginbottom* (1892).

The factors which the courts will bear in mind in appointing new trustees were outlined by Turner LJ in *Re Tempest*. These are:

- the wishes of the settlor and the beneficiaries;
- whether the appointee is likely to favour some beneficiaries at the expense of others; and
- whether the appointment is likely to promote or impede the execution of the trust.

Accepting the appointment

Acceptance may be express or implied. Express acceptance may be oral, written or by deed. There will be implied acceptance where, for example, a person who is appointed an executor and trustee in a will obtains probate of the will (see *Mucklow v Fuller* (1821) and *Re Sharman's WT* (1942)). Indeed, acceptance will be inferred from any interference with the trust property by the appointee, unless there is some other explanation for the interference. Thus in *James v Frearson* (1842) where the appointee gave directions concerning the sale of trust property this constituted acceptance. And in *Urch v Walker* (1838) assigning a lease to a beneficiary amounted to acceptance.

Where a person who is appointed a trustee decides to accept his appointment he is obliged to do the following:

- to disclose to the settlor or whoever has appointed him, any facts or circumstances liable to occasion a conflict between his interest and his trust duties (see *Peyton v Robinson* (1823));
- to acquaint himself with the material details of the trust. In particular, he 'ought to look into the trust documents and papers to

ascertain what notices appear among them of incumbrances and other matters affecting the trust', *per* Kekewich J in *Hallows v Lloyd* (1888);

- to initiate investigations and take legal action where there are grounds for suspecting that a breach of trust has been committed (see *Harvey v Olliver* (1877)).
- to ensure that legal title to the trust property becomes jointly vested in him and his co-trustees.

In the case of the initial trustees, the original trust deed itself usually fulfils the purpose of vesting. In the case of subsequent trustees, the process of vesting legal title in the new and continuing trustees has been simplified by the automatic vesting provisions in the TA. In particular, s 40(1) TA provides that where a new trustee is appointed by deed, the deed shall operate without any conveyance or assignment to vest the trust property in that trustee as joint tenant with the existing trustees.

However, under s 40(4) certain types of property are excluded from the automatic vesting provision in s 40(1), namely:

- land conveyed by way of mortgage for securing money owed to the trust;
- land held under a lease, which contains a covenant not to assign without consent unless such consent has been given;
- stocks and shares.

In effect these will only vest in the new trustees if the formalities for the vesting of such property are observed.

Where trust property consists of or includes equitable interests, on assuming office, the trustees must ensure that such interests are duly protected by notice or registration.

In addition, where the trust property or any part of it remains outstanding at the time of the trustee's appointment, he must take appropriate steps to obtain payment of the sum or secure the transfer of the property involved as soon as it falls due (see *Westmoreland v Holland* (1871)).

Disclaimer

Any person named as a trustee may turn down the appointment by disclaiming the trust before acceptance. A disclaimer may be in writing or even oral. It is, however, advisable that a deed should be employed for this purpose, because as Leach MR pointed out in

Stacey v Elph (1833) 'such deed is clear evidence of the disclaimer and admits of no ambiguity'. It was nevertheless accepted in this case that disclaimer may be implied from conduct and this is re-inforced by *Re Clout and Frewer's Contract* (1924) where it was held that a trustee may be deemed to have disclaimed where he has made no effort to take up his position for a considerable length of time.

The retirement of trustees

A trustee may retire or seek to be discharged from the trust in the following circumstances:

- where the trust instrument expressly provides for retirement;
- where all the beneficiaries are of full age and all consent to the retirement;
- where in the exercise of its inherent jurisdiction the court approves the retirement of a trustee;
- under s 36(1) provided there is somebody to fill the vacancy;
- under s 39 which enables a trustee to retire even where it is not contemplated that a new trustee will be appointed in his place. Retirement under this heading is possible only if:
  (a) there will be at least two trustees or a trust corporation to administer the trust when the trustee has been discharged;
  (b) the trustee executes a deed signifying his wish to retire; and
  (c) his co-trustees as well as any person with the power to appoint new trustees consent by deed to the discharge. (Note that under s 40(2) such a deed operates to divest the outgoing trustee of the trust property and vest it in the continuing trustees.)

Removal of trustees

Trustees may be removed from office in a number of circumstances:
- a trustee may be removed from office and replaced in the manner and on the grounds prescribed by s 36(1) and (2) TA.
- under s 41(1) TA, the judicial appointment of a new trustee sometimes entails the removal of an existing trustee.
- in the exercise of the court's inherent jurisdiction it has the power to remove a trustee from office without replacing him. This jurisdiction is especially useful where trustees commit breaches of trust. Thus in *Clarke v Heathfield (No 2)* (1985) trustees administering the funds of the National Union of Mineworkers sought to keep the

funds out of the hands of court-appointed sequestrators by transferring them abroad. This led the court to order their removal on the ground that their actions had put trust funds in jeopardy and made them unavailable for the purposes for which they had been contributed by union members.

Even where there has been no misconduct occasioning a breach of trust the court may nevertheless remove a trustee if it appears that it would be prejudicial to the proper performance of the trust for him to remain in office. Thus in *Letterstedt v Broers* (1884) the court found that all trust and respect between the trustees and beneficiaries had completely broken down and concluded that the welfare of the beneficiaries dictated that the trustees should no longer continue in office.

The main duties and powers of trustees

The nature of the trustee's responsibilities

The position of the trustee is one which carries heavy responsibilities. As Lord Hardwicke remarked in *Knight v Earl of Plymouth* (1747), 'A trust is an office [which] if faithfully discharged is attended with no small degree of trouble and anxiety' and it is therefore 'an act of great kindness in anyone to accept it'.

A trustee's functions normally entail the performance of duties and the exercise of powers. These duties and powers are defined primarily by the trust instrument. In addition, some duties and powers have either been laid down by statute or spelt out by the courts in the exercise of their general equitable jurisdiction.

Whereas the trustees duties are obligatory, his powers are essentially discretionary. As a fiduciary, the trustee must from time to time consider whether to exercise a particular power. See *Re Hays WT* (1981); but having considered the matter, it is open to him to decide against exercising the power.

Where a trustee decides not to exercise a power or to exercise it in a particular manner he is not bound to provide reasons for his decision (see *Re Beloved Wilkes Charity* (1851); *Re Londonderry's ST* (1965) and *Wilson & Anor v The Law Debenture Trust Corpn* (1994)). However, if the basis for the decision emerges and it is evident that he acted dishonestly, capriciously or without proper judgment the court may intervene to correct the decision (see *Klug v Klug* (1918); *Re Manisty's Settlement* (1974) and *Turner v Turner* (1984)).

The unanimity rule

Where there are several trustees, each one must actively take part in administering the trust. As far as trust duties are concerned, since these are obligatory in nature, all the trustees are bound to ensure that they are performed. The notion that trustees must participate fully in trust affairs is also reflected in the rule that where there are two or more trustees any decision to exercise a power must be unanimous. As Jessel MR remarked in this connection in *Luke v South Kensington Hotel Co* (1879), 'There is no law that I am acquainted with which enables the majority of trustees to bind the minority'. The effect of the unanimity rule is illustrated by *Re Mayo* (1943) where property was held by three trustees on trust for sale with a power to postpone sale. Two of them wished to postpone sale but the third favoured an immediate sale. It was held that the power to postpone sale could not be validly exercised since there was no unanimity and consequently the trustees were bound by the duty to sell imposed by the trust for sale.

The unanimity rule does not however apply:

- where there is any provision to the contrary in the trust instrument (see *Re Butlin's WT* (1976)); or
- where the trust in question is a charitable trust in which case the decisions of a majority of trustees will bind a dissenting minority (see *Perry v Shipway* (1859); and *Re Whitely* (1910)).

The trustee's entitlement to remuneration

Historically, the office of the trustee was gratuitous and as such the trustee was not expected to be paid for administering the trust. In *Robinson v Pett* (1734), for instance, Lord Talbot LC signified that 'It is an established rule that a trustee ... shall have no allowance for his care and trouble'.

Over the years, the responsibilities assumed by trustees have grown increasingly complex and time-consuming, often requiring the skills of professionals such as solicitors and accountants or the expertise of trust corporations. Such professionals and corporations are usually prepared to serve as trustees only if they are paid and it has now been accepted that trustees may be entitled to remuneration in any of the following situations:

- where the trust instrument contains a charging clause (see *Webb v Earl Of Shaftesbury* (1802)). Note if the trust is created by will, a charging clause is treated as a legacy and under s 15 Wills Act 1837 it will lapse if the trustee witnesses the will;

- where the court, in the exercise of its inherent jurisdiction orders the payment of remuneration (or an increase in the remuneration already payable) (see *Re Duke Of Norfolk's ST* (1981) and *Re Drexel Burnham Lambert* (1994));
- where an agreement is reached between the beneficiaries and the trustee specifying that he is to be paid for his services;
- where statutory provision has been made for the remuneration of a trustee. For example, under s 42 TA a trust corporation appointed by the court may be authorised to charge for its services. Equally s 1(5) Judicial Trustees Act 1905 and s 9 Public Trustee Act 1906 provide for the payment of remuneration to judicial trustees and the public trustee respectively;
- where trustees who are engaged in administering a trust which includes assets in a foreign country are entitled to remuneration under the laws of that country (see *Re Northcote's WT* (1949));
- where the rule in *Cradock v Piper* (1850) applies. This rule enables a solicitor-trustee or his firm to charge for acting on behalf of the solicitor-trustee and a co-trustee in a suit involving the trust provided the cost of representing the two is no more than would have been the case if the solicitor-trustee or his firm had represented his co-trustee alone.

Note also that under s 30(2) TA a trustee may re-imburse himself or pay or discharge out of the trust estate all expenses incurred in the execution of the trust (see *Stott v Milne* (1884) and *Hardoon v Belilos* (1901)).

The standard of care

In order to ensure that trusts are administered honestly and efficiently, the courts demand a high degree of diligence from trustees in carrying out their responsibilities.

An unpaid trustee (such as a friend or relation of the settlor) is deemed to have discharged his duty in this regard 'if he takes in managing trust affairs all those precautions which an ordinary prudent man of business would take in managing similar affairs of his own' *per* Lord Blackburn in *Speight v Gaunt* (1883).

The requirement is more stringent with regard to paid trustees. The position, as stated by Harman J In *Re Waterman's WT* (1952) is that 'a paid trustee is expected to exercise a higher standard of diligence and knowledge than an unpaid trustee' (see also *Bartlett v Barclays Bank Trust Co Ltd (No 1)* (1980)).

The trustee's duties

Fiduciary duties

We saw in Chapter 4 that trustees and other fiduciaries are duty-bound to ensure that they do not permit their personal interests to conflict with their duties. Equity has sought to safeguard against such conflicts equity by imposing on the trustee, a number of important prohibitions and restrictions.

Unauthorised profits

The most important of these safeguards is enshrined in Lord Herschell's assertion in *Bray v Ford* (1896) that a trustee 'is not, unless otherwise expressly provided, entitled to make a profit'.

In line with this principle, a trustee who receives a fee, commission or other payment (apart from remuneration to which he may lawfully be entitled in any of the situations outlined above) is liable to account to the beneficiaries for such a payment. This is seen from such cases such as *Sugden v Crosland* (1876); *Williams v Barton* (1927) and *Re Macadam* (1946) (which have already been considered in Chapter 4 in the context of fiduciaries as constructive trustees).

The trustee's obligation not to allow his interests to conflict with his duty has also found expression in the rule in *Keech v Sanford* (1726). According to this rule, where trust property consists of a lease, the trustee is bound on the expiry of the lease to seek to renew it for the benefit of the trust and not for his own benefit. This rule has been extended to situations where the trustee does not seek to renew the lease but to purchase the leasehold reversion (see *Protheroe v Protheroe* (1968)).

Also relevant in the present context is *Boardman v Phipps* (1967) which decided that a solicitor to a trust (and by implication a trustee) who derived some material benefit from exploiting confidential information that had come to him by virtue of his position would be liable to account for the benefit.

A point which emerges clearly from *Keech v Sanford* and *Boardman v Phipps* as well as cases such as *Regal (Hastings) Ltd v Gulliver* (1942) is that a trustee or any other fiduciary will be liable to account for whatever benefit he has obtained even where there has been no impropriety on his part. As Lord Russell observed in this connection in *Regal (Hastings)* 'The profiteer, however honest and well-intentioned, cannot escape that risk of being called upon to account. It appears, however, from the recent case of *Re Drexel Burnham* that trustees who seek to embark on a course of action which might lay them open to claims that they have profited from allowing their interests to override their duties may protect themselves by applying to the court for approval.

Purchase of trust property by trustee

Where a sale of trust property is proposed, the trustees, according to Wynn-Parry J In *Buttle v Saunders* (1950), 'have an overriding duty to obtain the best price which they can for their beneficiaries'. This is re-inforced by the 'self-dealing rule' which states that a sale of trust property to a trustee is voidable and may be set aside by any beneficiary. The justification for this is that a trustee who is both the seller and the buyer of trust property may be tempted to manipulate the terms of sale to his advantage or exploit knowledge about the property obtained in his capacity as trustee.

The trustee is caught by the self-dealing rule even if he acted in good faith and paid a fair price. As Lord Eldon LC put it in *Ex p James* (1803) 'the purchase is not permitted in any case, however honest the circumstances' (see also *Ex p Lacey* (1802)).

Purchase by retired trustees

A sale of trust property to a trustee may be set aside under the self-dealing rule even if it takes place after he leaves office as happened in *Wright v Morgan* (1926); unless the sale takes long after he ceases to be a trustee as in *Re Boles and British Land Co's Contract* (1902).

Indirect purchase through a third party

It is not permissible for the trustee to acquire trust property indirectly through its sale to a third party either as his nominee or with a view to repurchasing the property from the third party. In accordance with this, the courts have held that:

- where trust property is sold to a third party but before it is conveyed to him a trustee contracts to repurchase the property from him the trustee is not entitled to enforce the contract (see *Delves v Gray* (1902));
- where trust property has been sold and conveyed to a third party a trustee can repurchase it only if the original sale was in good faith and not with a view to reselling the property to the trustee (see *Re*

Postlethwaite (1888)). Where this was not the case, the beneficiaries are entitled to have the repurchase by the trustee set aside under the self-dealing rule;

- where trust property is sold to a company in which a trustee has a sizeable shareholding it has been held in *Re Thompson's Settlement* (1985) that this will be dealt with on the same footing as a sale to the trustee and will therefore be set aside.

Limits to the self-dealing rule

The courts will not set aside sales of trust property to trustees in the following contexts:

- where the trustee contracted to purchase the trust property before becoming a trustee but the sale was completed after he had become one (see *Re Mulholland's WT* (1949));
- where the trust is a bare trust under which the trustee who purchased trust property had no active duties to perform (see *Parkes v White* (1805) and *Clark v Clark* (1884)).
- where there are special circumstances which render it inappropriate to set aside the sale as was the case in *Holder v Holder* (1968). Here a testator left two farms to his widow and children. His executors included his son V who was also the tenant of the farms. V purported to renounce his executorship but this renunciation was ineffective as he had already taken a few minor steps in administering the estate (eg signing cheques and endorsing insurance policies). The farms were sold by auction by the other executors to V. Seven years later an order was sought to have the sale set aside under the self-dealing rule but the order was refused on the following grounds:

  (a) V had never effectively assumed the duties of executor and in particular had not been involved in arranging the auction or instructing the valuer who had valued the farms;

  (b) All the other beneficiaries knew that the reason why V had renounced the executorship was because he was interested in buying the farms and had acquiesced in V's purchase of the farms for which he had paid a fair price;

  (c) V had acquired no special knowledge of the farms in the capacity of an executor and there was no basis for the other beneficiaries to look to him to protect their interests.

Purchase of beneficial interest by trustee

It is necessary to distinguish between the purchase of trust property by the trustee and the purchase by the trustee of a beneficiary's interest in such property. This is because it has been established in cases like *Ex p Lacey* (1802) that the self-dealing rule does not apply to a trustee's purchase of the beneficial interest.

Such transactions are however governed by the 'fair-dealing rule'. According to *Megarry v C in Tito v Waddell (No 2)* (1977) the effect of the rule is that 'if a trustee purchases the beneficial interest of any of his beneficiaries, the transaction is not voidable *ex debito justitiae* but can be set aside by the beneficiary unless the trustee can show that he has taken no advantage of his position and has made full disclosure to the beneficiary and that the transaction is fair and honest' (see also *Coles v Trecothick* (1804), *Thomas v Eastwood* (1877) and *Dougan v Macpherson* (1902)).

Competing in business with the trust

A conflict may occur between the duties of a trustee and his personal interest where the trust estate includes a business and the trustee is found to be conducting a business of his own in competition with the trust. A case in point is *Re Thomson* (1930). Here the estate of a deceased testator included a yacht broking business which was a going concern. One of his executors sought to set up a yacht broking business of his own in the same town but an injunction was granted to prevent him from doing so because the court found that there was a distinct likelihood of a conflict between his business interests and his duty as an executor. Contrast with *Moore v M'glyn* (1894).

The duty to invest

Essence of the duty to invest

One of the trustees' main responsibilities is to ensure that the trust assets under their control are invested properly. In this context, investment entails 'the purchase [or retention] of property from which interest or profit is expected' *per* PO Lawrence J in *Re Wragg* (1919). This means, for instance, that the purchase of a house for the provision of rent-free accommodation for a beneficiary is not deemed to be an investment (see *Re Power's WT* (1947)).

The relationship between the TIA (1961) and express investment clauses

A trust instrument may contain an express clause, setting out the scope of the trustees' responsibility to invest and the types of securities in which they may invest.

Where the trust instrument is silent or makes provision for a few investments without expressly confining the trustees to these, the Trustee Investments Act (TIA) 1961 comes into play with its fairly extensive range of authorised investments from which the trustees are empowered to select.

It is, however, provided in s 1(3) that the TIA will apply only where there is no contrary intention in the trust instrument. Consequently, the Act will not constitute the basis for determining which investments the trustees are empowered to make in two notable instances, namely:

* where the trust instrument not only provides for a more limited range of investments than that contemplated by the TIA but also expressly directs the trustees not to exceed this range;
* where the investment clause is framed in terms which expressly empower the trustee to make investments which go beyond the range authorised by the TIA, for example:
  (a) where the trustees are expressly directed to invest in such securities as shares in a private company or income-bearing land (which are not authorised by the TIA); or
  (b) where the trustees are empowered to make any investment whatsoever which they think fit as if they were absolute and beneficial owners as happened in such cases as *Re Harari* (1949) and *Re Peczenik* (1964).

General principles to be taken into account in making investments

Trustees must exercise higher degree of care than in performing other duties

In *Learoyd v Whitely* (1887), Lord Watson made it clear that in making investment decisions, it is not enough for a trustee to act as an ordinary prudent man of business would in conducting his own affairs. A businessman of ordinary prudence may, and often does select investments of a more or less speculative nature; the same person acting as a trustee is required to spurn any investment which is attended with hazard. This suggests that the standard demanded of a trustee in making investments is higher than that applicable to the discharge of his other duties.

In addition to taking proper care in selecting investments, trustees are bound to take whatever steps are needed to safeguard such investments once they have been made. In particular, where the investment consists of shares in a company and the trustees hold a controlling interest in the company by virtue of these shares, they are obliged to see that the company is properly run. In *Bartlett v Barclays Bank Trust Co* (1980), the bank as trustee of a family trust held 99.8% of the shares in a private company which ran a property letting business. The bank was not represented on the board of directors nor did it seek detailed information of the company's affairs by demanding documents like minutes of board meetings, quarterly reports or detailed accounts. Instead it relied almost entirely on reports furnished by its representative at the company's annual general meeting. The bank raised no objection when the company embarked on a programme of speculative property development which resulted in considerable loss. Brightman J held that the bank was liable for the loss suffered by the trust, since it had not exercised adequate control over the company with a view to protecting the interests of the trust.

This does not, however, mean that trustees must be completely infallible in matters connected with investment. As Bacon VC acknowledged in *Re Godfrey* (1883) no investment can be guaranteed to be completely safe, since all human affairs are accompanied by some degree of risk and an investment will not be deemed to be attended with hazard so as to render it out of bounds to trustees just because it entails an element of risk. In line with this reasoning, it was held in *Re Chapman* (1898) that trustees who have acted honestly and in good faith in making investment decisions, will not be liable for any resultant loss, simply because the benefit of hindsight shows that the decision was wrong.

Trustees must diversify their investments
In order to minimise the level of risk, it is desirable for trustees to invest in a fairly diverse range of securities so that even if some of them fail to yield dividends others will do so. This principle of diversification is re-inforced by s 6(1) TIA.

Trustees must maintain a balance between income and capital
The trustees are under a general duty to act fairly as between different classes of beneficiaries. They must therefore avoid investments which tend to favour income beneficiaries at the expense of capital beneficiaries and vice-versa. In effect, investments should as far as possible be

designed to maintain the capital value of trust assets while also yielding a reasonable income. For example, it is not open to trustees to purchase objects like antiques or other chattels that are likely to appreciate in value without producing an income. Equally, trustees are precluded from making investments that are liable to yield a high income while the capital is either wasting away (eg short leaseholds or copyrights) or lacks security (eg a high interest unsecured loan (see *Khoo Tek Keong v Ch'ng Joo Tuan Neoh* (1934)).

Trustees should not ordinarily be guided by non-financial considerations
In the case of *Buttle v Saunders*, the court laid down the principle that in selling trust property, the trustees must pursue the best financial interests of the beneficiaries without regard to the underlying ethical implications.

This same principle was given expression in the realm of trust investments in *Cowan v Scargill* (1985) where Megarry VC declared that:

in considering what investments to make the trustees must put to one side their personal interests and views. Trustees may have strongly held social or political views. They may be firmly opposed to any investment in South Africa or any other countries or ... object to any form of investment in companies concerned with alcohol, tobacco, armaments or many other things. In the conduct of their own affairs of course, they are free to abstain from making any such investments. Yet if under a trust, investments of this type would be more beneficial to the trustees than any other investments, the trustees must not refrain from making the investment by reason of views they hold.

See also *Martin v City Of Edinburgh DC* (1988).
Where, however, the trust is one which falls within the charitable domain there are indications in the recent case of *Harries v The Church Commissioners* (1992) that the trustees may decline to invest in ventures and undertakings which might be profitable where these are incompatible with the basic charitable purposes of the trust. In so doing, the court signified that non-financial ethical considerations could be taken into account:

• where certain investments would conflict directly with the objects of the charity (eg a cancer charity investing in the tobacco industry); or
• where a particular investment was likely to alienate potential donors or beneficiaries.

The court also concluded that in other situations, trustees may also be guided by ethical considerations provided that this does not jeopardise the overall profitability of investments.

The mechanism for investment under the TIA

The authorised investments

The range of investments trustees are authorised to make under the TIA are set out in Schedule 1. These are classified broadly into narrower range (Part I); narrower range (Part II) and wider range (Part III) investments.

Part I: consists of securities which usually have a lower rate of yield but are relatively secure because they guarantee a fixed rate of income and a capital base which is not prone to fluctuation. Consequently, no investment advice is required by trustees before making such investments. Part I securities include Defence Bonds, National Savings Bonds, National Savings Certificates and deposits in the National Savings Bank.

Part II: sets out a long list of securities which are fixed as to the rate of income but which for the most part are liable to fluctuate in terms of their capital value. Such securities are generally more risky than those in Part I and hence trustees are required under s 6(1) to seek investment advice before proceeding with such investments. These investments include:

- the traditional gilt-edged securities (securities issued or guaranteed by the UK and other governments, local authorities, other public authorities and nationalised undertakings);
- debentures issued by companies registered in the UK;
- deposits in building societies; and
- mortgages of freeholds or leaseholds with an unexpired residue of at least 60 years.

Part III: securities within this category did not constitute authorised investments before the enactment of the TIA. Under Part III trustees are permitted to invest in:

- shares issued by public limited companies quoted on a recognised UK Stock Exchange. The company must have a minimum paid up capital of £1 million and must have paid dividends on all its shares in the five years preceding the investments;
- shares of (as distinct from deposits in) building societies;
- authorised unit trusts.

On the whole, wider range investments yield a higher rate of return than narrower range investments but are potentially more susceptible to the vicissitudes of the financial markets and are therefore relatively insecure. Trustees are thus required by s 6(1) to seek advice when making wider range investments.

Apportionment of the trust fund between narrower and wider range parts

It is open to trustees to tread the cautious path of confining all their investments to the narrower range, in which case the need for apportionment does not arise.

Where the trustees propose to invest in wider range securities the trust assets must be divided into two parts of equal value: a narrower range part and a wider range part. For this purpose, the assets must be valued in writing by a person the trustees believe is qualified to make a valuation (eg a stockbroker). Once this has been done, the narrower range part of the trust fund must be invested only in Part I and Part II investments. By contrast, the trustees may invest the wider range part of the fund entirely in Part III investments or may instead invest some of it in Part I and Part II investments and the balance in Part III investments.

Accruals

It sometimes happens that after the trust funds have been divided, some more property accrues to the trust estate. In such an event, it has to be determined whether such property (i) is an addition to the trust estate as a whole or (ii) has accrued to the trustee as owner of property already comprised in either part of the trust fund.

Where the property is in the nature of an addition to the trust estate, it will be apportioned equally between the narrower and wider range parts of the fund. This will be the case for example:

- where a debt owed to the trust estate is repaid after the division has been made; or
- where a reversion or remainder which forms part of the trust property falls into possession so that the income now becomes available to the trust estate.

By contrast, where the property accrues to the trustee as owner of property comprised in either part of the trust fund, the additional property shall not be apportioned but shall be treated as belonging to that part of the trust fund. For example if the wider range part of the trust fund includes shares in AB plc, any bonus shares issued by AB plc are deemed to accrue to the trustees as owners of property within the wider range part of the fund and will not to be apportioned between the two parts of the fund.

Withdrawals

After the division has been made, the need sometimes arises for the trustees to withdraw and appropriate money from the trust fund for purposes of the trust. For instance, the trustees may decide in the exercise of their power of advancement to pay a lump sum out of the trust fund to a beneficiary who has attained majority. Such a withdrawal may be made from either part of the trust fund without the need for a compensating transfer.

Where the object of making the withdrawal is to set up a separate fund, such as an accumulating fund for an infant beneficiary, the trustees may for purposes of investing the separate fund divide it into wider and narrower range parts. In this connection the separate fund may be divided equally or in the same proportions as the value of the two parts of the trust fund at the time of the withdrawal or in any intermediate proportion.

Special powers and special range investments

Apart from the power of investment conferred by the Act, a trust instrument as already seen may contain express powers of investment or of postponing conversion. Such powers may also be conferred by a court order or under the terms of other statutes. Such powers are known as *special powers* (see s 3(1)).

Where a special power provides for the trustees to hold property (including wider range but not narrower range property) otherwise than in accordance with the provisions of the TIA such property is known as special range property. Typical examples of special range property include shares in a private company and land.

Where it is prescribed that the trust should consist entirely of special range property, the TIA is inapplicable. However, where the trust contemplates that the trustees are to invest only part of the trust funds in special range property, the trustees must set apart the portion of the trust fund which they are directed to devote to special range investments and divide the remainder of the fund into a narrower range and a wider range part.

Investment advice

Before committing trust funds to Part II or Part III investments, the trustees are obliged by s 6(1) to obtain and consider proper advice from a person who the trustees reasonably believe is qualified in financial matters. The advice must be in writing or if given orally, confirmed in writing.

After the initial investment, s 6(3) makes it incumbent on the trustee to consider from time to time which investments to retain and to determine at what intervals and in what circumstances it is desirable to obtain advice on this matter. In effect, the trustees are expected to conduct periodic reviews of their investment portfolio and in so doing to obtain and consider proper advice. It does not however appear, judging from *Nestle v National Westminster Bank* (1992), that trustees are under a strict obligation to conduct such reviews, since the court concluded in this case that failure to do so is not in itself a breach of trust in the absence of evidence that such failure resulted in wrong investment decisions.

The special rules applicable to investments in mortgages

Trustees sometimes invest by lending trust funds to a borrower who undertakes to repay the sum lent with interest. To constitute an authorised investment under the TIA the loan has to be secured by a mortgage of land belonging to the borrower, either as a freehold owner or a leaseholder with an unexpired residue of at least 60 years. Moreover, the courts have long insisted that the loan must be secured by a first legal mortgage of the land. See *Swaffield v Nelson* (1876) and *Chapman v Browne* (1902).

Under s 8(1) TA trustees who are contemplating this type of investment are able to protect themselves, if, before making any advances, they:

- obtain a valuation of the property securing the loan from a person they reasonably believe is a competent surveyor or valuer;
- take proper account of the contents of the report received from the valuer or surveyor in determining whether the land represents a suitable investment;
- ensure that any amount advanced does not exceed two-thirds of the value as determined by the valuation.

Considering an equivalent provision in s 4 TA (1888), Eve J stated in *Palmer v Emerson* (1911) that it is a relieving section and not a section which imposes further obligations on trustees. At the same time, it has been emphasised in *Re Stuart* (1897) that the provision constitutes the standard by which reasonable conduct will be judged. This means that if the trust estate suffers a loss as a result of investing in a mortgage, the trustees will be relieved from liability for the loss only where they can show that they acted with due care by obtaining and acting on advice in the manner contemplated by s 8 TA (see also *Shaw v Cates* (1909), *Re Solomon* (1912) and *Learoyd v Whitely* (1887)).

Section 9 TA provides a limited measure of relief for a trustee who has advanced trust funds on the security of a mortgage. The effect of this section is that if the mortgage would in all other respects have been a proper investment for a lesser sum than that actually advanced by the trustee, his liability will be restricted to the difference between the sum advanced and the lesser sum. Where, for example, the security put forward by the borrower is property valued at £12,000, the maximum amount which the trustee can lend under s 8 is £8,000. Assuming he is persuaded by the borrower to lend £10,000 and the property subsequently depreciates in value to £6,000, so that the trust fund loses £4,000 the trustee's liability will be restricted to £2,000 (ie the difference between the £10,000 which was actually lent and the £8,000 which could properly have been lent) (see *Re Walker* and *Shaw v Cates*).

Investments in land

The purchase of land does not fall within the list of authorised investments contained in the TIA. Consequently, the trustees are not allowed as a general rule to invest in the purchase of land.

Investment in land is permissible, however, either:

- where this is expressly authorised by the trust instrument (in which case the land is treated as special range property); or
- where investment in land is provided for by other statutes, most notably the Settled Land Act. Under s 73(1)(xi), trustees are empowered to invest the proceeds of the sale of settled land in the purchase of freehold land or leasehold land with an unexpired residue of at least 60 years. By virtue of s 28(1) Law of Property Act 1925, a corresponding power is conferred on a trustee who holds land under a trust for sale.

The court's jurisdiction to widen the trustees investment powers

Where the trustees propose to make investments which are neither provided for in the trust instrument nor authorised by statute they can only do so with the court's approval.

Originally, the courts were not prepared to approve any such proposal even where this would be in the interest of the beneficiaries except in cases of emergency (see *Re Tollemache* (1903)). Statute has since intervened to enable the courts to enlarge the powers exercisable by trustees including their investment powers. Trustees seeking wider investment powers may apply to the court under s 57 Trustee Act or s 1 Variation of Trusts Act (1958). An application under s 57 is less problematic since the trustees are not obliged to secure the consent of the beneficiaries. Recourse must, however, be had to the Variation of Trusts Act where subsisting beneficial interests in the trust property are liable to be affected (see *Anker-Petersersen v Anker-Petersen* (1991)).

Even though s 15 TIA made it clear that the statutory jurisdiction of the courts to confer wider powers of investment on trustees was not to be affected by the enactment of the TIA, the prevalent judicial view in the 1960s was that the range of investments authorised by the TIA was sufficient. In the light of this assumption, the principle was laid down in cases such as *Re Kolb's WT* (1962) and *Re Cooper's Settlement* (1962) that no application by trustees for enlarged investment powers would be approved, unless there were special circumstances.

Even if this assumption was true in the 1960s when the *Re Kolb* line of cases was decided, by the latter part of the 1970s it had become increasingly evident that the range of investments authorised by the Act had not kept pace with major changes in investment practice occasioned by recent developments in the legal and economic spheres. Significantly, the Law Reform Committee in its 1982 report on the Powers and Duties of Trustees described the TIA as tiresome, cumbrous and expensive in operation and recommended that it should be reformed in various respects.

Like the Law Reform Committee, the courts themselves came to appreciate that the range of investments in the TIA is inadequate and by the early 1980s had developed a much more flexible attitude to applications for wider investment powers than that which was adopted in the *Re Kolb* line of cases. This is evident from *Mason v Farbrother* (1983) which involved a pension fund trust for employees of the Co-operative Society. When the fund was set up the trustees were given limited powers of investment. By 1982, as a result of prudent management and inflationary trends the trust fund had grown substantially. The trustees now sought wider investment powers under s 57. The court had no hesitation in holding that there were special circumstances of the type alluded to in *Re Kolb* which would warrant the conferment of enlarged investment powers on the trustees.

The court was prepared to go even further in *Trustees Of The British Museum v AG* (1984) where it was held that in the light of great changes in investment conditions and practice in the years since the TIA was enacted, the principle in the *Re Kolb* line of cases should no longer be followed. Here, the investment powers of the trustees were set out in a scheme created in 1960. The trustees applied for wider investment powers, particularly the power to invest abroad. It was common ground that the trustees were eminent and responsible, had highly skilled advice and the fund consisted of £5-6 million which made the trust more like an institutional investor. The application was approved by Megarry VC. In so doing, he insisted that in the prevailing climate it was no longer appropriate to maintain as had been done in *Re Kolb* that special circumstances must exist before such an application could be granted. Rather each case had to be dealt with on its particular merits and in determining the merits of a given case, factors to be considered would include; the standing of particular trustees, the objects of the trust and the size of the trust fund as well as the width of permissible investments, the scope for division and diversification and the efficiency of the provision for advice and control (see also *Steel v Wellcome Custodian Trustees Ltd* (1988)).

The duty to distribute

The trustees must distribute the trust estate to those who are properly entitled to it. Failure to do so renders them liable for breach of trust (see *Eaves v Hickson* (1861)).

Where the trustees are in doubt regarding the identity or whereabouts of prospective beneficiaries, the matter may be resolved by making preliminary enquiries and placing advertisements in the manner contemplated by s 27 TA.

Where the entitlement of a beneficiary is not in doubt but it is uncertain whether he is still alive, the problem may be overcome by applying for a Benjamin Order (see *Re Benjamin* (1902) and *Re Green's WT* (1885)).

Where the trustees cannot resolve any matter concerning the distribution of the trust estate on their own, they may apply to the court for directions. Moreover, where despite all the best efforts of the trustees the beneficiaries cannot be ascertained or it is otherwise impossible or impracticable for the trustees to carry out the distribution, they may pay the trust fund into court as a last resort (see *Re Gillingham Bus Disaster Fund* (1885)).

The duty to keep accounts and provide information

The duty to keep accounts is laid down in *Pearse v Green* (1819). There is, however, no requirement that the accounts must be audited, although under s 22(4) TA, the trustees may arrange for an independent accountant to audit the accounts.

Apart from accounts and other financial statements, beneficiaries may also call for general information concerning the affairs of the trust (see *O'Rourke v Darbishire* (1920)). The trustees are, however, entitled not to furnish information which will disclose to the beneficiaries the manner in which they have exercised a discretionary power (see *Re Londonderry's Settlement* (1965)).

The trustee's powers

In addition to the duties imposed on them, trustees are usually invested with far-reaching discretionary powers which enable them to exercise their judgment in a wide range of matters concerning the trust. The precise powers available to the trustees in any given case are determined in the first instance by the trust instrument. In addition to such express powers, the trustees have at their disposal a number of important statutory powers unless the trust instrument directs otherwise. We shall concentrate on three of these powers namely maintenance (s 31 TA); advancement (s 32 TA); and delegation (ss 23-25 TA). Thereafter we shall refer briefly to various other powers exercisable by trustees.

The power of maintenance

A trustee is ordinarily precluded from paying over to an infant beneficiary any income arising from his beneficial interest while he remains an infant. It is incumbent on the trustees to retain such income and accumulate it with the capital until the infant attains majority at the age of 18.

Instead of accumulating the income, the trustees may see the need to apply the entire income or part thereof towards meeting the routine, recurring expenses of the infant eg school fees, food, clothing, lodging etc. Before statute intervened, the trustees could do so only where the trust instrument contained an express power of maintenance. Under s 31 TA, however, trustees can now exercise a statutory power of maintenance where the trust instrument is silent. The section provides as follows:

- Where trustees hold an interest in property for an infant beneficiary, whether the interest is vested or contingent, they may in their discretion pay to the infant's parents or guardian or otherwise apply towards the infant's maintenance, education or benefit, such part of the income of the property as they think reasonable. This power is exercisable, whether or not:

(a)   there is any other fund applicable to the same purpose; or
(b)   there is any person bound by law to provide for the infant's education or maintenance.

- During the infancy of the beneficiary, as long as his interest continues, the trustees shall accumulate any income not expended on his maintenance and invest it in authorised investments. However, it is open to the trustees in any given year, to carry over and apply income accumulated in preceding years towards the maintenance or education of the beneficiary in a subsequent year.
- Where the beneficiary attains majority or marries at an earlier age and (i) has a vested interest in the income or (ii) is entitled to the property from which the income arose in fee simple or fee tail the trustees shall hold such accumulations on trust for the beneficiary absolutely. For example, if £10,000 is held on trust for B either in fee simple or for life and B is 13, if the sum is invested and yields £1,000 a year, on reaching 18, B will be absolutely entitled to the accumulated sum of £5,000.
- If the beneficiary's interest is not yet vested, when he attains majority, he does not become entitled to the accumulated income. From that time, however, the trustees must pay him the income from the capital together with the income produced by any accumulated income until his interest becomes vested. If the beneficiary's interest fails before it becomes vested either because he dies or for any other reason, the income accumulated during his infancy will be treated as an accretion to the capital. For example, if £10,000 is given to trustees 'on trust for B if he attains the age of 25' assuming again that B is 13 and that the trustees invest the money which yields £1,000 a year, B will not be entitled to the accumulated income of £5,000 at the age of 18. From that date, however, he will become entitled to the income on the £10,000 capital and on the £5,000 accumulated income until he attains the age of 25 (unless there is a provision to the contrary in the trust instrument as happened in *Re Turner's WT* (1936)). If B dies at 23, his interest fails and the £5,000 will be treated as an accretion to the capital so that whosoever is entitled to the capital on B's death will receive £15,000.
- If an infant beneficiary dies before attaining majority or getting married even if his interest was vested, any income not expended on his maintenance will be treated as an accretion to the capital (see *Re Delamere's ST* (1984)).

Conditions for the exercise of the power of maintenance

* There must be nothing in the trust instrument pointing to a contrary intention on the settlor's part (see *Re Ransome; IRC v Bernstein; Re McGeorge* and *Re Turner's WT*).
* The beneficiary in respect of whom the power is exercisable must be below 18.
* The trust property or a share of it must be held on trust for the beneficiary.
* The beneficiary must be entitled to the *intermediate income* ie the income yielded by the trust property between the date of the gift and the date on which he attains majority or the date on which the event which operates to vest his interest occurs. The beneficiary will not be so entitled where for instance trustees are directed to hold £10,000 on trust for an infant beneficiary but the settlor expressly specifies that until the infant attains majority the income should be paid to some other person.

The rules which determine whether a particular gift carries the intermediate income are found in s 175 LPA and s 31(3) TA as supplemented by the decisions of the courts. The applicable rules can be summarised as follows:

Vested gifts
Where the interest of the beneficiary is vested it will ordinarily carry the intermediate income unless the trust instrument provides otherwise (as in the last example, above).

Contingent gifts
A gift is contingent where it is expressed to be conditional on the occurrence of a specified event the happening of which is uncertain. As far as contingent gifts made by will are concerned, the combined effect of s 175 LPA, s 31(3) TA and the decided cases is as follows:

* a contingent specific bequest or devise carries with it the intermediate income;
* a contingent gift of residuary personalty or residuary realty carries with it the intermediate income;
* a contingent general bequest or devise or contingent pecuniary legacy will not generally carry the intermediate income which goes to person entitled to the residue until the vesting event occurs. This is, however, subject to three exceptions namely:
  (a) where the testator is the father of an infant beneficiary or stands in *loco parentis* to him and no further provision is made for the infant in the will;

(b) where the testator is not the father of the infant nor in loco parentis but the will reveals an intention that the legacy is to be used to maintain the child;

(c) where the will specifically directs that the legacy should be set apart from the rest of the testator's property.

Deferred gifts

A deferred gift is one which is limited to take effect at a specified time or on the occurrence of a specified future event which in the natural order of events must occur. Such a gift may be contingent (eg the residue of my estate to B, five years after my death provided he attains the age of 21). On the other hand, it may be vested (eg £10,000 to B to be paid to him on my death or to be paid to him in two years time). The position with regard to such gifts is as follows:

- deferred specific bequests or devises carry the intermediate income;
- deferred gifts of residuary realty do not carry the intermediate income unless the gift in question is also contingent in nature;
- deferred gifts of residuary personalty and deferred gifts in the form of general and pecuniary legacies do not carry the intermediate income.

Improper exercise of the power of maintenance

Although it is at the discretion of the trustees to determine whether to use trust income for maintenance or to accumulate such income, they are required to take proper care in exercising this discretion. In particular, they are required by the proviso to s 31(1) to have regard to such factors as the infant's age, his requirements, other income available for his maintenance and the general circumstances of the case. Failure to take proper care in exercising the discretion may render the trustees liable to repay any income which is lost as a consequence (see *Wilson v Turner* (1883)).

Maintenance from capital

While s 31 specifies that provision for maintenance must be made out of the income, the courts have the power under s 53 TA to order the disposal of an infant's beneficial interest and the application of the capital and income towards his maintenance or towards the acquisition of some other capital investment.

Authorisation of maintenance by the court

In addition where s 31 is inapplicable because the power of maintenance has expressly or impliedly been excluded in the trust instrument, the court may in the exercise of its inherent jurisdiction authorise the use of the trust income for maintenance as seen from such cases as *Re Collins* (1886).

The power of advancement

What is advancement?

Trustees are commonly empowered to apply trust capital for the 'advancement or benefit' of beneficiaries. In its original sense advancement entails making financial provision out of trust capital towards the establishment in life of a beneficiary before the beneficiary becomes entitled to demand such capital. The power of advancement has been construed in very wide terms by the courts and the following applications of trust funds have been held to constitute valid exercises of the power:

- buying an Army commission for a beneficiary (*Lawrie v Barnes*);
- purchasing a house for a doctor-beneficiary (*Re Williams WT* (1953));
- providing money to pay off a beneficiary's debts (*Lowther v Bentinck* (1874));
- paying for the passage of a beneficiary who is emigrating to another country (*Re Long's Settlement* (1868));
- assisting a beneficiary to start a career at the Bar (*Roper-Curzon v Roper-Curzon* (1871); or to set up in business (*Re Kershaw* (1868));
- providing out of the capital for the payment of medical and nursing home expenses of an elderly and incapacitated beneficiary (*Stephenson v Wishart*);
- applying capital towards donations to charity on behalf of a beneficiary who was a young man of immense wealth (*Re Clore* (1966)); and
- the redistribution of capital by resettling such capital due to a beneficiary under a new trust so as to take advantage of savings on estate duty (*Pilkington v IRC* (1964)).

The statutory power of advancement (s 32)

An express power of advancement may be conferred on trustees by the trust instrument. If no such express power is found in the trust instrument, the trustees may avail themselves of the statutory power of advancement under s 32 TA unless they are precluded from doing so under the terms of the trust.

Under s 32 the trustees may pay or apply any capital money subject to a trust for the advancement or benefit of a beneficiary whether the beneficiary has:

- an absolute vested interest; or
- a vested interest which is liable to be defeated (eg by the exercise of a power of appointment); or
- an interest which is contingent on the attainment of a specified age or the occurrence of a particular event or one which is subject to a gift over on his death under a specified age or on the occurrence of some other event.

This statutory power is exercisable for example:

- where £10,000 is given to trustees to hold on trust for B absolutely and B happens to be an infant. Notwithstanding the fact that B has a vested interest in the fund, the trustees are precluded from paying any part of the income or capital directly to B. They may, however, apply part of the capital towards his advancement by virtue of this section;
- where £10,000 is given to trustees to hold on trust for B, a bachelor, provided he marries, B's interest is contingent but the trustees may exercise the power of advancement in his favour even though B is single;
- where £10,000 is given to trustees to hold on trust for B if he attains the age of 21 and if he dies before then to hold on trust for C, the trustees may make an advancement in favour of B;
- where £10,000 is bequeathed to trustees for the benefit of such of the testator's children as his wife shall appoint and in default of appointment to B, the trustees may prior to any such appointment exercise the power of advancement in favour of B who has a vested interest that is liable to be divested.

Conditions for the exercise of the statutory power
In exercising the statutory power of advancement the trustees must ensure:

- that the money paid or applied in favour of a beneficiary shall not in total exceed half of the vested or presumptive share or interest of that beneficiary in the trust property. Accordingly:

(a) where trustees hold £10,000 on trust for B if he attains the age of 21, they are entitled to advance £5,000 to him;

(b) where trustees hold £10,000 on trust for B1, B2, B3 and B4 in equal shares and all the beneficiaries are infants, the trustees are entitled to advance £1,250 to each of them;

(c) where the trustees are directed in T's will to hold £12,000 on trust to be divided among all T's sons who are called to the Bar by the age of 30 and T is survived by four sons under 30, the trustees may advance £1,500 to each of them;

(d) where the trustees are directed in T's will to hold £12,000 on trust for the benefit of the first of T's sons to qualify as a doctor and T is survived by three sons the position is more problematic. Strictly speaking the presumptive share of each son is £12,000 since any son that qualifies is entitled to the entire amount. It would, however, appear that the trustees will not advance £6,000 to any of the sons but will for the purpose of the exercise of the power treat the presumptive share of each son as £4,000 and therefore advance no more than £2,000.

- where after an advancement has been made in his favour, a beneficiary becomes absolutely entitled to a share in the trust capital, this advancement shall be taken into account as part of his share. Thus, for example, if T gives £15,000 to trustees to hold on trust for T's children, B1, B2 and B3, each of them is entitled on attaining majority to £5,000 out of the capital. Assuming that when B1 was 17, the trustees had advanced £1,000 to enable him secure an apprenticeship and acquire the tools of his trade his entitlement to capital will be reduced by the sum advanced to £4,000.

- the power will not be exercisable to the prejudice of any person entitled to a prior life or other interest, unless such person is of full age and consents in writing to the advancement (as happened for instance in *IRC v Pilkington*). For example, where property is held on trust for A for life, remainder to B and C in equal shares, A is entitled to the income from the property in his lifetime and would therefore be prejudiced if any part of it is advanced to B or C. It is in order to safeguard A against this that his consent is required.

It must be noted that if A's interest arises under a protective trust, the effect of giving his consent would ordinarily be to determine his life interest and bring into being a discretionary trust. This result has, however, been avoided by the provision in s 33(1) to the effect that consent to the exercise of the power of advancement does not constitute a determining event.

The trustee's responsibility for ensuring proper utilisation of sums advanced

It is provided in s 32 that the trustees may 'pay or apply any capital money', which suggests that they may either transfer the money directly to the beneficiary or apply it on his behalf.

Where the trustees hand over the money to the beneficiary, they are not entitled to stand back and leave it open to the beneficiary to spend the money as he chooses but must seek to ensure that he applies it for the specified purpose. Failure to do so may amount to a breach of trust and may render the trustees liable to account for any money which has been misapplied. In this connection the Court of Appeal made it clear in *Re Pauling's ST* (1964) that trustees cannot prescribe a particular purpose and then raise and pay money over to the beneficiary leaving him entirely legally and morally free either to apply it for that purpose or dissipate it on other things without any responsibility on their part to inquire after its application.

Settled land not covered by the statutory power of advancement

For the purpose of s 32, the trustees are empowered to make advances of any capital consisting of money or securities or property held on trust for sale (including land held on trust for sale as seen from *Re Stimpson's Trust* (1931)). The power does not however apply where the capital consists of land held under the SLA or the proceeds of sale of land or other capital money for the purposes of the Act.

Exercise of the power of advancement by the courts

Just as the courts have affirmed in such cases as *Re Collins* that they have an inherent jurisdiction to order provision to be made out of the trust income for the maintenance of an infant beneficiary (*Re Collins*) so also have they held in such cases as *Barlow v Grant* (1684) and *Re Mary England* (1830) that they have an inherent jurisdiction to order payments by way of advancement or maintenance out of the capital.

Furthermore, under s 53, the courts may also arrange for the conveyance of property to which an infant is beneficially entitled with a view to the application of the capital or income which is yielded for the maintenance, education or benefit of the infant.

The power of delegation

Traditionally, trustees were regarded as being under an obligation to perform their functions personally and the trustee was accordingly required by equity not to delegate any matter relating to the administration of trust. As Langdale MR asserted in *Turner v Corney* (1841) 'Trustees who take on themselves the management of trust property for the benefit of others have no right to shift their duty to other persons'. The operative principle in this connection was *delegatus non potest delegare*.

It has, however, been recognised from the outset that trustees could justifiably derogate from this principle in certain circumstances. On the one hand, it has always been open to the settlor to confer the power of delegation in the trust instrument. On the other hand, even where this has not been done, the courts have for centuries empowered the trustees to delegate various aspects of their responsibilities to agents. Thus, in *Ex p Belcher* (1754), for instance, Lord Hardwicke signified that trustees could employ a broker to sell a consignment of tobacco by auction and allow him to receive the purchase price; while in *Speight v Gaunt* (1883), the House of Lords held that it was permissible for a trustee to appoint a broker to purchase corporation stock as an investment. In giving effect to the power to delegate, the courts laid down a number of conditions, namely that:

- the delegation must be justified by some legal necessity or be in accordance with ordinary business practice (*Ex p Belchier*);
- the trustee could only delegate his ministerial duties and was precluded from delegating his discretions (*Fry v Tapson* (1884));
- the trustee was obliged to take reasonable care in selecting the agent and to assign to him only tasks which were of a kind normally undertaken by that class of agent (*Rowland v Witherden* (1851); *Fry v Tapson*);
- after appointment the trustee was required to exercise proper supervision over the agent, ensuring in particular that any money or property received by the latter was invested or paid to the trust as soon as reasonable (*Mathew v Brise* (1845); *Rowland v Witherden*).

The restricted power of delegation available before 1925 was considerably broadened by ss 23 and 25 TA which provide for delegation by trustees in a variety of circumstances:

The basic power of delegation is set out in s 23(1), which specifies;

- that trustees may, instead of acting personally, employ a solicitor, banker, stockbroker or other agent to transact any business/do any

act required to be done in the execution of the trust including the receipt and payment of money;
* that trustees who exercise this power shall be entitled to recover all charges and expenses incurred by them in so doing and shall not be liable for any defaults of the agent if he was employed in good faith.

The leading case in which the effect of s 23(1) was explored is *Re Vickery* (1931) where Maugham J declared that it revolutionised the position of trustees as regards the employment of agents. His judgment indicates that the sub-section has relaxed the pre-existing rules on delegation in two highly significant respects:

* in the first place, he indicates that it is no longer necessary for the trustees to justify their decision to delegate by showing that there was a legal necessity or that such delegation accords with normal business practice;
* secondly he suggests that the combined effect of the provision in s 23(1) that a trustee shall not be liable for the default of an agent if employed in good faith and the provision in s 30(1) that a trustee shall not be answerable for losses caused by agents unless they happen through his own wilful default is that where an agent is appointed under s 23(1) the trustees are to be judged by a subjective standard which is considerably less rigorous than that contemplated by the pre-1925 rules. According to this reasoning it no longer depends on whether the trustees had acted reasonably in appointing and supervising the agent as was the case before 1925, but rather on whether he was employed in good faith. This operates to the advantage of the trustees in that even if their choice of agent or the manner in which they allowed him to carry out his task does not appear reasonable from an objective standpoint this will not render them liable for his defaults unless they were motivated by bad faith.

Commenting on the decision in *Re Vickery* notable commentators like GH Jones in his article 'Delegation by Trustees: A Reappraisal' (1959) 22 MLR 381 and Hanbury & Martin pp 561-566 have justifiably called into question the construction placed on s 23(1) in *Re Vickery*, not least because it affords the indolent but well-meaning trustee a degree of immunity which he scarcely deserves.

The trustee is empowered by s 23(2) to appoint an agent for the purpose of administering any part of the trust estate situated outside the UK or executing or exercising any discretion or power vested in them in relation to such property.

This provision goes beyond s 23(1) in one important respect. This is because s 23(1) merely authorises trustees to appoint agents to transact particular business or do specific acts whereas s 23(2) while providing for delegation of ministerial acts also empowers trustees to delegate their decision making responsibilities or discretions (see *Green v Whitehead* (1930)).

A third sub-section of s 23 provides that without prejudice to his general power to employ agents a trustee may:

- authorise a solicitor to receive any money or other property due to the trust by producing a deed containing a receipt signed by the trustee;
- authorise a solicitor or banker to receive money payable to the trust under an insurance policy by producing the policy with a receipt signed by the trustee.

A proviso to this sub-section imposes on the trustee the same liability which would have attached to him before 1925, for any loss occasioned by his permitting such money or property to remain under the control of the solicitor or banker for longer than is reasonably necessary to enable it to be transferred to the trustee (contrast this with the lesser degree of liability apparently contemplated by s 23(1)).

Under s 25, the trustees are invested with a wide power of temporary delegation. Unlike s 23(1) which contemplates the appointment of agents to perform purely ministerial acts, s 25 enables a trustee to delegate all his responsibilities. Initially this was permissible only where a trustee was proceeding outside the UK for over a month. However, by virtue of ss 9 and 11 Powers Of Attorney Act (1971), this restriction has been removed.

According to s 25:

- a trustee may by power of attorney delegate for a period not exceeding 12 months the execution or exercise of any or all of the duties, powers or discretions vested in him;
- this power is available whether he is a sole trustee or one of several trustees (although in the latter case, if there is only one other trustee he cannot delegate to that trustee unless the latter is a trust corporation);
- the delegating trustee is required to ensure that the power of attorney is attested by at least one witness;
- he is also required before or within seven days of executing the power of attorney to give written notice of its existence and details

to the other trustee(s) and any person empowered to appoint new trustees;
* the delegating trustee remains liable for the acts and defaults of the delegate as if they were his own;
* even in those instances in which the power of attorney authorises the delegate to execute and exercise all the trustees duties, powers and discretions it is not open to him to delegate the general administration of the trust by executing a power of attorney under s 25 in favour of some other person.

Finally mention must be made of the Enduring Powers Of Attorney Act (1985). This Act is intended to ensure that if a donor who has executed a power of attorney becomes incapable his incapacity will not terminate the power of attorney.

According to s 2(8) of this Act, a power of attorney executed by a trustee under s 25 TA will not be an enduring power of attorney because it is only effective for a maximum of 12 months and in any case mental incapacity would warrant the replacement of the delegating trustee.

By contrast s 3(3) of the Act provides that the donee of an EPA may execute or exercise all or any trusts, discretions or powers vested in the donor as trustee. This provision was inserted to address a particular mischief in the pre-existing law, but its unintended effect has been to enable a trustee to delegate his duties and powers indefinitely where this would not have been open to him under s 25 TA. This has been described as a 'legislative blunder by Oerton (1986) 130 SJ 23, 25 and the matter is currently under consideration by the Law Commission.

Other powers exercisable by trustees

These include:

* The power of sale conferred by statutes such s 1(1) TIA which contemplates the sale of trust property for investment purposes; s 16 TA which empowers trustees to raise money by selling trust property for any purpose authorised by the trust instrument or by statute. and s 33 Administration of Estates Act 1925 which authorises the sale of the assets of a person who dies intestate; and the distribution of the proceeds to beneficiaries.
* The power to issue receipts under s 14 TA for money, securities or other property. In the case of money or personal property a receipt by one trustee suffices but where the money constitutes the proceeds of the sale of settled land or land held on trust for sale, it must be issued by at least two trustees (s 14 TA).

- The power to insure trust property under s 19 TA.
- The power to compound liabilities under s 15 TA. As emphasised in *Re Earl of Stafford* (1980) the power conferred by s 15 must be exercised in the interests of the beneficiaries regard being had to the benefits and costs of settling the claim as compared with proceeding with litigation.

Variation of trusts

Introduction

Trustees are required to carry out the trust according to the express terms set out in the trust instrument as supplemented by the various implied terms imposed by statute. Where the beneficiaries are all of full age and absolutely entitled to the trust property and are all of one accord, this presents no difficulties, since they can simply bring the trust to an end under the rule in *Saunders v Vautier* (1841) and reconstitute it under whatever terms they consider appropriate. In other instances, however, any departure from or variation of the terms of the trust will be allowed only where it is sanctioned by the court either acting in the exercise of its inherent jurisdiction or on the basis of some statute.

Variation in the exercise of the courts inherent jurisdiction

As a facet of the courts inherent jurisdiction to oversee the proper administration of trust property, the courts are competent to vary the terms of a trust. Historically, however, this jurisdiction was exercised very sparingly. Consequently, before Parliament intervened to confer a wide-ranging statutory jurisdiction on them, the courts were willing to sanction such variations only in a limited number of well-defined situations outlined by Lord Morton in *Chapman v Chapman*:

- The courts were prepared to authorise variations which would enable trustees to change the nature of property held on trust for infant beneficiaries from real property to personal property and vice-versa which the trustees were incompetent to do of their own accord because of pre-1925 rules governing succession to the property of infants (see *Inwood v Twyne*).

- The courts were also prepared to act where the trust instrument provided for accumulations out of income in favour of an infant during his minority, while making inadequate provision for his maintenance during the accumulation period (see *Re Collins*).
- Where an unexpected development or event occurred, which was unprovided for by the settlor and which threatened to undermine the basis of the trust, the courts were prepared to authorise certain acts/transactions not provided under the trust, with a view to salvaging the situation. As observed in this connection by Romer LJ in Re New:

in a case of this kind, which may reasonably be supposed to be one not foreseen or anticipated by the author of the trust, where the trustees are embarrassed by the emergency that has arisen and the duty upon them is to do what is best for the trust estate ... the court in a proper case would have jurisdiction to sanction ... such acts on behalf of the trustee.

In line with this, the court in *Re Jackson* (1882) signified its willingness to allow the mortgage of trust property to raise funds to carry out vital repairs on the property.

The courts have, however, emphasised in such cases as *Re Tollemache* (1903) that for a variation to be authorised under this heading it was not sufficient that the proposed transaction would be advantageous to the beneficiaries; it also had to be established that it was necessitated by an emergency.

- The courts could also approve a variation in the exercise of its inherent jurisdiction where there was a dispute as to the terms of the trust or the rights and interests created thereunder and the dispute was settled by a compromise re-defining the terms of the trust or the interests of the parties.

Variations under this fourth heading became especially common where the trustees acting in consonance with the adult beneficiaries wished to vary the beneficial interests provided for under a trust but could not invoke *Saunders v Vautier*, because they were also infant beneficiaries or beneficiaries yet unborn. An application would usually be made to the judge in chambers to approve the variation on behalf of such infants and unborn beneficiaries and approval was sometimes given even in instances where there was no genuine dispute to be compromised. In *Chapman* itself, an application was made by the trustees on this footing for the variation of the trust by the deletion of a particular clause (Clause 3). The House of Lords found that the terms and effect of this clause were not in dispute and the variation was sought simply because of its tax-saving implications. In view of this the court declined to approve the proposed variation insisting that its jurisdiction under this fourth heading was not general but confined to variations which in the real sense of the word were designed to compromise real disputes. It was largely in response to this decision that Parliament enacted the Variation Trusts Act which we shall examine in greater detail below.

Variations authorised by statute

Section 96(1) Mental Health Act (1983)

This gives the Court of Protection the power to make a settlement of property of a mental patient and further provides that the Court may vary any such settlement in whatever manner it sees fit, if any material fact was not disclosed when it was made or if circumstances have changed substantially.

Sections 23 and 24 Matrimonial Causes Act (1973)

By virtue of these provisions the courts enjoy wide powers to make orders affecting the property of parties to matrimonial proceedings. The court may among other things effect the variation of ante-nuptial and post-nuptial settlements as well as any subsisting settlement orders. Furthermore, it may order capital provision to be made by cash payment or property transfer or by the making of a settlement for the benefit of the other spouse and children.

Section 53 Trustee Act (1925)

This enables the court, where an infant is beneficially entitled to property to order such property to be conveyed or transferred with a view to applying the capital or income produced for the maintenance, education or benefit of the infant, notwithstanding that this is not provided for by the terms of the trust. For instance in *Re Meux* (1959) where property was settled on A for life, remainder to B, an infant, the court granted an application under s 53 for the appointment of a person to convey B's interest to A absolutely, in consideration for a sum to be paid by to trustees for B's maintenance. Also in *Re Gower's* Settlement (1934) the court authorised the mortgage of an infant remainderman's interest with a view to providing for his maintenance.

Section 57 Trustee Act (1925)

This enables the courts to enlarge the administrative powers of trustees beyond the scope provided for by the terms of the trust. It provides that where in the management or administration of trust property it is expedient to sell, lease, mortgage or otherwise dispose of such property or to undertake any purchase, investment, acquisition, transfer or other transaction but the trustees have no power to do so under the trust instrument or by law, the court may confer the necessary power on the trustees.

As noted above the courts could in their inherent jurisdiction vary the terms of the trust to allow such transactions only in the event of an emergency. By contrast, it is now open to the courts, relying on s 57 to authorise such transactions on the grounds of expediency rather than emergency.

The section has been invoked to confer additional powers on trustees in respect of a broad range of matters. For example:

* widening the trustees' investment powers (*Mason v Farbrother, Anker-Petersen v Anker-Petersen*);
* authorising the sale of land where parties who under the terms of the trust had to consent to its sale had refused (*Re Beale* (1932));
* authorising the sale of settled chattels where the trust instrument prohited such sale (*Re Hope* (1929));
* authorising the sale of the residuary estate where the trust instrument directed that it should not be sold until it fell into possession (*Re Cockerell's ST* (1956));
* permitting the purchase of a residence for the rent-free occupation of a beneficiary (*Re Power* (1947));

It is not, however, in every instance where it is proposed to vary the terms of a trust that recourse can be had to s 57. The type of variation permitted by the section must be one which relates to the administrative or managerial functions of the trustees and not one which is intended to redefine or refashion the beneficial interests created by the trust (see *Re Downshire's Settled Estates* (1953)).

Section 64 Settled Land Act 1925

This section prescribes that any transaction affecting or concerning settled land which is not authorised by the settlement or by law may be undertaken by the tenant for life on the order of the court, if it is one which could have been effected by an absolute owner and will in the court's opinion be for the benefit of the settled land or any person interested under the settlement.

In the light of s 28(1) LPA, the jurisdiction of the courts under s 64 SLA covers not only settled land but also land held on trust for sale (see *Re Simmons* (1956)).

As emphasised in *Re Downshire* it is open to the courts in the exercise of their jurisdiction under s 64 to sanction, not only variations which enlarge administrative or managerial powers of the courts, but also those which entail the alteration of beneficial interests. In the instant case, the proposed variation which was upheld under the s 64 was intended to alter the beneficial interests in a manner which would reduce tax liability.

The section has also been invoked in a variety of other cases such as *Re Scarisbrick's Resettlement Estates* (1944) and *Re Mount Edgcumbe ST* (1950). In the former it was used to authorise the tenant for life to raise money by the sale of capital investments to enable him to continue to reside in Scarisbrick Hall in circumstances where this was essential to its preservation. Similarly, in the latter case, it was used to authorise the application of £10,000 out of capital monies in replacing furniture and heirlooms in a mansion house which formed part of the settled estate, where the mansion house had been destroyed during the Second World War and had just been rebuilt.

The Variation of Trusts Act (VTA) (1958)

The VTA was designed to strengthen the jurisdiction of the courts to sanction proposed variations on behalf of beneficiaries or potential beneficiaries. According to s 1(1) of the Act, the courts are now empowered to approve arrangements varying or revoking all or any of the terms of the trust and enlarging the trustees' powers to manage or administer any property subject to the trust. Because the provision is framed in such wide terms, it allows the judges to authorise departures from the trust instrument in instances where they would previously have felt unable to do so either on the basis of their inherent jurisdiction or on the strength of s 57 TA. This prompted Lord Evershed MR to remark in *Re Steed's WT* (1960) that the VTA has given the court a 'very wide and indeed revolutionary discretion'.

At that same time the courts have distinguished between arrangements varying the terms of the trust which will be approved under the VTA and other arrangements which operate to resettle the property completely which they have no jurisdiction to approve under the Act.

In this connection, the material consideration, according to Megarry J in *Re Ball's Settlement* (1968) is whether the proposed arrangement alters the substratum of the trust.

The four categories

The Act empowers the court to approve any proposed variation on behalf of four categories of persons namely:

(i) Any person who is unborn; eg, where property is held on trust for A for life, remainder to A's eldest son and A as yet has no children.

Note, however, that where there is little or no possibility of a future beneficiary coming into existence (eg to trustees on trust for F, for life, remainder to her children and F attains the age of 65 without children) the court without needing to approve a variation under the VTA authorise may the trustees to deal with the property on the footing that no children will subsequently be born (*Re Pettifor's WT* (1966)).

(ii) Any person who is an infant or who is incapable of assenting to the variation because of some other incapacity such as unsoundness of mind; eg, where a trust is declared for the benefit of to C for life remainder to D (D being A's five year old daughter); see *Re Whittall* (1973) and *Re CL* (1969).

(iii) Any person who has a discretionary interest under a protective trust, provided the interest of the principal beneficiary has not been determined; eg where property is left to A for life on protective trusts, remainder to A's eldest child and A has a wife, as long as the protective trust subsists, the courts may approve the variation on the wife's behalf even if she is an adult and even if the variation will not benefit her in any way.

(iv) Any person (whether ascertained or not) who may become entitled to an interest as being at a future date or on the occurrence of a future event a person of a specified description or a member of a designated class

For example where property is held on trust for A remainder to his wife, the court may approve the variation on behalf of any future wife he may marry even if at the time the trust was created he was engaged to B (see *Re Clitheroe* (1959)). Equally where property is held on trust for C for life remainder to his next of kin and C is still alive, the court may approve such a variation on behalf of such next of kin (see *Re Suffert* (1961) and *Re Moncrieff* (1962)).

With regard to category (iv), there is, however, a proviso which stipulates that the court will not be competent to consent on behalf of any person who would fit the description or would be a member of designated class if the date had arrived or the event had occurred on the day the application was made to the court. Thus in the first example if A proceeds to marry B and an application is thereafter made to the court to vary the trust, the court cannot approve on B's behalf if she is of full age and in the second example if at the date of the application D would qualify as C's next of kin if C were dead, it is clear from *Re Suffert* and *Re Moncrieff* that the courts will not be competent to approve the variation on D's behalf.

Benefit

Where a proposed variation is presented to the court for approval on behalf of persons in categories (i) (ii) and (iv) it must be established that the requirement is for the benefit of such persons. No such requirement exists in connection with variations on behalf of persons in category (iii).

Usually it is sufficient to show that there will be some financial benefit in favour of such persons such as savings in various forms of tax which thus releases a larger sum for distribution among such persons when their interests ultimately vest in possession (see *Re Druce's ST* (1962); *Re Sainsbury's Settlement* (1967); *Gibbon v Mitchell* (1990) and *Re Clithero*.

It was, however, emphasised by Megarry J in *Re Holt's Settlement* (1969) that benefit in the present context 'is plainly not confined to financial benefit, but may extend moral or social benefit'. This is most clearly illustrated by the case of *Re Weston's Settlements* (1969), where a settlor having settled property on his sons and their issue now sought the courts approval for an arrangement under which the trusts would be transferred from settlements based in England to off-shore settlements in Jersey and the appointment of new trustees resident in Jersey. This would have achieved a tax saving of £163,000 but would have necessitated the settlor's sons who were still children moving from England to go and live in Jersey. It was held that notwithstanding the substantial financial gain involved the arrangement ought not to be approved since according to Lord Denning 'I do not believe that it is for the benefit of children to be uprooted from England and transported to another country simply to avoid tax' (contrast, however, with *Re Seales Marriage Settlement* (1961)).

Also relevant is *Re CL* where the court approved a variation on behalf of a wealthy elderly widow who was a mental patient whereby she gave up her life interest in trust funds in favour of her two adopted daughters for no consideration. Although the variation would operate to deprive the widow of income otherwise due to her this income was greatly in excess of her spending requirements and was liable to substantial taxes. While she did not benefit materially from the variation she benefited morally since she would in all probability have met with her approval if she had been of sound mind.

Also in *Re T's Settlement* (1964), the terms of the trust specified that an infant beneficiary would become absolutely entitled on reaching majority to the trust fund but a variation was approved under which her interest would become vested at a later date on the ground that she was immature and irresponsible and it would therefore be in her best interests not to have immediate access to the trust fund.

Account to be taken of settlor's intention

The courts must not only ensure that the proposed variation is in the interests of the person on whose behalf approval is sought but must enquire whether it runs counter to the settlor's intention. As explained by Evershed MR in *Re Steed's WT* it should 'look at the scheme as a whole and when it does so consider, as surely it must, what really was the intention of the benefactor'. Here T devised property for the plaintiff on protective trusts for her life and on her death to any person to whom she might appoint. She wished to eliminate the protective trust to take an absolute interest in the property. The only potential beneficiaries were any husband she might marry in future and their issue, although as things stood she was unlikely to get married and was past childbearing age and an application was made for the arrangement to be approved on their behalf. The court declined to do so. The court found that the reason why the plaintiff wanted absolute ownership was so that she could pass the property on to her brother and his family who were constantly sponging on her, and held that this would be inconsistent with the testator's intention in providing for her by means of a protective trust which was to ensure that she did not fall prey to the temptation to pass it on to her brother.

Position where adult beneficiary does not consent to variation

The court has no responsibility under the VTA to secure the consent of any adults except those who fall within categories (iii) and (iv). If it comes to the courts attention that an adult beneficiary outside these categories has not been consulted it may adjourn proceedings until his consent is obtained. If an adult beneficiary has been consulted and refuses to consent, the court would decline to approve the variation. And if the variation has mistakenly been approved without his consent, it appears from *IRC v Holmden* (1968) that the non-consenting beneficiary will not be bound by the variation and may seek an injunction preventing the trustees from departing from the original terms of the trust.

Consenting beneficiaries not required to execute any document

Under s 53(1)(c) LPA the disposition of a subsisting equitable interest must be in writing signed by its owner. In those instances where recourse is had to the VTA with a view to re-defining beneficial interests under a trust, it might have been assumed that pursuant to this provision all adult beneficiaries who consented would be required to execute a document. This argument was canvassed in *Re Holt's Settlement,* but did not find favour with Megarry J who concluded that no such document was required in order for the variation to be effective.

Revision Notes

Appointment of trustees

Any person capable of owning property may be a trustee. In addition to human beings corporate entities, notably the Public Trustee and Trust Corporations can be appointed as trustees. An infant cannot be appointed as an express trustee and an alien cannot serve as a trustee where the property concerned is a British ship.

There is no minimum or maximum limit to the number of persons who may be appointed as trustees of personalty. With regard to real property held under a settlement or trust for sale, there should be at least two trustees as a sole trustee cannot give a valid receipt if the property is sold. Also the number of trustees shall not exceed four.

The initial trustees are usually appointed by the settlor or testator and hold the trust property as joint tenants so that on the death of one the trust property vests in the survivors.

Where for any reason none of the initial trustees is available to assume office, equity will not allow the trust to fail for want of trustees. This is the case both in respect of testamentary trusts (*Re Smirthwaite; Dodkin v Brunt*) and inter vivos trusts (*Jones v Jones; Mallot v Wilson*).

Subsequent trustees may be appointed in addition to or in place of the initial trustees either under the terms of the trust instrument or in accordance with s 36 TA. An appointment under s 36 must be in writing.

An appointment can be made under s 36(6) where it becomes necessary to appoint additional trustees to serve alongside the existing trustees. Such additional trustees may only be appointed where this will bring the total number of trustees up to no more than four.

An appointment can be made under s 36(1) and (2) when it becomes necessary to replace a trustee who (i) is dead; (ii) remained outside the UK for 12 months; (iii) desires to be discharged; (iv) refuses to act; (v) is unfit to, or incapable of acting; (vi) is an infant; or (vii) has been removed from office in accordance with the trust instrument.

Such new trustees are to be appointed (i) by the persons given the power to do so by the trust instrument; (ii) by the surviving or continuing trustees for the time being; or (iii) by the personal representatives of the last surviving trustee.

Note also s 36(8) which provides that a continuing trustee includes a refusing or retiring trustee if he wishes to act. Does this mean that the trustees who are to remain in office cannot appoint a successor without the concurrence of an outgoing trustee? See *Re Coates To Parsons* and *Re Stoneham's ST*.

The court may appoint new trustees in addition to or in place of existing trustees under s 41 TA. The court will intervene where it is expedient to make an appointment but this proves difficult, inexpedient or impracticable under the trust instrument or s 36.

Such judicial appointments have been made in the types of situations which arose in *Re Smirthwaite, Re Parsons, Re Lemann's WT, Re Phelps WT, Re May's WT* and *Re Tempest*.

On the other hand, the courts will not intervene simply on the ground that the beneficiaries do not approve of the choice of new trustees made by the persons empowered by the trust instrument or s 36 to make the appointment (*Re Higginbottom; Re Brockbank*).

Acceptance of appointment may be by deed, in writing or verbally or may be by conduct. Examples of acceptance by conduct are seen in *Mucklow v Fuller, Re Sharman's WT, James v Frearson* and *Urch v Walker*.

On accepting office, the trustee is required to:

- disclose any possible conflict of interest (*Peyton v Robinson*);
- acquaint himself with the trust (*Hallows v Lloyd*);
- investigate suspected breaches of trust and take legal action where a breach has been committed (*Harvey v Oliver*);
- ensure that title to the property becomes duly vested in him jointly with the other trustees. In this connection, note the automatic vesting provisions in s 40 TA.

A trustee who does not wish to accept office may issue a disclaimer at any time before acceptance. No specific form of disclaimer is required by law and in certain instances it may be inferred from conduct (*Re Clout And Frewer's Contract*). It is however advisable for the avoidance of doubt for disclaimer to be by deed (see *Stacey v Elph*).

Retirement of trustees

A trustee may retire or be discharged from office:

- where all the benefiaries are of full age and consent to his retirement;
- under the terms of the trust instrument;
- under s 36(1) if someone else is available to fill the vacancy;

- under s 39 TA provided there are at least two trustees or a trust corporation left to administer the trust. The trustee must execute a deed declaring his wish to retire and his co-trustees and any person empowered to appoint new trustees must also consent by deed before the retirement is effective.

Removal of trustees

A trustee may be removed from office and replaced by someone else under s 36(1) for such reasons as absence abroad, unwillingness to act, unfitness, incapacity to act or infancy.

He may also be removed in the process of a judicial appointment of new trustees under s 41. Even if the court does not propose to appoint new trustees it can remove a trustee in the exercise of its inherent jurisdiction (see *Clarke v Heathfield (No 2)*; *Letterstedt v Broers*).

The trustees duties and powers

These are defined primarily by the trust instrument. A variety of duties and powers also arise from statute or are imposed by equity.

The trustee cannot choose whether or not to perform his duties since they are obligatory. His primary responsibility with regard to his powers is to consider their exercise from time to time (*Re Hay's WT*). If there are several trustees, these powers can only be exercised if there is unanimous agreement among the trustees (*Re Mayo, Luke v South Kensington Hotel*, unless the trust instrument provides otherwise or the trust is a charitable trust).

In the discharge of his responsibilities, the trustee is required to act with due care and diligence. If he is an ordinary trustee the standard demanded of him is that of a prudent man of business in the conduct of his affairs (*Learoyd v Whitely*). If he is being paid to serve as a trustee the standard is even higher (*Re Waterman, Bartlett v Barclays Bank*).

A trustee will only be entitled to receive payment if this is provided for:
- by a charging clause in the trust instrument;
- by an order of the court (*Re Duke Of Norfolk's ST*; *Re Drexel Burnham*);
- under an agreement with the beneficiary;
- in a statute (eg s 42 TA which deals with the remuneration of trust corporations and s 9 Public Trustee Act which deals with the remuneration of the Public Trustee);

- in accordance with the laws of a foreign jurisdiction where trust property is located in that jurisdiction; and
- under the rule in *Cradock v Piper* which operates for the benefit of solicitor-trustees.

In addition to any remuneration he may receive, the trustee is entitled to re-imburse himself out of the trust estate for expenses incurred by the trustee in executing the trust (s 30(2) TA, *Stott v Milne, Hardoon v Belilos*).

Fiduciary duties

In his capacity as a fiduciary the trustee must not allow his interests to conflict with his duties.

In the first place, the trustee is not allowed to make any unauthorised profit from his office (*Sugden v Crosland; Williams v Barton; Re Macadam*) nor is he allowed to take advantage of a benefit which he should have secured for the trust estate, such as the renewal in his own name of a lease previously held by him on behalf of the trust (*Keech v Sanford; Protheroe v Protheroe*).

Secondly, if the trustee purchases trust property for himself, he is caught by the self-dealing rule, under which the beneficiaries are entitled to set aside the sale within a reasonable time even if the trustee paid a fair price and did not take undue advantage of his position (*Ex p James; Ex p Lacey*). He cannot get around the rule by retiring from the trust and purchasing the property a short while later (*Wright v Morgan*); or by purchasing it indirectly through a third party (*Delves v Gray, Re Postlethwaite*), or by arranging for it to be purchased by a company in which he has a substantial stake: (*Re Thompson*).

The sale to a trustee will not be set aside under the self-dealing rule:

- where the contract of sale was made before he became a trustee (*Re Mulholland's WT*);
- where the trust was a bare trust under which the trustee had no active duties (*Parkes v White; Clark v Clark*); or
- where there are special circumstances (*Holder v Holder*).

Where the trustee purchases a beneficiary's interest in trust property rather than the trust property itself, such a transaction is subject to the fair-dealing rule. Under this rule, the beneficiary cannot set aside the sale if the trustee made full disclosure to him and the transaction was fair and honest (*Tito v Waddell (No 2); Coles v Trecithick; Thomas v Eastwood; Dougan v Macpherson*).

Thirdly, the trustee will not be allowed to set up on his own account, a business which is in competition with a business which forms part of the trust estate (see *Re Thomson*; but contrast with *Moore v M'Glyn*).

The duty to invest

The trustee is bound to ensure that trust property or funds are properly invested. This entails the the purchase or retention of property from which interest or profit is to be expected (*Re Wragg*), and accordingly excludes the acquisition of assets for non-profit making purposes such as the purchase of a house for a beneficiary to live in (*Re Power*).

In carrying out the duty to invest, the trustees must adhere to certain general guidelines:

• they must take care to avoid investments which are attended by risk. Note the standard laid down in *Learoyd v Whitely*;
• they must seek to diversify their investments;
• they must maintain a balance between the beneficiaries entitled to income and those entitled to the capital;
• they must eschew non-financial considerations in deciding which investments to select or retain (*Cowan v Scargill*; *Martin v City Of Edinburgh DC*; *Harries v The Church Commissioners*).

The TIA 1961 provides a detailed statutory regime for regulating investment by trustees. The operation of the Act may, however, be restricted or completely dispensed with under the terms of the trust instrument (see *Re Harari*; *Re Peczenik*).

The investments authorised by the TIA fall into three categories:

Narrower Range (Part I): eg Defence Bonds, National Savings Bonds and Certificates and deposits in the National Savings Bank.

No investment advice is needed for Part I investments.

Narrower Range (Part II): eg traditional gilt-edged securities issued or guaranteed by the government, local authorities and other public authorities; debentures issued by companies; deposits in building societies and mortgages of freehold land or leasehold land with an unexpired residue of 60 years.

Wider Range (Part III): including shares in public companies quoted on a UK Stock Exchange, provided the company has a minimum paid up share capital of at least 1 million and has paid dividends on its shares for the preceding five years.

For Part II and Part III investments, advice must be sought under s 6(1) TIA. Moreover, under s 6(3) advice should be sought from time to time on which of these investments to retain.

Trustees may opt to confine all their investments to the narrower range. If they wish to invest in wider range securities the trust fund must be apportioned into two parts of equal value; a narrower range part and a wider range part. After apportionment the narrower range part cannot be invested in wider range securities but the wider range part can be invested in narrower range securities.

The trustees may be authorised in the trust instrument or empowered by statute to invest in securities other than those enumerated in the TIA (eg land or shares in a private company). This is known as a special power and any such security acquired in the exercise of the power is special range property and is dealt with outside the TIA.

Apart from the requirements in the TIA which apply to all authorised investments, special provision is made for investment in mortgages s 38 TA 1925 which lays down the need to obtain the advice of a competent valuer or surveyor. The effect of non-compliance with this requirement is seen from cases like *Palmer v Emerson, Re Stuart, Re Solomon, Re Walker* and *Shaw v Cates*.

Although investment in land is not authorised by the TIA, the trust instrument may authorise such an investment. In addition, where land held under a settlement or trust for sale is sold, the trustees may invest the proceeds in freehold land or leasehold land with an unexpired residue of 60 years or more.

Finally, the trustees may wish to enlarge the powers of investment conferred on them by the trust instrument or the TIA. In the years after the enactment of the Act, the courts were reluctant to grant applications for enlarged investment powers (*Re Kolb's WT; Re Cooper's Settlement*). In more recent years, however, the courts have adopted a much more liberal attitude when dealing with such applications (*Mason v Farbrother; Trustees Of The British Museum v AG; Steel v Wellcome Custodian Trustees*).

The power of maintenance

Trustees may be given a power in the trust instrument to apply trust income towards the maintenance of infant beneficiaries. If not they can exercise the statutory power of maintenance in s 31 TA.

In order for the statutory power of maintenance to be exercisable:

* the trust property or a share in must be held on trust for the beneficiary;

- the beneficiary must be below 18. Where he is 18 or above, he will usually be entitled to the capital and any accumulated income on the trust property if his interest is vested. Where he is 18 or above but his interest is not vested, he will not be entitled to the capital or accumulated income until his interest becomes vested but can demand the income yielded by the capital plus accumulated income;
- there must be nothing in the trust instrument to the contrary such as an express direction to accumulate (*Re Ransome*; *IRC v Bernstein*; *Re McGeorge*; *Re Turner's WT*). If the terms of the trust instrument preclude the exercise of the power of maintenance, the trustees can only employ the trust income for the purpose of maintenance if the court in the exercise of its inherent jurisdiction authorises them to do so (see *Re Collins*).
- the infant beneficiary must be the person who is entitled to the intermediate income. His entitlement will depend on whether his interest is vested, contingent or deferred.

Where these conditions are satisfied, the trustees in exercising the power of maintenance, must have regard to matters such as the infant's age, requirements, other income available for his maintenance etc and are obliged to ensure that the income provided for maintenance is used for the intended purpose (*Wilson v Turner*).

The power of advancement

A trust instrument may sometimes empower the trustees to apply trust capital for the advancement of beneficiaries. This power is now statuorily provided for in s 32 TA. The power of advancement is capable of being exercised in a many different contexts as seen from the decided cases referred to on pp 168-169 above.

The exercise of the statutory power of advancement is subject to three conditions:

- the trustees shall not advance to any beneficiary an amount in excess of one-half of his presumptive share;
- a beneficiary who becomes absolutely entitled to his share in the trust capital after an advancement has been made in his favour will have the amount advanced deducted from his share;
- the power cannot be exercised to the prejudice of a person entitled to a prior life or other interest in the trust property or fund unless the person is of full age and consents in writing.

With regard to the third condition, it is significant that if the person entitled to a prior interest is the principal beneficiary under a protective trust, the consent of the principal beneficiary to the advancement is not a determining event.

A trustee who exercises a power of advancement is bound to ensure that the sum advanced is used by the beneficiary for the intended purpose (*Re Pauling's WT*).

Finally, the court may in the exercise of its inherent jurisdiction authorise payments out of the capital by way of advancement where the trust instrument does not alow such payments (*Re Collins; Barlow v Grant; Re Mary England*).

The power of delegation

For many years, trustees were under a duty to act personally and could not delegate any matter connected with the running of the trust (*Turner v Corney*).

By the 19th century, the principle that trustees could delegate some of their tasks had become well entrenched in English law but the courts imposed a number of strict conditions designed to discourage unnecessary delegation and ensure that trustees exercised proper control over the agents to whom they delegated trust business (*Ex p Belchier Speight v Gaunt; Fry v Tapson; Rowland v Witherden; Mathew v Brise*).

With the enactment of the TA 1925, the trustee's powers of delegation were extended considerably and the strict supervision which trustees were obliged to exercise over their agents were substantially relaxed. In particular s 23(1) which is the general provision dealing with delegation empowers trustees to employ agents to do any act required to be done in the execution of the trust and stipulates that they shall not be liable for defaults of agents employed in good faith even if they fail to supervise him effectively (see *Re Vickery* but note also the criticisms of Jones and Hanbury and Martin).

The above provision is supplemented by s 23(2) which empowers trustees to appoint agents to administer trust property situated abroad; and s 25 which allows trustees to delegate by means of a power of attorney, the exercise of any or all of their duties, powers and discretions for up to 12 months. In addition, the Enduring Powers of Attorney Act 1985 appears to provide another avenue for enlarging the trustee's power of delegation.

Variation of trusts

Where the beneficiaries are of full age and absolutely entitled to the entire trust property they may bring the trust to an end and reconstitute it under whatever terms they wish (*Saunders v Vautier*). In every other case, no variation or deviation from the original terms of a trust is allowed unless sanctioned by the court.

Variation under the court's inherent jurisdiction

Until comparatively recently the terms of a trust could only be varied under the courts inherent jurisdiction in a limited number of situations, eg:

* where the trust instrument directed income to be accumulated in favour of an infant without providing adequately for his maintenance (*Re Collins*);
* where an unexpected emergency arose which threatened to jeopardise the trust (*Re New; Re Jackson; Re Tollemarch*).
* where a dispute relating to the terms of the trust or the entitlement of beneficiaries was settled by a compromise which altered the terms of the trust, the court would as a matter of course approve the compromise. This practice was, however, called into question by the House of Lords in *Chapman v Chapman* which decided that the courts would not approve a compromise varying the terms of a trust where the trust instrument gave rise to no dispute.

Variations authorised by statute

The courts are empowered to sanction variations of trusts in a variety of specific contexts by such statutory provisions such as s 96 Mental Health Act 1983, ss 23 and 24 Matrimonial Causes Act 1973, s 53 TA and s 64 Settled Land Act.

In addition, s 57 TA empowers the court in general terms to authorise the exercise by trustees of a broad range of powers which they would not otherwise be entitled to exercise under the trust instrument or the law where this is considered expedient by the court. The courts have had occasion to rely on s 57 in a variety of cases like *Anker-Petersen v Anker-Petersen, Mason v Farbrother, Re Beale, Re Hope, Re Cockerell's ST* and *Re Power*.

Section 57 is, however, restricted in scope by the fact that it can be invoked only where the proposed variation relates to an administrative or managerial function but not when the variation will have the effect of redefining or restructuring the beneficial interests under the trust (*Re Downshire's Settled Estates*).

Where a proposed variation will have a bearing on the beneficial interests, the application must be made under the Variation of Trusts Act. Under the VTA, the court is empowered to approve arrangements varying or revoking all or any terms of the trust on behalf of four categories of persons:

(i)   unborn persons;
(ii) infants and persons incapable of assenting to the variation;
(iii) any person with a discretionary interest under a protective trust which has not been determined; and
(iv) any person who may become entitled as being a person who may at a future date or on the occurrence of a future event come within a specified description or class.

Where approval is sought on behalf of persons in categories (i), (ii) and (iv) the variation must be shown to be for the benefit of such persons. In this connection, it emerges from cases such as *Re Weston's Settlement* and *Re CL* that benefit in this context is not confined to the financial benefit which might accrue to the person if the variation is approved but also includes moral and social benefits.

In determining whether to approve a variation under the VTA, the court will take account of the intention of the settlor or testator who created the trust, so long as this can be ascertained (see *Re Steed's WT*).

Finally, it is the responsibility of the parties applying for the variation to ensure that all adults with interests in the trust property give their approval to the proposed variation. If they fail to do so and the variation is approved without obtaining the consent of any such beneficiary he is not bound by it (*Re Holmden*).

7 Breach of trust

General

A breach of trust occurs where a trustee either fails to perform any of the duties imposed on him or abuses any of the powers conferred on him by the trust instrument or equity. The breach may be in the nature of a positive act (eg misappropriation of trust funds) or may consist of some default or omission to act (eg failure to recover debts due to the trust estate).

Where a trustee profits from committing a breach of trust he will be liable to the beneficiaries for any profit he makes and also for any loss caused to the trust estate as a consequence of the breach. This is the case not only where he fraudulently deviated from his duties or exceeded his powers but also where genuinely believed he was acting in the best interest of the trust estate. In *Re Brogden* (1888), for instance, a marriage settlement contained a covenant to pay £10,000 to the trustees at the end of a five years. When this sum fell due the trustees of the settlement chose not to sue the covenantor's estate for this sum. Their reason was that his estate formed the basis of a family partnership and legal action would undermine the business. In spite of this, the court found the trustee liable for failing to take all possible steps on behalf of the trust estate to recover the sum. It has, however, been accepted in cases like *Lee v Brown* (1798) and *Brown v Smith* (1878) that where a trustee commits a mere technical breach which occasions no harm to the trust estate he will not be liable if his act is one which would have been authorised by the court.

Remedies for breach of trust

Where a breach of trust has been committed or appears to be imminent, the beneficiaries may pursue the following remedies:

- an injunction to restrain the breach;
- a personal remedy exercisable against the trustee; and
- a proprietary remedy exercisable against the trustee or some other party who has received the property from him.

Injunction

Where a beneficiary suspects that a trustee intends to commit a breach of trust, he may seek an injunction to prevent the anticipated breach. See *Dance v Goldingham* (1873) and *Wheelwright v Walker* (1883): injunctions to prevent the sale of trust property for less than could reasonably be obtained; *Riggal v Foster* (1853): injunction to restrain trustees from mortgaging trust property unnecessarily; and *Fox v Fox* (1870): injunction to prevent the distribution of the trust estate contrary to the terms of the trust instrument.

The personal remedy against the trustee

Where a breach of trust has already been committed which produces a profit for the trustee or results in a loss to the trust, the beneficiaries are entitled to pursue a personal action against the errant trustee to recover the profit or make good the loss.

The statutory basis upon which the trustee's personal liability is founded is s 30(1) TA 1925. The main thrust of s 30(1) is that while a trustee is personally liable for breaches committed by him, he will not as a rule be vicariously liable for breaches of his fellow trustees or losses suffered by the trust due to the dishonesty or neglect of other persons to whom trust business has been delegated. It is only where there has been some wilful default on the part of the trustee that he will be liable for the breaches of co-trustees and the shortcomings of delegates.

This principle was established long before s 30(1) was enacted, in the old case of *Townley v Sherborne* (1634). In this case, a trustee, over a period of time, jointly signed receipts for rents collected on trust property but allowed the money collected to remain in the hands of his co-trustees. When some of the money was misapplied by the co-trustees, he was held to be liable not simply because he happened to be a trustee but because of his wilful default in failing to ensure that the rent collected was properly controlled by all the trustees.

Liability for wilful default may also arise where a trustee knows that his co-trustees have committed, are committing, or are planning to commit a breach of trust but does nothing (see *Boardman v Mosman* (1779); *Booth v Booth* (1838) and *Wilkins v Hogg* (1861)).

Liability of incoming trustee for breaches by his predecessors
A new trustee will not be liable for breaches committed by other trustees before he assumed office. However, it was decided in *Re Strahan* (1856) that if it comes to his knowledge, after assuming office that any such breach has been committed, the incoming trustee is obliged to take whatever action is necessary against the errant trustee, including legal action.

Liability of retired trustees
Where a trustee retires, this does not extinguish his liability for breaches he committed while in office. Conversely, a trustee is not normally liable for breaches committed by other trustees after he leaves office. It is, however, clear from *Head v Gould* (1898) that a retired trustee will be liable for a breach by his successors if he retired so as to pave the way for the breach to be committed.

The position where trustees are jointly liable
Where a breach is committed by the trustees acting together or is committed by one trustee but facilitated by the wilful default of the other, their liability is joint and several. All the trustees or any one or more of them may be sued to recover the loss (see *AG v Wilson* (1864); *Fletcher v Green* (1864) and *Re Harrison* (1891)).

Contribution
Where the beneficiaries opt to pursue their action against one trustee, he is entitled to claim a contribution from any co-trustee who is also

liable for the breach. For many years the rule was that the contributions of all the trustees had to be equal, irrespective of the extent to which they were at fault for the breach. This has now been altered materially by s 2(1) Civil Liability (Contribution) Act 1978 under which the court now has a discretion, in the event of a breach to determine what it will be fair and just for each trustee to contribute having regard to the extent of the trustee's responsibility for the breach.

Indemnity

A trustee may be relieved from his liability to contribute towards the cost of repairing a breach of trust where he is entitled to be indemnified by a co-trustee.

The issue of indemnity has frequently arisen where a breach has been committed by two trustees, one a solicitor and the other an ordinary trustee. Cases like *Chillingworth v Chambers* (1896) and *Re Lindsay* (1904) indicate that where the solicitor exerted such a controlling influence over his co-trustee that the latter relied entirely on the former's professional judgment in matters connected with the trust, the solicitor will be obliged to indemnify the co-trustee for any breach. On the other hand, it was decided in *Head v Gould* (1898) that the solicitor will not be bound to indemnify his co-trustee if the latter actively participated in the alleged breach and did not participate merely in consequence of the advice and control of the solicitor.

Apart from cases involving solicitors, a trustee may claim an indemnity against a co-trustee who acted fraudulently in procuring the breach. Thus in *Re Smith* (1896) two trustees acting together invested trust funds in a loss-making venture. One trustee was bribed to make the investment but the other genuinely believed that the investment was sound. The court directed that the bribed trustee should bear the entire liability for the breach. By contrast, the courts are reluctant to allow a trustee to claim an indemnity where the co-trustee against whom it is sought is adjudged not to have acted fraudulently. This is seen from *Bahin v Hughes* (1886) which decided that a trustee was not entitled to an indemnity, where he had abdicated all his responsibilities under the trust to his co-trustee who acting honestly but erroneously committed a breach.

The measure of liability

Once it is shown that a trustee is guilty of a breach, it becomes necessary to establish the extent of his personal liability. Broadly speaking, the measure by which his liability will be determined is the profit he has made or the loss suffered by the trust estate as a consequence of the breach. The Court of Appeal even went as far as to hold in *Target Holdings Ltd v Redferns* (1994) that the obligation to make good the loss caused by a breach exists even if it would still have occurred without the breach.

Purchase of unauthorised investments

Where the trustees make an investment which is not authorised by the trust instrument or by statute, they will be liable for the difference between the cost of the investment and the price at which it is subsequently sold. This will be so, even if the investment was sold under a court order and would have fetched a higher price had the sale been delayed until a later date (see *Knott v Cottee* (1858)).

If the beneficiaries are all *sui juris* it has been recognised in cases like *Re Jenkin's and Randall's Contract* (1903) and *Wright v Morgan* (1926) that they can adopt the unauthorised investment instead of requiring the trustees to sell it. This presents no difficulty if at the time the beneficiaries elect to adopt the investment, its value is higher than the price the trustees paid for it. On the other hand, if the value of the investment has fallen below the purchase price, it is not entirely clear whether the beneficiaries are entitled to recover the difference from the trustees. Cases like *Thornton v Stokill* (1855) suggest they cannot; whereas other cases like *Re Lake* (1903) suggest they can.

Improper retention of unauthorised investments

Where the trustees improperly retain an unauthorised investment, when they could have sold it at an earlier stage, they will be liable for the difference between the price at which it is subsequently sold (or its value at the date of the judgment if it remains unsold) and the price which would have been realised if it had been sold at the proper time (see *Fry v Fry* (1859)).

Improper sale of authorised investments

Where the trustees have improperly sold an authorised investment, the beneficiaries may insist that they must replace the investment. Alternatively, as seen from *Re Bell's Indenture* (1980) the court may require the trustees to pay the difference between the price at which it was sold and the cost of replacing it at the date of the judgment.

If after the improper sale, the proceeds are invested in an unauthorised security which is thereafter sold for no less than it was purchased, *Re Massingberd's Settlement* (1890) decided that the trustees will still be liable for the difference between what has been realised from the unauthorised investment and what would have been yielded if the authorised investment had been retained.

Omission to invest within a reasonable time

Where the trustees are under a duty to invest trust funds, they must do so within a reasonable time. Before a suitable investment is found, it is contemplated by s 11(1) TA 1925 that they will pay the funds into a bank account where it will yield interest.

Furthermore, if the trustees are required by the terms of the trust instrument to invest in a specified type of asset but either make no investment at all or invest in some other asset, it has been held in *Byrchall v Bradford* (1822) and *Pride v Fooks* (1840) that they will be liable to purchase as much of the specified asset as they could have been done if they had made the investment at the appropriate time.

On the other hand, the courts have long accepted that where trustees are simply under a general duty to invest and delay unduly in making a suitable investment, their only liability is to produce the trust fund they should have invested (see *Shepherd v Mouls* (1845) and *Robinson v Robinson* (1851)). More recently, in *Nestle v National Westminster Bank* (1992) the Court of Appeal opined that the trustees might in such circumstances have to make good the difference between the uninvested fund and its projected value if it had been properly invested by a prudent trustee.

Setting off losses against profits

Where a breach has been committed resulting in a loss to the trust estate but the guilty trustees also entered into some other transaction which produced a profit for the trust, the general rule is that the profit cannot be set off against the loss (see *Dimes v Scott* (1828) and *Wills v Gresham* (1854)).

However, a set-off will be allowed, where the court finds that the profit and loss resulted either from the same transaction or from the same policy decision to pursue a particular course of investment (see *Bartlett v Barclays Bank Trust Co (No 1)* (1980)).

The position regarding payment of interest

A trustee whose breach of trust causes a loss to the trust estate is generally required to make good the loss with interest. As observed in *Wallesteiner v Moir (No 2)* (1975):

it is well established in equity that a trustee who misapplies trust funds will be liable not only to replace the misapplied fund but also to do so with interest from the date of misapplication.

It is a matter for the court to determine what rate of interest is appropriate and whether simple or compound interest will be charged. In the 19th century, a rate of 4% was widely considered by the courts to be acceptable, increased to 5% if the breach was fraudulent. More recently, the courts have sought to keep abreast of current commercial interest rates by charging interest at 1% above the prevailing bank rate (see *Wallensteiner v Moir, Belmont Finance Corporation v Williams Furniture Ltd (No 2)* (1980) and *Guardian Ocean Cargoes Ltd v Banco do Brasil (No 3)* (1992). As an alternative, it has been suggested in *Bartlett v Barclays Bank* that the proper rate of interest to be awarded was that allowed from time to time on the court's short-term investment account.

The position where a breach results in tax-savings

Where a breach of trust involves misappropriation or misapplication of trust funds or property by trustees this may lead to a downward adjustment of the tax payable by the beneficiaries on the trust estate. The courts have made it clear in cases such as *Re Bell's Indenture* (1980) and the *Bartlett* case, that in such an event, the trustees will not be allowed to claim that the money which has been saved on tax, should be deducted from the amount which they are liable to pay for the loss occasioned by their breach.

Defences to an action for personal liability

Several defences are available to trustees who commit a breach.

Participation or concurrence in the breach

A beneficiary who participates or concurs in a breach of trust is not entitled to sue for the breach. For example, the leading case of *Re Pauling's ST* (1964) recognised that trustees who improperly advance trust funds to a beneficiary at the beneficiary's request may have a good defence if sued by the beneficiary for breach of trust.

For this defence to succeed, it must be shown, not only that the beneficiary was aware of the breach, but also that he concurred of his own free will, without any undue influence or pressure and with a full understanding of what he was concurring in. Once this is established, it is not necessary to show that the concurring beneficiary received some personal benefit from the breach (see *Re Paulings ST and Holder v Holder* (1968)).

The fact that a beneficiary has concurred in a breach, will not avail a trustee as a defence if he is sued by another beneficiary who had nothing to do with the breach (see *Brice v Stokes* (1805); *Wilkinson v Parry* (1828) and *Fletcher v Collis* (1905).

Release and acquiescence

Where a breach has been committed and thereafter, a beneficiary releases the trustees from liability or acquiesces in the breach, this will have the same effect as if he had at the outset concurred in the breach. As Lord Eldon declared in *Walker v Simmonds* (1818) 'I agree that either concurrence in the act or acquiescence without original concurrence will release the trustees [from liability]'.

As in the case of concurrence in the breach, it must be shown that the beneficiary's release or acquiescence was based on a full knowledge and understanding of the circumstances connected with the breach and was not the result of undue influence or pressure (see *Farrant v Blanchford* (1863) and *Re Garnett* (1885)).

Impounding the beneficiary's interest

Where a trustee commits a breach at the instigation or with the concurrence of a beneficiary, the court may order the beneficiary's interest to be impounded either under its inherent jurisdiction or under s 62 TA. Where such an order is made, the affected beneficiary will not be able to recover from the trustees any loss incurred by him as a result of the breach. Moreover, the liability to make good the loss suffered by other beneficiaries will fall on the affected beneficiary rather than the trustees and will as far as possible be met out of his beneficial interest.

The inherent jurisdiction

Under this heading, the courts have distinguished between cases in which the beneficiary instigated or requested the breach and cases in which he simply consented to it. If the beneficiary instigated the breach, an order impounding his beneficial interest may be made, even if he did not benefit from the breach (see *Trafford v Boehm* (1746); *Fuller v Knight* (1838) and *Chillingworth v Chambers* (1896)). By contrast, if the beneficiary did not instigate but consented to the breach, an order will be made only if he personally benefitted from the breach (see *Booth v Booth* (1838) and *Chillingworth v Chambers*).

Section 62 TA

On the strength of this statutory provision, the court may order the interest of any beneficiary in trust property to be impounded where he has instigated, requested or consented to a breach of trust irrespective of whether he derived any benefit from the breach. However s 62 cannot be invoked in cases of consent to the breach unless the consent was given in writing.

Finally, an impounding order will be refused where a beneficiary has instigated or consented to an act which is not in itself a breach but the act is then performed by the trustees in a manner which amounts to a breach. For example, if a beneficiary suggests to the trustees that they should invest trust funds in mortgages and the trustees in doing so do not take care to ensure that property offered as security is of sufficient value to cover the trust money advanced under the mortgage, there will be no basis for impounding the beneficiary's interest (see *Re Somerset* (1894)).

Relief from liability under s 61 TA

Under this section, the court may in its discretion relieve a trustee wholly or partly from personal liability for breach of trust provided that:

• the trustee acted honestly and reasonably; and
• it would be fair for him to be excused.

The onus rests on the trustee to establish that his actions were honest and reasonable. It is clear from such cases as *Re Turner* (1897), *Re Stuart* (1897) and *Re De Clifford* (1900) that in discharging this burden, the trustee must show that he has acted as prudently as he would have done in dealing with his own affairs.

As Byrne J pointed out in *Re Turner* the courts have not attempted to lay down general rules or principles to be strictly adhered to in determining whether a trustee should be relieved from liability for breach of trust, but have preferred to deal with each case according to its own circumstances. The effect of this approach is illustrated by the following cases.

On the one hand, in *Perrins v Bellamy* (1899), trustees of a settlement who erroneously believed they had a power of sale and sold certain leaseholds on their solicitor's advice were relieved from liability to the tenant for life whose income was reduced by the sale. Also in *Re De Clifford* trustees who entrusted trust money to the solicitor to the trust to be used for paying debts and for other trust purposes were relieved from liability when the solicitor became bankrupt without having paid all the debts.

These may be contrasted with other cases like *Re Turner* and *Re Barker* (1898). In *Turner*, there were two trustees, a solicitor and an ordinary trustee. The solicitor arranged for the investment of trust funds in certain mines in which he had an interest and the investment turned out to be useless. The court refused to relieve the ordinary trustee from liability for the breach since he had abdicated his responsibilities to the solicitor-trustee and failed to take any steps to ensure that the investment was sound. In *Barker*, a trustee of a family trust, acting on the advice of a commission agent who was a family friend, failed to sell unauthorised investments for 14 years. She was held to be liable for breach of trust, since the court considered it unreasonable for her to have retained the investment for so long.

Actions which are statute-barred

Where a beneficiary discovers a breach of trust but delays unduly in suing, the trustee may be able to claim the protection of s 21(3) Limitation Act 1980, which provides that 'an action by a beneficiary to recover trust property or in respect of any breach of trust ... shall not be brought after the expiration of six years from the date on which the right of action accrued'.

The operation of this six year limitation period is, however, subject to a number of important exceptions and qualifications. In the first place, the proviso to s 21(3) specifies that where a beneficiary is entitled to a future interest in the trust property his right of action will not be treated as having accrued until his interest falls into possession. This means, for instance, that if property is held on trust for A for life remainder to B, and a breach of trust is committed in A's lifetime, B's action will not be statute-barred until six years after A's death.

Secondly, where a beneficiary is able to show that was unable to pursue his claim within the six year period because he was under a disability (such as infancy or mental incapacity), s 28 of the Act enables the court to extend the limitation period to take account of this. Equally, where the beneficiary was unaware of his right of action at the time it accrued, due to some mistake or because it was fraudulently concealed from him by the trustee or his agent, s 32 provides that the period of limitation shall not begin to run until he has discovered the mistake or concealment or could with reasonable diligence have discovered it.

Finally, s 21(1) makes it clear that the limitation period in s 21(3) shall not avail the trustee, where the action by the beneficiary is either an action:

- in respect of any fraud or fraudulent breach of trust to which the trustee was a party or privy; or
- to recover from the trustee trust property or the proceeds of trust property in the possession of the trustee or previously received by the trustee and converted to his use.

The proprietary remedy of tracing

Where it is alleged that loss has been occasioned to the trust estate owing to a trustee's breach of trust a personal action would be of no avail if the trustee does not have sufficient funds from which the loss can be recovered. Where this happens, the principal course of action open to the beneficiaries is to pursue the proprietary remedy of tracing or following the trust funds or assets which have been lost.

The remedy is available primarily against the trustee who has misappropriated trust funds which he has applied towards acquiring property in his own name or who has intermingled trust funds or assets with his own personal resources. It may also be employed against any other party who has received such funds or assets in breach of trust (eg an overpaid beneficiary or an innocent volunteer to whom the funds or assets have been transferred).

Tracing as a right *in rem*

Because the remedy of tracing is proprietary in character, it is enforceable *in rem* and not merely *in personam*. The chief advantage of this is that the rights of the beneficiaries will not be extinguished by the insolvency of the trustees or any other person against whom the right exists. On the contrary, their rights will in such an event be accorded priority over those of general/unsecured creditors of the trustee or other insolvent person.

Tracing under the common law

In most instances, parties seeking to pursue the remedy of tracing base their claims on equity and we shall elaborate on the rules governing tracing in the realm of equity below. Tracing is also available as a common law remedy. In this latter connection it is primarily a mechanism for protecting a parties' immediate right to possession.

The context in which the right to trace commonly arises under the common law is where there is a contract of agency, bailment or hire-purchase under which property/funds are entrusted by one party to another and such property/funds have been lost or misappropriated. In *Taylor v Plumer* (1815) for instance, the defendant entrusted money to W to purchase exchequer bonds for him but W used the money to purchase bullion and American investments for himself and absconded. When W was apprehended the defendant seized the bullion and investments from him. W's assignees in bankruptcy subsequently claimed the seized assets from the defendant but the court held that the defendant's money was traceable into the investments and bullion and the claim therefore failed.

Tracing under common law differs materially from tracing in equity because it is not available if the asset being claimed is no longer ascertainable in its own right but has been mingled with other funds or been employed together with other funds in the purchase of property. This limitation to the common law remedy which was imposed in *Taylor v Plumer* and confirmed by the Court of Appeal in *Re Diplock* (1948) was recently re-iterated in *Agip (Africa) Ltd v Jackson* (1990), where it was stated by Millett J that:

money can be followed at common law in and out of a bank account provided it does not cease to be identifiable by being mixed with other money derived from the same account.

No wholly convincing reason has been advanced for the common law position and some cases such as *Clayton's Case* (1816) and *Banque Belge v Hambrouck* (1921), favour the view that monies paid into a mixed fund should properly be regarded as ascertainable and hence traceable at common law as it is in equity. As Lord Atkin opined in the latter case:

if in 1815 [when *Taylor v Plumer* was decided] the common law halted outside the banker's door, by 1879 equity had the courage to lift the latch, walk in and examine the books. I see no reason why this means of ascertainment should not now be available for common law and equity proceedings.

Tracing in equity

There is little scope for recourse to tracing under the common law in the context of breach of trust. If the claim is against the trustee, the beneficiaries are hindered by the fact that in the eyes of the common law, beneficiaries have no recognised interest in trust property as against the trustee. Even if the action is against a third party to whom trust assets have been wrongfully transferred, an action for tracing would only be entertained under the common law if the trustee joined in the suit.

For a claim to trace to succeed in equity, three basic conditions must be fulfilled, namely:

- the claim must be founded on an initial fiduciary relationship;
- there must be some property in a traceable form;
- the order to trace must not yield inequitable results.

The initial fiduciary relationship

An initial fiduciary relationship must exist before a tracing order will be made in equity. As Jessel MR declared in *Re Hallett* (1880), 'the moment you establish the fiduciary relation the modern rules of equity as regards following trust property apply'.

Such a fiduciary relationship is easy to discover where property is held on trust and the beneficiary has cause to seek a tracing order against the trustee. Such an order may also be granted where a trustee improperly transfers trust property to a third party since what is material is the *initial* fiduciary relationship with the trustee which extends to the transferee (see *Re Diplock*). The transferee will not, however, be subject to a tracing order if he is a bona fide purchaser for value without notice (see *Re J Leslie Engineers Co Ltd* (1976)).

The equitable remedy of tracing is also available in the context of other fiduciary relationships. As Jessel MR pointed out in this connection in *Re Hallett*, there is no distinction between the liability of the trustee and that of an agent, a collector of rents or anybody else in a fiduciary position.

Thus, for instance, in *Re Diplock*, the fiduciary relationship which gave rise to a tracing order was that existing between executors of a will and the residuary beneficiary. In *Sinclair v Brougham* (1914) the fiduciary relationship relied on was that between a building society and its depositors. And in *Chase-Manhattan Bank v Israel-British Bank* (1980) the material fiduciary relationship was between two banks, one of which had paid a large sum of money to the other twice over under a mistake of fact.

Property in a traceable form

Unless there is property into which the beneficiaries can trace the remedy will not be available. Assuming for instance, T, a trustee of £10,000 uses this sum to purchase shares on his own account, the beneficiaries can trace into the shares in lieu of the £10,000; but if T dissipates this money on a holiday and is declared bankrupt soon thereafter, a tracing order would be fruitless and equity will not act in vain.

The rules which the courts have laid down in determining whether there is property in a traceable form and the extent to which the right to trace can be exercised in respect of such property will be dealt with under the following headings.

The position with regard to unmixed funds

Where the trustee (T) has kept the trust funds distinct from his own assets without at any stage mixing both funds this presents no problems as long as T remains solvent. However, if T becomes bankrupt, it is often necessary to deal with competing claims made by the beneficiaries on the one hand and other creditors on the other. Such claims may arise in the following circumstances.

Where the trust fund remains intact

Assuming, for instance, that T holds £10,000 of trust funds in a separate trust account which he has not touched and £8,000 of his own money in a personal account and that he then becomes bankrupt the beneficiaries will be entitled to the £10,000 in the trust account to the exclusion of T's other creditors who must content themselves with the £8,000 in T's personal account.

Where trust money has been withdrawn and squandered

If T has withdrawn the £10,000 from the trust account and spent it on a round-the-world cruise, while leaving the £8,000 in his personal account untouched, B cannot rely on the remedy of tracing as a basis for claiming the £8,000 in priority to T's other creditors. B will rank *pari passu* with these other creditors and be entitled to a share out of the £8,000 in proportion to them.

Where trust money has been applied in the purchase of specific property

If T withdraws the £10,000 and uses it to purchase an asset such as a car, a house or shares, B will be able to rely on the right to trace to defeat any claims to the asset by T's creditors. As Jessel MR signified in *Re Hallett's Estate*, in such circumstances, B 'has a right to elect either to take the property purchased or to hold it as security for the amount of trust money laid out in the purchase'.

It follows that where the property has increased in value since purchase, B will be entitled to the benefit of this increase. Where its value has decreased, say to £4,000, B will still have a personal claim against T for the remaining £6,000 but stands in the same position as T's other creditors in respect of this sum.

The position where the trustee mixes trust funds with his own

Where T transfers money from the trust account into his personal account which already contains his own money (or sells trust property and puts the proceeds into his personal account), equity will as a rule allow B to trace into the mixed funds.

Where the dispute is between B and T

As between T and B the position is well summed up in Jessel MR's rhetorical observation in *Re Hallett* that:

Supposing the trust money was 1,000 sovereigns and the trustee put them in a bag and by mistake or accident, or otherwise, dropped a sovereign of his own into the bag ... [c]ould anybody suppose that a judge in equity would find any difficulty in saying that the cestui que trust has a right to take 1,000 out of the bag. It would make no difference if instead of one sovereign it were another 1,000 sovereigns.

Moreover the onus is on the trustee to satisfy the court as to which part of the mixed fund belongs to him, for as Ungoed-Thomas J stated in *Re Tilley's WT* (1967):

if a trustee amalgamated trust property with his own, the beneficiary will be entitled to every portion of the property which the trustee cannot prove to be his own.

Where the dispute is between B and T's creditors
Where a trustee becomes bankrupt after wrongfully mixing trust funds with his own funds, the tracing remedy is usually employed by beneficiaries as a means of obtaining priority over other creditors. Where the funds are lawfully mixed, however, this remedy will not be available to the beneficiaries. Thus in *Space Investments Ltd v Canadian Imperial Bank Of Commerce Trust Co (Bahamas) Ltd* (1986) a bank-trustee was authorised under an express power to deposit trust funds with itself. When it was subsequently wound up, it fell to be determined whether the beneficiaries could trace into the bank's general assets to recover the funds which had been so deposited. The Privy Council held that if the bank had misappropriated the funds for its own benefit, the tracing remedy would have been available but since the mixing was done lawfully, the bank only had a personal liability to repay with the result that the beneficiaries had no priority over unsecured creditors.

Where trustees have acted wrongfully in mixing trust funds with their own funds, the entitlement of beneficiaries to trace into the mixed fund can be dealt with under the following headings.

Where no withdrawals have been made after mixing
If the trustee (T) mixes £10,000 belonging to the trust with £8,000 in his personal account and becomes insolvent without drawing from this account, leaving debts of £18,000, the beneficiary (B) will have a first charge on the money in the account. This entitles B to recover the £10,000 belonging to the trust before other creditors who are therefore left with £8,000 (see *Re Hallett*).

Where T has withdrawn money from the mixed fund and squandered it
If T, having mixed £10,000 of trust funds with his own £8,000 withdraws £12,000 from the fund which he dissipates before becoming bankrupt, the position as established by *Re Hallett* is that T will be deemed to have drawn out his own money first before touching any part of the trust money. This operates to B's advantage at the expense of other creditors since it means that B will be able to claim the £8,000 left in the account as representing trust funds, to the exclusion of the creditors.

Where T has withdrawn money from the mixed fund squandered it and then paid in a further sum of his own into the fund

Assuming in the previous instance, T mixed the funds in January 1994, had squandered the £12,000 by April 1994 and proceeded in May 1994 to pay into the account an additional £3,000 of his own money, and then become bankrupt, the issue arises as to whether B can trace into the £3,000 in priority to T's other creditors.

In *Roscoe v Winder* (1915) it was held that B can only trace into the lowest intermediate balance (ie the £6,000 remaining in the account before the injection of the additional £3,000). With regard to the additional £3,000 B stands in no better position than T's other creditors.

A contrary approach was, however, favoured by Lord Templeman who suggested in the *Space Investments Ltd* case that where it is impossible to trace misappropriated trust funds into a specific asset, equity allows the beneficiary to trace the trust money into all the assets of the trustee and to recover the trust money by exercising a charge over all the assets. The effect of this would be that B, in our example, would have an equitable charge over the £9,000 in the trust account and may thus have recourse to this money in priority to T's other creditors.

The uncertainty inherent in these divergent approaches has recently been resolved by the Court of Appeal in *Bishopsgate Investment Management Ltd v Homan* (1994) where the 'least intermediate balance' approach was preferred. See also the Privy Council decision in *Re Goldberg* (1994).

Where mixed funds have been applied in the purchase of specific property

In determining B's entitlement to trace where T has mixed trust funds with his own money in a single account and then drawn money from this account to purchase property regard must be had to the following hypothetical possibilities.

T mixes £8,000 of his own money and £10,000 of trust money and withdraws the £18,000 to purchase property

In such circumstances it appears from *Re Hallett* and *Sinclair v Brougham* that B will be deemed to have a first charge over the property purchased to the extent of the £10,000 due to the trust estate.

Where the property purchased has since increased in value the position is not entirely clear. On the one hand, going by the *dicta* in *Re Hallett/Sinclair v Brougham* and the views of such scholars as Maudsley (1959) 75 LQR 234, 246, the charge in B's favour simply entitles him to recover the trust money, with interest and not to claim any part of the increased value. (Contrast with the position where the property has been purchased entirely with trust funds.)

The contrary view, representing the law in the US, which was adopted in Australia in *Scott v Scott* and approved per obiter in the English case of *Re Tilley's WT* is that B will be entitled to claim a part of the increased value relative to the proportion in which trust funds and T's money have been laid out in purchasing the property. Preference for this latter solution has been expressed by such writers as Pettitt and Hanbury and Martin who consider it illogical and startling that T should be allowed to profit from the trust by claiming the entire increase in value.

A third solution has been put forward by Riddal who suggests that the appropriate course in some circumstances would be to order T to hold the whole increase on trust for B, particularly where it is shown that T would not have been in a position to buy the property without recourse to the trust funds.

Where the value of the property purchased has diminished, B will have a charge on the property in priority to other creditors and if its current value is less than the £10,000 due to the trust estate he will have a personal claim against T but will rank *pari passu* with other creditors with regard to this claim.

T mixes £8,000 of his own money and £10,000 of trust money and withdraws £15,000 to purchase property leaving a balance of £3,000 in the account

As seen above *Re Hallett* establishes that where a mixed fund is involved T will be presumed to have expended his own money first, with the result that it is open to B to claim the balance of £3,000.

With regard to the remaining £7,000 due to the trust estate, B can claim a first charge over the property which will be more than sufficient to meet his claim if it maintains its value.

Where the property appreciates in value, whether or not B will be entitled to a share of the increased value will depend on which of the contending positions outlined above will ultimately prevail.

Where on the other hand the property depreciates in value, say to £5,000, B in addition to his entitlement to the £3,000 left in the mixed account will be entitled to the assert his right to trace into this property in priority to T's other creditors (see *Re Hallett*).

T mixes £8,000 of his own money with £10,000 of trust money, uses £7,000 of the mixed fund to purchase property and then withdraws and squanders the balance

In a situation of this nature, the adoption of the presumption in *Re Hallett* would work to B's disadvantage. This is because if T is presumed to have spent his own part of the fund first, it would mean that of the £11,000 squandered by him £10,000 will be traceable as trust money with the result that B would be unable to trace into the property purchased by T. It has, however, been decided in *Re Oatway* (1903) that in such situations the presumption that the trustee spent his own money first will be displaced thus enabling the beneficiary to trace into any part of the mixed fund that remains identifiable. This means that in our example, B's entitlement to trace will now be exercisable by reference to the property purchased with the £7,000 taken from the mixed fund.

The position where the trustee mixes funds from two trusts

Assuming T who is a trustee of Trust A and Trust B mixes funds from the two trusts in a current bank account and thereafter withdraws some money from this account which he fritters away, it is necessary to determine how the balance will be appropriated.

In the first place assuming the account in question also contained money belonging to T, the rule in *Re Hallett* comes into play as between T and the beneficiaries under the two trusts such that T will be deemed to have spent his own money first. For example, if A has an account containing £5,000 of his own money and in January 1994 transfers £10,000 belonging to Trust A to this account; in February 1994 transfers £10,000 belonging to Trust B to the same account and in March 1994 withdraws and spends £5,000, the effect of the presumption is that Trust A and Trust B will be entitled to recover the £10,000 due to each fund out of the remaining £20,000.

The matter becomes more complicated if in the above instance T withdrew and spent £15,000 rather than £5,000 leaving a balance of £10,000 in the account. The issue here is whether Trust A or Trust B will be entitled to this balance. It has been held in such cases as *Re Hallett*, *Hancock v Smith* (1889), *Re Stenning* (1895) and *Re Diplock* that any dispute between Trust A and Trust B falls to be determined by reference to the rule in *Clayton's Case*. According to this rule the first payment into the account (ie the £10,000 belonging to Trust A) will be deemed to have been withdrawn first, the operative principle being first in, first out. This means in effect that the £10,000 remaining in the account will be deemed to belong to Trust B, while the beneficiaries under Trust A will have to be content with asserting a personal claim against A.

The operation of this rule in the present context has been subjected to considerable criticism and the Court of Appeal has recently emphasised in *Barlow Clowes International v Vaughan* (1992) that it will be displaced as a basis for determining such competing claims where the courts are able to deduce a contrary intention, express or presumed.

Where, on the other hand, a mixed fund derived from Trust A and Trust B is applied towards the purchase of specific property, different considerations apply. In *Sinclair v Brougham* the position was stated thus by Lord Parker:

Suppose property is acquired by means of money part of which belongs to one owner and part to another, the purchaser is in a fiduciary position to both, each owner has an equal equity and is entitled to a charge on the property for his own money and neither can claim priority over the other. It follows that their charges must rank *pari passu* according to their respective amounts.

The position where trust funds are given to innocent volunteers

Where T acting in breach of trust transfers trust property or funds to V who takes as an innocent volunteer, V, not being a bona fide purchaser for value without notice takes subject to the trust. In such an event, B is required in the first instance to pursue a claim for breach of trust against T. Where T is insolvent or otherwise unable to meet B's claim, it is clear from the decision in *Re Diplock* that equity will allow B to trace the funds or property in to V's hand even though there is no fiduciary relationship between B and V, provided there is property in a traceable form and the result will not be inequitable.

The position is fairly straightforward where V, having received property or funds from T, keeps it separate from his own property. Where this happens, the courts will in all likelihood hold that B can recover the property/funds. Equally, where V puts the amount received from T in an account containing his own money (or sells the property received and puts the proceeds in such an account) without making any subsequent withdrawals B will also be entitled to recover the trust funds or proceeds of sale from the account (see *Banque Belgique v Hambrouck*).

Where such mixing has occurred and thereafter V withdraws sums of money from time to time for various purposes, then according to such authorities as *Re Stenning*, and *Re Diplock*, the rule in *Clayton's Case* will determine the order in which the mixed fund has been expended. Thus, for example, if V who already had £5,000 in his account, received another £5,000 from T on 1 March and then paid in another £3,000 of his own money into the account on 1 April and finally withdrew £8,000 on 15 April, spending £4,000 on a holiday and the other £4,000 on repaying a long-standing debt, there will be a balance of £5,000 in the account. Out of this 5,000 B cannot exercise his right to trace in respect of the £3,000 which represents the amount paid in by V on 1 March but he can trace into the remaining £2,000.

Where, on the other hand, part of the mixed fund is withdrawn for a purpose such as the purchase of specific property and it can be shown that V's intention was to use the funds received from T for the purchase, the money so used will be traceable by B into the property (*Re Diplock*). If it is the entire fund that has been withdrawn and applied in the purchase of property, B will also be entitled to trace into the property purchased but his claim will rank *pari passu* with that of V according to the proportion of the mixed fund representing their respective shares (see Lord Parker in *Sinclair v Brougham*).

No inequitable results

Even where an initial fiduciary relationship is established and there is identifiable property into which the beneficiary can trace, the courts have the discretion not to grant the remedy where inequitable results would follow. The courts are especially anxious to ensure that there are no inequitable results where the party against whom the order is sought is an innocent volunteer. This point was emphasised in *Re Diplock* with particular reference to situations in which the innocent volunteer has applied trust funds received by him in good faith in making improvements or alterations to property belonging to him. The remedy of tracing was felt to be inappropriate in such instances in so far as it would create a charge on such property which would impose an unfair burden on the innocent volunteer.

Closely allied to the proposition that tracing will not be allowed where the result will be inequitable is the doctrine of change of position which has only recently found its way into the sphere of tracing. This doctrine proceeds on the premise that:

the right of a person to restitution from another because of a benefit received is terminated or diminished, if after the receipt of the benefit, circumstances have so changed that it would be inequitable to require the other to make full restitution.

The possibility that this doctrine could afford a defence in a tracing action was acknowledged by the House of Lords in *Lipkin Gorman v Karpnale Ltd* (1991). Its effect in this context will be that where an innocent recipient of trust funds has spent the money received on improving his property or has irretrievably spent money on the assumption that he is entitled to the sum received he may be relieved from making restitution, wholly or in part.

Revision Notes

A trustee who commits a breach of trust will be liable to the beneficiaries for whatever profit he has made or whatever loss has been suffered by the trust estate. Liability may be imposed even where the trustee believed that what he was doing was in the best interest of the trust (*Re Brogden*). A trustee may, however, escape liability for a mere technical breach which the court would have authorised had leave been sought (*Lee v Brown; Brown v Smith*).

Remedies for breach

Injunction

This remedy is available where it is anticipated that a trustee intends to commit a breach of trust (see eg *Dance v Goldingham; Wheelwright v Walker; Riggal v Foster; Fox v Fox*).

The personal remedy

Where a breach of trust has actually been committed, the beneficiary may bring a personal action against the trustee. Section 30(1) TA provides that the trustee will be liable for breaches committed by him, but not vicariously liable for the breaches of co-trustees or the dishonesty or neglect of agents carrying out trust business except if there has been wilful default on his part. What constitutes wilful default is seen from such cases as *Townley v Sherborne, Boardman v Mosman, Booth v Booth*, and *Wilkins v Hogg*.

It has been established that an incoming trustee will not be liable for any breach of trust committed before he assumed office but that if he becomes aware of such a breach he must take steps to remedy it (*Re Strahan*). For his part, an outgoing or retiring trustee will be liable for breaches he committed while in office but not for those committed by other trustees after he leaves office, unless it was within his contemplation that his departure would pave the way for the breach to be committed (*Head v Gould*).

Where two or more trustees are involved in committing a breach they are liable jointly and severally and the beneficiaries may sue all or any of them. If only one trustee has been sued for the breach, he may claim a contribution from any other trustee who is also liable. Under the Civil Liability (Contribution) Act 1978, the courts are now able to set the contribution of each trustee to reflect the extent of his responsibility for the breach.

In some cases where two trustees are jointly liable for a breach of trust, one trustee is entitled to an indemnity from the other. For example, an indemnity may be claimed against a solicitor-trustee by his co-trustee who has placed complete reliance on the solicitor in matters connected with trust business but not by a co-trustee, who relying on his own judgment, has actively participated in the breach (*Chillingworth v Chambers; Re Lindsay; Head v Gould*).

Again, where two trustees have jointly committed a breach of trust, and one of the two acted fraudulently, the other trustee may be entitled to an indemnity against him (*Re Smith*). Such an indemnity will not, however, be available if the court is satisfied that the trustee against who it is sought has not acted fraudulently or dishonestly (*Bahin v Hughes*).

Where a trustee is guilty of a breach the manner of quantifying his personal liability will depend on the nature of the breach:

- Trustees who make an unauthorised investment are liable to pay the difference between the cost of the investment and the price at which it is sold (*Knott v Cottee*). If all the beneficiaries are of full age, it is accepted in cases like *Wright v Morgan* that they may adopt the investment instead of demanding its sale. If they adopt the investment but its value at the time is less than the price the trustees paid for it, judicial opinion is divided on whether they can claim the difference from the trustees (contrast *Thornton v Stokill* with *Re Lake*).
- Trustees who improperly retain an unauthorised investment will be liable to pay the difference between the price at which it is sold or its value at the judgment date if not sold and the price it would have fetched if sold at the appropriate time (*Fry v Fry*).
- Trustees who improperly sell an authorised investment may be required to replace it; or may be directed to pay the difference between the price at which it was sold and what it would cost to replace it (*Re Bell's Indenture*).
- Trustees who are required by the trust instrument to invest trust funds in a specified type of asset but fail to do so are liable to purchase as much of that asset as they could have done if the investment had been made at the appropriate time (*Byrchall v Bradford, Pride v Fooks*).

In the case of trustees who were not obliged under the trust to invest in specific assets, cases such as *Shepherd v Mouls* and *Robinson v Robinson* suggest that if they do not perform their duty to invest their only liability is to replace the uninvested fund (contrast, however, with *Nestle v National Westminster Bank*).

- trustees are not ordinarily allowed to set off a profit made from one transaction against losses resulting from another transaction entered into in breach of trust (see *Dimes v Scott; Wills v Gresham* but note the exception in *Bartlett v Barclays Bank*).

Where a trustee is liable for a loss to the trust estate in any of the circumstances outlined above, it must usually be repaid with interest (*Wallensteiner v Moir (No 2); Belmont Finance Corporation v Williams Furniture Ltd; Guardian Ocean Cargoes Ltd v Banco Do Brasil; Bartlett v Barclays Bank*).

Where a breach of trust results in tax savings for the trust estate or a beneficiary, the trustees will not be allowed to claim that this should be deducted from the amount they are liable to pay for the breach (*Re Bell's Indenture; Bartlett v Barclays Bank*).

The following defences are open to a trustee where it is claimed that he is personally liable for a breach of trust:

- the beneficiary's participation or concurrence in the breach (*Re Pauling's ST; Holder v Holder; Fletcher v Collis*);
- the beneficiary's release or acquiescence (*Walker v Simmonds; Farrant v Blanchford; Re Garnett*);
- an application for the court to impound the interest of a beneficiary who has requested/instigated/consented to the breach either under its inherent jurisdiction or under s 62 TA.

Inherent jurisdiction

Where breach is requested/instigated, there is no need to prove that beneficiary benefitted from it (*Trafford v Boehm; Fuller v Knight, Chillingworth v Chambers*).

Where the beneficiary merely consented to it it must be shown that he benefitted from the breach (*Booth v Booth; Chillingworth v Chambers*).

Section 62 TA

This provides that whether the breach was instigated or consented to by the beneficiary it need not be proved that he benefitted from it. However, s 62 will not apply in consent cases unless such consent was in writing.

A beneficiary's interest will not be impounded if he asks the trustees to perform an act which is not a breach but the act is carried out by them in a manner occasioning a breach (*Re Somerset*).

- An application for relief under s 61 TA is available at the discretion of the court where, in committing a breach of trust, a trustee has acted honestly and reasonably and it would be fair for him to be excused (see *Re Turner; Re Stuart; Re De Clifford; Perrins v Bellamy* and *Re Barker*).
- A claim that the beneficiary's action is statute-barred under s 21(3) Limitation Act 1980 is available as a defence where a beneficiary brings an action for breach of trust after the expiry of six years from the date on which his right of action accrued.

But note that:

- in the case of a future interest the right of action does not accrue until it falls into possession;
- the stipulated six year period does not begin to run against a beneficiary who is under a disability until the disability ceases or is removed;
- the stipulated six year period does not begin to run against a beneficiary who as a result of some mistake or fraudulent concealment was unaware that the cause of action had arisen until he discovers or with reasonable diligence could have discovered the mistake or concealment;
- the trustee cannot rely on s 21(3) in his defence if the action by the beneficiary against him is either based on fraud to which the trustee is party or privy; or for the recovery of trust property or its proceeds in the possession of the trustee or previously received by him and converted to his use.

The proprietary remedy of tracing

This is available where a personal action would be of no avail. It is in the nature of a right *in rem* which may be pursued not only against a trustee who has committed the breach but also against any person to whom he has transferred trust property or assets in breach of trust.

Tracing is available in equity only if:

(i)   there is an initial fiduciary relationship;
(ii)   there is property in a traceable form; and
(iii)   it will not lead to inequitable results.

The initial fiduciary relationship

This requirement is easily satisfied as between trustee and beneficiary under an express trust. Also as seen from such cases as *Re Diplock; Sinclair v Brougham* and *Chase-Manhattan Bank v Israel British Bank*, a tracing order may also be made in the context of other types of fiduciary relationships.

Property in a traceable form

In determining whether there is property in a traceable form it is necessary to consider a number of different possibilities as follows.

Unmixed funds

• where the trust fund remains intact and is kept separately, the beneficiaries are entitled to trace into it to the exclusion of the trustee's other creditors.
• where the trust fund was withdrawn and without being mixed with the trustees own money was used to purchase a specific asset, it emerges from *Re Hallett's Estate* that the beneficiary is entitled either to trace into that asset and retain it or to treat it as security for the trust money used to purchase it.
• where the trust fund is withdrawn and squandered without being mingled with the trustee's own funds, the beneficiary's right to trace in priority to other creditors of the trustee is lost.

Where trust funds are mixed with the trustee's funds

Where a trustee becomes bankrupt after mixing trust funds with his own, the beneficiary has no prior right to any part of the mixed fund if the mixing was authorised by the terms of the trust (*Space Investments Ltd v Canadian Imperial Bank Of Commerce Trust Co*).

If the mixing was not done lawfully, the following situations must be distinguished:

• where no withdrawals are made after mixing the beneficiaries will have a prior claim to the part of the mixed fund belonging to the trust (*Re Hallett*);
• where the trustee withdrew money from the mixed fund and squandered it, according to the decision in *Re Hallett*, he is deemed to have spent his own money first, with the result that the beneficiaries will have a prior claim to the balance in the account up to the amount taken out of the trust fund;

- where the trustee has mixed trust funds with his personal funds, withdrawn part of the mixed fund and thereafter paid in additional money of his own, the beneficiaries shall be entitled to trace into the least intermediate balance before the later payment of the trustees own money into the fund (*Roscoe v Winder* and *Bishopsgate Investment Co Ltd v Homan*);
- where the mixed fund has been used to purchase specific property, it is clear from *Re Hallett* and *Sinclair v Brougham*, that the beneficiaries shall have a first charge over the property purchased to the extent that trust money has been used to purchase it.

One matter that has not been completely settled is whether, if the property purchased appreciates in value, the beneficiaries can claim a proportionate share of the increased value. It appears from *Re Hallett* and *Sinclair v Brougham* that the charge which they have over the trust property extends only to the amount of trust money used in its purchase and no more. By contrast in the US and Australia (*Scott v Scott*) the preferred view is that the beneficiaries are entitled to a proportionate share of the increased value and this has been endorsed albeit per obiter in *Re Tilley's WT*.

Finally, where the trustee after mixing trust funds with his own, purchases property with part of the mixed fund and squanders the balance, the principle in *Re Hallett* that the trustee is deemed to have spent his own money first (with the implication that it is trust money which has been squandered) is dispensed with. In such instances, *Re Oatway* establishes that the beneficiaries will have a charge over the property purchased out of the mixed fund, thereby preserving their priority over other creditors with regard to that property.

Where trust funds from two trusts are mixed

In a situation of this nature, if the mixed fund also contains money belonging to the trustee himself, the rule in *Re Hallet* will apply and he will be deemed to have spent his own money first.

As between the two trust funds whose monies have been mixed, the position is determined primarily by reference to *Clayton's Case*, unless as happened in *Barlow Clowes International v Vaughan*, this rule is displaced by the express or implied intention of the parties. The effect of the rule is that the first of the two trust funds to be paid into the account is deemed to have been withdrawn first, so that the beneficiaries under the second trust will be entitled to trace into the balance of the account in priority to the beneficiaries of the first trust.

On the other hand, where the entire mixed fund has been used to purchase specific property, the two trust funds will rank *pari passu* in proportion to the amounts derived from their respective funds (*Sinclair v Brougham*).

Where trust funds are given to an innocent volunteer

In such an event, if the trust money remains intact, the beneficiaries can recover it from the innocent volunteer through the process of tracing.

Where after the trust money is received, it is mixed with the innocent volunteer's own money and withdrawals subsequently made from the mixed fund leaving a balance, the position of the innocent volunteer and the beneficiaries with regard to the balance is dealt with by reference to *Clayton's Case*. Equally, if property is purchased using the mixed fund the entitlement of the parties will fall to be determined in accordance with *Sinclair v Brougham*.

The requirement that there should be no inequitable results

Like all equitable remedies, the remedy of tracing is discretionary and will not be awarded if in the court's view to do so would lead to inequitable results (see *Re Diplock*). Note also the indication in *Lipkin Gorman v Karpnale* that it may be possible for the party against whom a tracing order is sought, to rely on the defence of change of position.

Index

Administration of charities
Charity Commissioners 99, 100,
110, 116, 123, 156
exempted charities.......................100
Advancement
presumption of 62-65, 92
statutory power............................168
171, 191
Agent 5-6, 10
Analogies 49, 101, 129
Animals.................8, 19, 112, 127, 132
Appointment, power of 6, 8, 10,
141, 143,
146, 169, 174
Associations,
unincorporated 68-70, 93

Bankruptcy 6, 10, 86,
141, 204, 206,
208, 210, 211, 221
Beneficiary
advancement 168, 170,
191, 192
breach of trust 171, 196, 201,
217, 219, 220
interest of 3, 9, 18, 41, 55,
153, 166, 181, 188,
202, 203, 219, 220
Bona vacantia.......................................69
Breach of trust
indemnity.............................198, 218

Cestui que trust 2, 3, 79, 209
Common law
tracing at 206, 207
Constructive trust
definition of 70, 71, 93, 94
principle of 71, 74, 80

types of 59, 89
Covenant 50, 52, 56,
145, 195
Cy-pres doctrine 122

Directors 76, 77, 155
Discretionary trust 7, 10, 20,
22, 24, 29, 40, 170
Donationes mortis causa.....................52

Equitable
remedies 207, 223
Equity
common law and..............2, 4, 9, 30,
50, 206, 207
definition......................................70
maxims 19, 45, 65, 140
scope of 56, 207
Express trusts
creation of 13

In loco parentis.......................62, 64, 91,
92, 166, 167

Judicial trustees 149

Legacies 30, 32, 33, 102,
121, 125, 128, 148, 166, 167

Marriage
settlement of 49, 50, 56,
66, 182, 195
Obligation...............1, 2, 4, 8, 9, 11, 13,
15, 19, 31, 39, 41,
62, 63, 68, 71, 85,
150, 160, 172, 199

Precatory words.........................14, 15

Private trust 13, 14, 16, 18, 20,
22, 24, 26, 28, 30, 32,
34, 36, 40, 42, 99, 100, 129

Secret trust
basis of.. 34
half-secret 30, 42

Specific performance 4, 46, 50

Trust
agency and 5, 10, 79
concept of 1, 72

constituted..................................45-48
constructive 26, 32, 59-98
contract and 4-5, 9-10,
corporations and 139, 140, 144,
146, 185, 187
declaration and 13, 19, 21,
29, 36, 37, 39,
41, 46, 55,
59, 66, 87, 101
deviation from 93, 195
discretionary 6, 8, 10, 20,
22, 24, 29, 40, 88,
164, 170, 181, 194
fixed 7, 20, 21, 24, 40

implied 60, 61, 144,
145, 176, 222
marriage and 50, 56,
66, 84, 195
minors and 148, 177
perpetual......................................100
public 100, 114-118,
120, 132, 139, 185, 187
resulting................................28, 59-98
unlawful...65

Trustee
additional 140, 142, 158,
179, 185, 222

appointment of 6, 7, 76, 99,
123, 139, 146, 149,
169, 172, 175, 178,
182, 185, 187, 192
bare 152, 188
breach of trust by 80, 147, 163,
195-220
custodian 110, 140, 163, 190
de son tort 78, 79, 95
death of 52, 86, 140, 169, 185
discharge of.......... 13, 141, 146, 147,
149, 154, 185, 187, 203
duties of....................................13, 76,
122, 147-164, 187, 189,
192, 195, 200, 219
insurance 174
investment by 153-154, 157
172,189, 198,
203, 204, 218, 219,
liability of 78, 82, 155, 160, 161,
169, 171, 173, 175,
204, 217, 219
powers of 6-8, 10, 24,
159, 161, 164-176,
179, 180, 187, 189
receipts and 79, 82, 95,
140, 173, 175, 185, 197
removal of 139, 142,
146, 147, 174, 185, 187
remuneration of 76, 94, 139,
148, 150, 187, 188
retirement of 139, 142, 146,
151, 186, 187, 197
reversionary interests.................150

Variation of trusts 139, 161,
162, 176, 177, 179,
181, 184, 193, 194

Wills
mutual...............71, 72, 82, 84, 85, 96